Graph Data Processing with Cypher

A practical guide to building graph traversal queries using the Cypher syntax on Neo4j

Ravindranatha Anthapu

BIRMINGHAM—MUMBAI

Graph Data Processing with Cypher

Publishing Product Manager: Arindam Majumder
Content Development Editor: Priyanka Soam
Technical Editor: Sweety Pagaria
Copy Editor: Safis Editing
Project Coordinator: Farheen Fathima
Proofreader: Safis Editing
Indexer: Subalakshmi Govindhan
Production Designer: Aparna Bhagat
Marketing Coordinators: Priyanka Mhatre, Nivedita Singh

First published: November 2022

Production reference: 1301122

Published by Packt Publishing Ltd.
Livery Place
35 Livery Street
Birmingham
B3 2PB, UK.

ISBN 978-1-80461-107-4

www.packt.com

I would like to dedicate this book to my lovely wife, Sreevani Rajuru, for all her encouragement and patience during this journey

Contributors

About the author

Ravindranatha Anthapu has more than 25 years of experience in working with W3C standards and building cutting-edge technologies, including integrating speech into mobile applications in the 2000s. He is a technology enthusiast who has worked on many projects, from operating system device drivers to writing compilers for C language and modern web technologies, transitioning seamlessly and bringing experience from each of these domains and technologies to deliver successful solutions today. As a principal consultant at Neo4j today, Ravindranatha works with large enterprise customers to make sure they are able to leverage graph technologies effectively across various domains.

About the reviewer

Koji Annoura has over 40 years of experience as a full stack developer. He has been working in Agile software development since 2009 and is one of the founders of the Tokyo Neo4j User Group in Japan.

He is a Neo4j Ninja, Graph Community MVP, and Neo4j Speaker, and he founded the Apache Hop User Group Japan in 2021. He has been involved in the Agile transformation of many companies and teams and has been involved in the implementation of Agile and Scrum. He likes Star Trek (Trekie) and has given presentations about the Klingon language. More information on the Neo4j Ninja program can be found here: `https://community.neo4j.com/t5/ninjas-program/ct-p/ninjas`.

Sean William Grant is a product and analytics professional with over 20 years of experience in technology and data analysis. His experience ranges from geospatial intelligence with the United States Marine Corps, product management within the aviation and autonomy space, to implementing advanced analytics and data science within organizations. He is a graph data science and network analytics enthusiast who frequently gives presentations and workshops on connected data. He has also been a technical advisor to several early-stage startups. Sean is passionate about data and technology, and how it can elevate our understanding of ourselves.

Table of Contents

Part 1: Cypher Introduction

1

2

Part 2: Working with Cypher

3

4

5

Filtering, Sorting, and Aggregations   125

6

List Expressions, UNION, and Subqueries   153

Part 3: Advanced Cypher Concepts

7

Working with Lists and Maps   177

8

Advanced Query Patterns   201

9

Query Tuning   227

10

Using APOC Utilities   245

11

Cypher Ecosystem   283

12

Tips and Tricks   289

Index   303

Other Books You May Enjoy   312

Preface

Cypher is a declarative language to query graph databases. As graph databases are becoming more mainstream, there is a dearth of content and guidance for developers to leverage the database capabilities fully. This book is an attempt to fill that information gap. It is well suited to describe graph traversal patterns in a simple and readable manner. While it is easy to learn and understand, it can be very difficult to master.

This book provides a guided tour of Cypher language from understanding the syntax of the language, building a graph data model, loading the data into graphs, building queries, and profiling the queries for best performance. It introduces APOC utilities that can augment the Cypher queries to build complex queries. It also introduces visualization tools such as Bloom to get the most out of the graph when presenting the results to the end users.

By the end of this book, you should be a seasoned Cypher query developer with a good understanding of the query language and how to get the best performance out of it.

Who this book is for

This book is targeted at database administrators, database developers, graph database developers, and graph database architects. This book will also help someone migrate from a DBA role to a graph data engineer or data scientist role.

If you are working with graph databases and need to learn Cypher, or are a basic Cypher developer who wants to get better at data modeling and tuning queries to build performant Cypher queries, then this is the book for you.

What this book covers

Chapter 1, Introduction to Neo4j and Cypher, introduces Cypher and Neo4j. We discuss what the Cypher language is and how it is used to query the Neo4j graph database. We also take a look at how Cypher is different from other query languages and what sets it apart for querying graph databases.

Chapter 2, Components of Cypher, introduces the Cypher syntax with some examples. We will review the important aspects of the Cypher syntax and semantics in building graph traversal queries. We will discuss important keywords and the role they play in building the queries. We will take a look at the graph data model and how Cypher queries follow the data connections.

Chapter 3, Loading Data with Cypher, explains how to load the data into Neo4j using Cypher. We will discuss the various options available to create/update/delete the nodes, labels, relationships, and properties. We will discuss loading CSV, text and JSON files into Neo4j using Cypher.

Chapter 4, Querying Graph, discusses how querying works with Cypher. It discusses leveraging indexes on nodes and relationships to anchors and traversals. It also discusses conditional traversals, using multiple relationship types, returning paths, nodes, relationships, and so on. It also talks about returning the data as column-formatted data.

Chapter 5, Filtering, Sorting, and Aggregations, discusses how to filter the data using where conditions on nodes and/or relationship properties, and how to sort the data and use aggregation functions such as SUM, AVG, COUNT, and so on.

Chapter 6, List Expressions, UNION, and Subqueries, talks about using list expressions to reduce and process lists. It also explores how UNIONs can be used to return combined results from multiple queries along with leveraging subqueries to filter and process data.

Chapter 7, Working with Lists and Maps, explains how lists and maps are core elements in Cypher. This chapter discusses how we can handle lists and maps both as an input and as an output. It shows how easy it is to handle lists and maps as part of the querying process. It shows how to handle basic lists with Strings and also how to access individual elements at random or iterate through them.

Chapter 8, Advanced Query Patterns, discusses advanced concepts such as OPTIONAL MATCH to handle scenarios where the graph path may or may not exist. It also discusses the query chain using WITH and UNWIND. It also talks about executing subqueries using the CALL keyword and handling the responses in the main query.

Chapter 9, Query Tuning, talks about options to tune the Cypher queries. It talks about working with EXPLAIN PLAN to understand the query execution plan. It also talks about using PROFILE to understand how the query is executing and the amount of data being processed to understand the reasons for bottlenecks.

Chapter 10, Using APOC Utilities, talks about using APOC utilities to extend the built-in capabilities of Cypher. It gives more options to be able to load CSV and JSON data, schedule timers, make ad hoc batch data modifications, and so on.

Chapter 11, Cypher Ecosystem, talks about the Cypher ecosystem. It introduces you to tools and packages available to do more advanced data processing along with visualizing the results as graphs, tables, and so on.

Chapter 12, Tips and Tricks, talks about the best practices to get the most out of Cypher queries, which includes how to leverage data modeling and patterns. It also discusses the tips and tricks to identify performance bottlenecks and how to go about addressing them.

To get the most out of this book

There is no need to have RDBMS querying experience or a good understanding of graphs to get the most out of this book. Familiarity with databases and SQL will help in understanding some of the Cypher concepts and tuning approaches.

Software/hardware covered in the book	Operating system requirements
Neo4j Desktop and Neo4j Database Server	Windows, macOS, or Linux

> **Note**
> All the Cypher code used in this book has been tested on Neo4j version 4.4.8 but should work with the latest Neo4j 5.0 release.

If you are using the digital version of this book, we advise you to type the code yourself or access the code from the book's GitHub repository (a link is available in the next section). Doing so will help you avoid any potential errors related to the copying and pasting of code.

You can join the Neo4j community at `https://community.neo4j.com` to get answers to most Cypher or Neo4j-related questions. There is a huge developer community that answers all the basic syntax to modeling-related questions.

Download the example code files

You can download the example code files for this book from GitHub at `https://github.com/PacktPublishing/Cypher-Querying`. If there's an update to the code, it will be updated in the GitHub repository.

We also have other code bundles from our rich catalog of books and videos available at `https://github.com/PacktPublishing/`. Check them out!

Conventions used

There are several text conventions used throughout this book.

`Code in text`: Indicates code words in the text, folder names, filenames, file extensions, pathnames, dummy URLs, user input, and Twitter handles. Here is an example: "we are using the `apoc` procedure to add `EncounterClass` to an encounter node. Since we are trying to add labels dynamically, we have to use the `apoc` option."

A block of code is set as follows:

```
CREATE (p {name: 'Tom'})
RETURN p
```

When we wish to draw your attention to a particular part of a code block, the relevant lines or items are set in bold: "The Cypher query looks like this:

```
MATCH (d:Drug)<-[:HAS_DRUG]-()<-[:HAS_ENCOUNTER]-(p)
WITH DISTINCT d, p
WITH d.description as drug, count(p) as patients
WHERE patients > 100
RETURN drug, patients
```

Bold: Indicates a new term, an important word, or words that you see onscreen. For instance, words in menus or dialog boxes appear in **bold**. Here is an example: "In particular, the addition of a new **Encounter** node and the **HAS_END** relationship are a bit different from how we approach data in the RDBMS world."

> **Tips or important notes**
> Appear like this.

Get in touch

Feedback from our readers is always welcome.

General feedback: If you have questions about any aspect of this book, email us at customercare@packtpub.com and mention the book title in the subject of your message.

Errata: Although we have taken every care to ensure the accuracy of our content, mistakes do happen. If you have found a mistake in this book, we would be grateful if you would report this to us. Please visit www.packtpub.com/support/errata and fill in the form.

Piracy: If you come across any illegal copies of our works in any form on the internet, we would be grateful if you would provide us with the location address or website name. Please contact us at copyright@packt.com with a link to the material.

If you are interested in becoming an author: If there is a topic that you have expertise in and you are interested in either writing or contributing to a book, please visit authors.packtpub.com.

Share Your Thoughts

Once you've read *Graph Data Processing with Cypher*, we'd love to hear your thoughts! Scan the QR code below to go straight to the Amazon review page for this book and share your feedback.

https://packt.link/r/1-804-61107-7

Your review is important to us and the tech community and will help us make sure we're delivering excellent quality content.

Download a free PDF copy of this book

Thanks for purchasing this book!

Do you like to read on the go but are unable to carry your print books everywhere? Is your eBook purchase not compatible with the device of your choice?

Don't worry, now with every Packt book you get a DRM-free PDF version of that book at no cost.

Read anywhere, any place, on any device. Search, copy, and paste code from your favorite technical books directly into your application.

The perks don't stop there, you can get exclusive access to discounts, newsletters, and great free content in your inbox daily

Follow these simple steps to get the benefits:

1. Scan the QR code or visit the link below

https://packt.link/free-ebook/9781804611074

2. Submit your proof of purchase

3. That's it! We'll send your free PDF and other benefits to your email directly

Part 1:
Cypher Introduction

This part introduces you to Neo4j and the origins of Cypher. By the end of this part, you will be able to set up a Neo4j database and understand how Cypher is used to interact with the Neo4j database. It also introduces the core concepts of Cypher and graph databases.

This section comprises the following chapters:

- *Chapter 1, Introduction to Neo4j and Cypher*
- *Chapter 2, Components of Cypher*

1

Introduction to Neo4j and Cypher

Neo4j is the world's leading graph database. Its architecture is optimized to store, retrieve, and traverse graphs as nodes and relationships. It takes a property graph approach, which is beneficial for fast traversals and operations.

Neo4j uses Cypher as its query language, which makes it easy to represent traversals. Cypher is a declarative language for describing visual patterns in graphs using ASCII-art-like syntax. This makes it easy to read and comprehend how the data is connected as nodes and relationships in graphs.

In this chapter, we will cover the following topics:

- Introducing Neo4j and graph database concepts
- Installing the Neo4j Desktop
- A visual tour of Neo4j Desktop
- Using Neo4j Desktop
- Working with local DBMSs

If you are already familiar with these basic concepts and are comfortable using Neo4j Desktop and Browser, you can skip this chapter and move on to the next ones.

Technical requirements

You need a Windows, Mac, or Linux machine to be able to download and install Neo4j Desktop. Neo4j Desktop comes pre-packaged with all the required software dependencies.

Introducing Neo4j and graph database concepts

In this section, we will take a look at how data is stored as a graph in Neo4j. We will first introduce what a graph is, what a graph consists of, and how we can query graphs.

Neo4j uses a property graph data model to store the data. The following diagram shows a sample graph created in Neo4j:

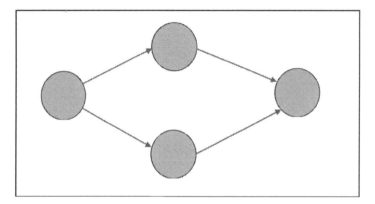

Figure 1.1 – Sample graph

Neo4j property graphs can consist of the following features:

- Nodes, which describe the entities of a domain.

- Nodes can have zero or more labels, but a node with no labels is not a normal occurrence. A node with multiple labels represents multiple facets that the node is part of. For example, a node that has labels such as **Employee** and **Manager** means this node is an employee who is also a manager.

- A relationship is a connection between two nodes.

- Relationships always have a direction, which is represented using an arrow symbol. The node at the starting point of the arrow is called the start node and the node at the end is called the target node.

- Relationships should have a type, which describes the relationship between the two nodes.

- Both nodes and relationships can have properties, which are key-value pairs.

Let's take a look at what nodes represent in a graph.

Understanding nodes in graphs

A **node** is used to represent an entity in the data domain. A sample node in an HR data domain might be as shown in the following figure:

Figure 1.2 – A node in a graph

This node represents a person in an HR data domain. It has two labels. A label can be thought of as something that describes what this node data represents. Here, the labels are **Employee** and **Manager**. This can be interpreted as the node representing an employee who is also a manager, with the **firstName**, **lastName**, and **joinDate** properties.

Let's take a look at what relationships represent in a graph.

Understanding relationships in graphs

A **relationship** describes how a source node and a target node are related. It is possible for a node to have a relationship with itself.

A relationship has the following aspects:

- It joins a **source node** and a **target node**, symbolizing the relationship between these nodes.
- It has a direction, which can be either incoming or outgoing. It represents the relationship direction of the nodes it is connecting.
- It has a **type**, which represents the nature of the connection between the nodes.
- It can have properties (key-value pairs), which further describe the relationship.

The following diagram represents relationships between employee nodes in HR data:

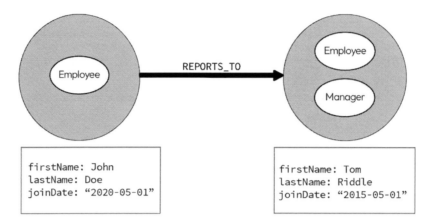

Figure 1.3 – Relationships between employee nodes

Figure 1.3 represents an employee named **John Doe** who reports to a manager named **Tom Riddle**. The REPORTS_TO string is the type of relationship between the two nodes. The direction of the relationship shows the direction of reporting structure. A relationship can also have properties that can further quantify the type of relationship between the two nodes.

Cypher

Nodes typically represent entities, such as concepts, events, places, and so on. Relationships connect the nodes that represent the context of how those two nodes are related. They can be considered as building blocks of the graph. The real strength of a property graph lies in its simplicity when it comes to representing and traversing patterns in graphs in an efficient manner.

Cypher is a query language based on graph traversal descriptions. These patterns are used to match the desired graph paths. When the matching pattern has been found, it can be used for further processing.

A simple pattern in Cypher is shown as follows:

```
(p:Person {name: "Tom"})-[:LIVES_IN]->
        (city:City {name: "Edison"})-[:PART_OF]->
        (country:Country {name: "United States"} )
```

The pattern here is self-explanatory and human-readable. A person named Tom lives in a city named Edison, which is a part of the country named the United States. You can see here that nouns represent the nodes and verbs represent the relationships.

We will take a deeper look at Cypher syntax in the coming chapters.

Installing Neo4j Desktop

Neo4j Desktop is a client application that makes it easy for developers to quickly start working with Neo4j databases. This makes it easier to set up and play with Neo4j databases, along with becoming familiar with other tools for developers. Neo4j Desktop allows the user to create multiple servers as needed and work with them in a seamless manner. This makes it easier to update the configuration of **DataBase Management Systems** (**DBMSs**), manage plugins, view the logs, backup and restore data, and upgrade the existing DBMS instances.

Downloading Neo4j Desktop

Neo4j Desktop can be downloaded from the Neo4j website, `https://neo4j.com/download/`.

The system requirements to install the Neo4j desktop are shown in the following table:

Software requirements:	
macOS	10.10 (Yosemite)
Ubuntu	12.04+
Fedora	21
Debian	8
Windows	8.1+, with PowerShell 5.1+

Figure 1.4 – System requirements for Neo4j Desktop

Neo4j comes bundled with Java 17, Java 11, and Java 8, along with Neo4j Browser and the Bloom visualization plugin.

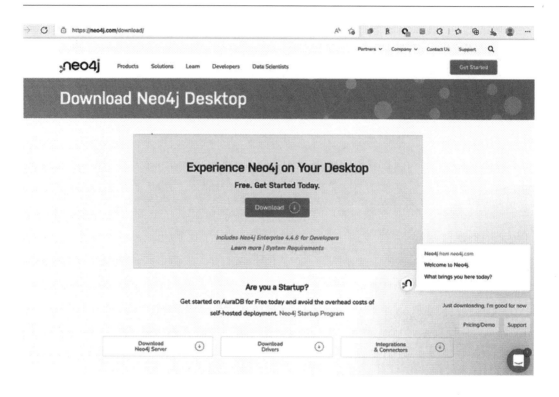

Figure 1.5 – Neo4j Desktop download

Next, follow the steps to download Neo4j Desktop:

1. Click on the **Download Desktop** button to register and download Neo4j Desktop. This will take you to the registration screen.

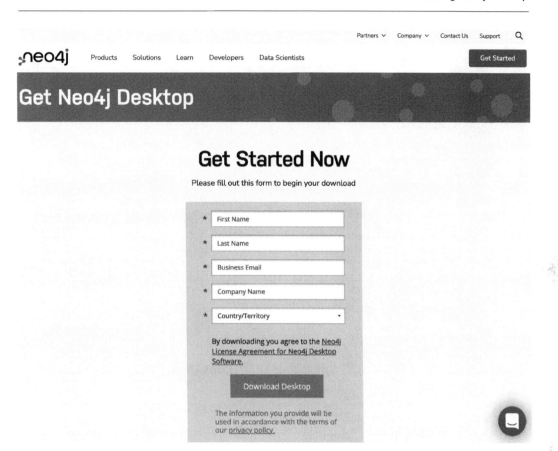

Figure 1.6 – User registration screen

2. Fill out the form with your details. You will need to register with an email to download. You will receive an activation key once registration is complete, as shown in the following figure. This activation key will also be emailed to the email address you have provided.

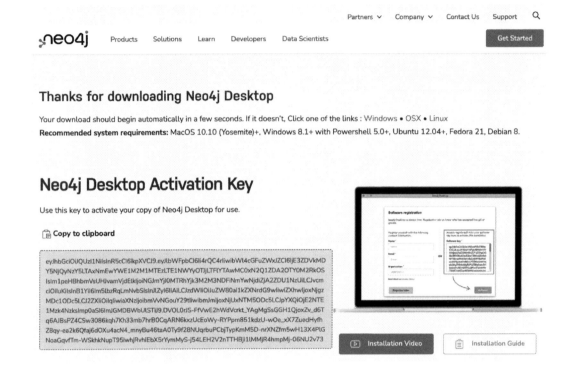

Figure 1.7 – Neo4j Desktop Activation Key

Now that we have downloaded the Neo4j Desktop binary and acquired the activation key, let us continue with installation.

The installation steps are as follows:

1.   Double-click on the downloaded file to start the installation.

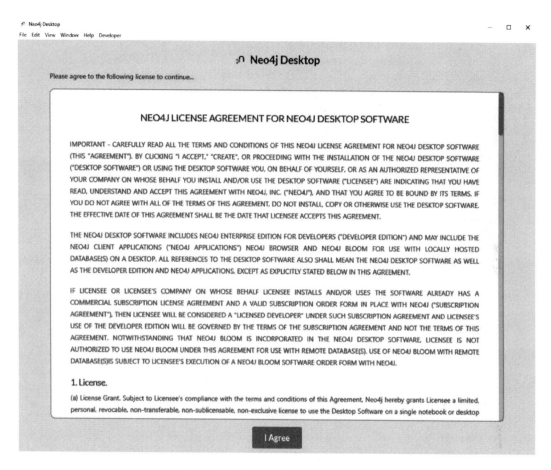

Figure 1.8 – End user license agreement

2. Accept the terms and conditions by clicking on the **I Agree** button. You are only asked to do this the first time Neo4j Desktop is installed.

Figure 1.9 – Selecting an installation location

3. Select the installation location and click **Confirm**.

Software registration

Neo4j Desktop is always free. Registration lets us know who has accepted this gift of graphs.

Register yourself with the following contact information.

Name *

> Name

Email *

> Email

Organization *

> Organization

Read about our privacy policy.

OR

Already registered? Add your software key here to activate this installation.

Software key *

> Software keys look like a long block of hexadecimal characters.

Register later

Activate

Figure 1.10 – Activating Desktop with a software key

4. Take the software key, paste it into the software key box, and click on **Activate**.

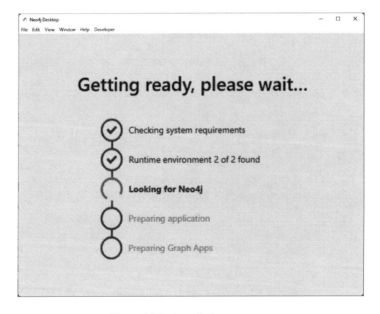

Figure 1.11 – Installation progress

Neo4j Desktop will continue setting up a first-time environment and creates a starter database when installation is complete. Neo4j Desktop is now ready for use.

A visual tour of Neo4j Desktop

Let's have a visual tour of the Neo4j Desktop. The following screenshot shows the screen after Neo4j Desktop has launched successfully. The arrows and text point to various sections of the Desktop UI. We will explore each of those sections shortly.

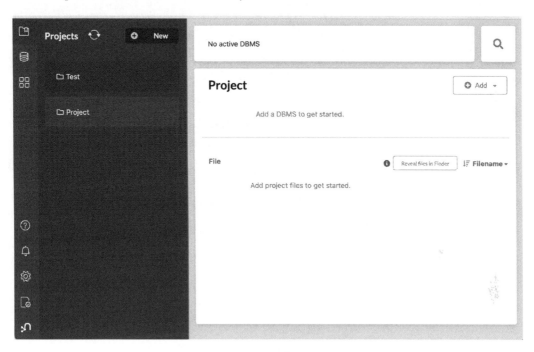

Figure 1.12 – Neo4j Desktop start screen

Let's move on to the **Projects** menu next.

Projects menu

A project in Neo4j Desktop is a representation of a development folder. You can create local database instances, known as DBMSs, or connect to remote DBMSs, and add files within your project. This allows you to manage multiple projects, and it is easy to move databases and files between different projects using the drag and drop method. At any given point in time, you can have only one active local DBMS or **remote connection**.

DBMSs menu

A DBMS is a Neo4j server instance that contains a minimum of the system database and a default database. When a DBMS is created, a default database named Neo4j is made. This can be renamed, or a new database can be created.

This screenshot shows all the versions of Neo4j servers that are available to create instances using Neo4j Desktop, along with how many instances of each version exist.

Figure 1.13 – DBMSs menu

Neo4j Desktop includes a free Neo4j Enterprise license for developers to explore all the enterprise capabilities, such as multiple databases, role-based access controls, and so on.

Graph applications

When you click on the graph applications icon in Neo4j Desktop, it will show a list of the graph applications installed.

The following figure shows the graph applications that are available in Neo4j Desktop:

Figure 1.14 – Graph applications

Neo4j Desktop comes with the Neo4j Browser and Bloom applications pre-packaged to help you interact with graphs.

When you click on **Graph Apps Gallery**, it will take you to the site to explore and install other graph apps.

Help menu

When the help menu is clicked, Neo4j Desktop shows all the forms of help available, as shown in the following screenshot:

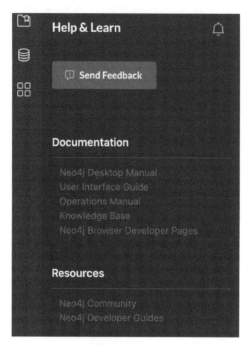

Figure 1.15 – Help menu

This section contains the links for Neo4j documentation and resources for developers.

Settings menu

When you click on the settings menu icon, Neo4j Desktop shows the menu that controls Neo4j Desktop operations. The following figure shows which aspects of Neo4j Desktop users can control and change.

Figure 1.16 – Application settings menu

Users can control whether to send crash reports and usage statistics to Neo4j. If **Store DBMS passwords** is checked, then the user ID and passwords are stored securely, so that you don't need to enter them every time the Neo4j server is restarted.

In some enterprise environments, you might have to configure a proxy for Neo4j Desktop to be able to go to the internet to download updates and install graph apps and the latest Neo4j server software.

Now that we have talked about the UI control elements of Neo4j Desktop, the next section will discuss using these elements to create a Neo4j instance and manage it.

Using Neo4j Desktop

In this section, we will take a look at how we can use Neo4j Desktop to create a Neo4j instance and manage it.

Creating a local DBMS

Let's go through the steps to create a local DBMS:

1. To create a local DBMS, a project should be created and selected.

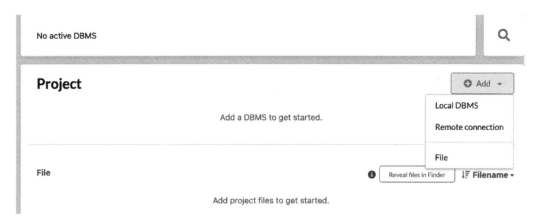

Figure 1.17 – Creating a local DBMS

2. Click on the **Add** button and select **Local DBMS** to create a local DBMS instance.

Figure 1.18 – Select the Neo4j version

3. You can change the name from **Graph DBMS** to anything that makes sense. You will need to provide a password. This would be the password for the Neo4j admin user.

4. In the **Version** dropdown, Neo4j Desktop shows the latest downloaded version as the selected one and, if there are newer versions, they are also shown in the dropdown with a download icon next to them. This means this version is not available locally and needs to be downloaded. If you would like to use any of those versions, then click on the download icon. This will download that version of the Neo4j software before creating the local DBMS instance.

5. Once the required version is selected, click the **Create** button to create the local instance.

Next, we will take a look at how we can manage the instance we have created.

Managing a local DBMS instance

Once we have created the local database instance, we can then manage that instance. We can start/stop the instance, change the configuration, and add plugins. Here, we will take a look at how to manage the local Neo4j instance we created.

Reviewing DBMS details

Once the instance is created, an entry is shown in the selected project. The following screenshot shows the instance details:

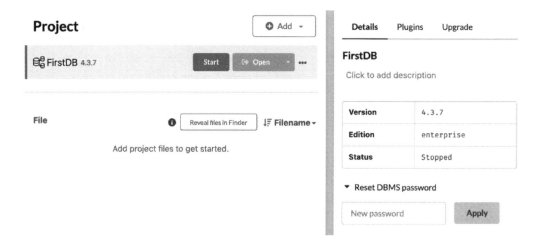

Figure 1.19 – Local instance details

When you click on the name of the instance, it shows the details on the right-hand side. The description box can be used to add details about this DBMS instance. If you need to change the password, it can be done under the **Reset DBMS password** option.

Managing DBMS plugins

For this instance, we can add or remove plugins. To do this, click on the **Plugins** tab. It displays all the installed plugins and the available plugins to install. The following screenshot captures this aspect:

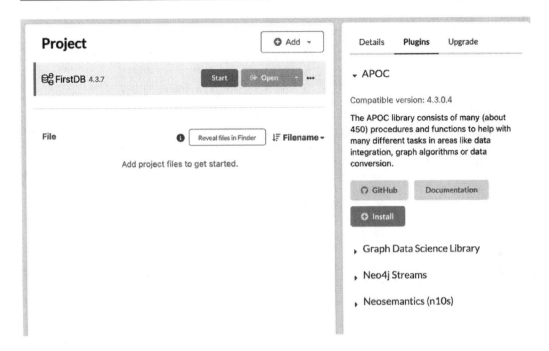

Figure 1.20 – Plugins installation

The list of the plugins available is dependent on the version of the Neo4j instance. When you click on the name of the plugin, it shows the details of that plugin and any related links. You can click on the **Install** button to install a plugin. Neo4j Desktop will install the plugin and make the required changes to the server configuration.

Upgrading the server

It is possible to upgrade the version of the instance we have created. When you click on the **Upgrade** tab, it shows the options available. The following screenshot captures this aspect:

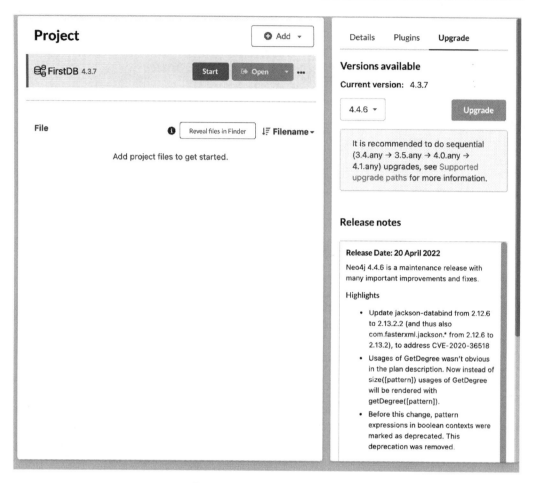

Figure 1.21 – Upgrade options

Here, you will find a dropdown of all possible versions of this instance that can be upgraded. When a version is selected, the release notes for that version are shown. By clicking the **Upgrade** button, you can upgrade the selected DBMS instance.

Working with a local DBMS

This section discusses how you can work with a local **Database Management System** (**DBMS**) instance. We can perform multiple operations on an instance. We can start a stopped instance and once an instance is started, we can launch the browser and work with the database instance.

Starting the instance

When an instance is selected in a project, it will show the buttons to start the instance. The following screenshot showcases this:

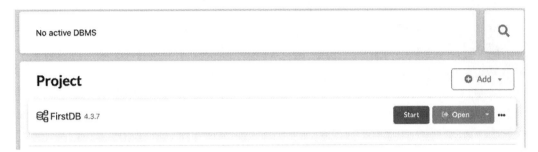

Figure 1.22 – Starting the instance

Click on the **Start** button to start the instance.

Opening the browser

When the instance is available to query, the **Open** button will be activated. The following screenshot demonstrates this:

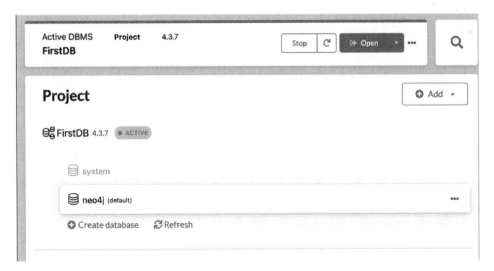

Figure 1.23 – Opening the browser

Click on the **Open** button to open the browser. If you need to create another database, you can use the **Create Database** button to create a new database on this instance. By default, a database named neo4j will be created.

Working with the browser's UI

The browser looks as shown in the following screenshot. It can be used to query the database.

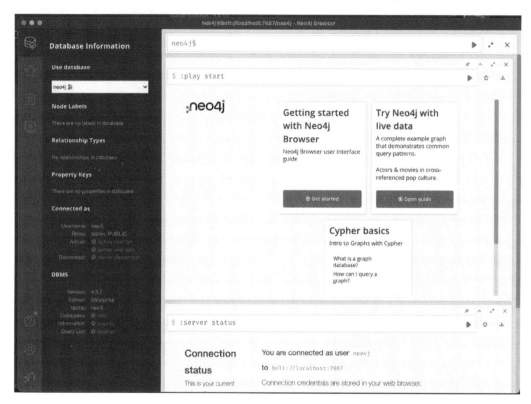

Figure 1.24 – Neo4j Browser

The Neo4j Browser interface is used to execute Cypher queries against a database:

1. On the left side of the Neo4j Browser interface, you can see the database details. The dropdown shows the active database that is selected. It can be changed by clicking on the dropdown and selecting the required database.

2. Below the dropdown, you can see the number of nodes, node labels, relationships, relationship types, and property types. You can click on the name of the node labels or relationship types to sample data.

3. Below the database stats section, there are the current user details and user management shortcuts to create, update, or delete local users. It also gives a shortcut to disconnect from DBMS.

4. The **DBMS** section shows the current DBMS version and shortcut links to get the DBMS details, such as a list of databases available, current queries being executed, and system information.

The query area is where Cypher queries are written. Click on the blue arrow to execute the query. The results will be shown below the query area.

Using Browser help

To get help with browser usage, you can enter `:help` in the query area. Neo4j Browser will show all the commands available with descriptions, as shown by the following figure:

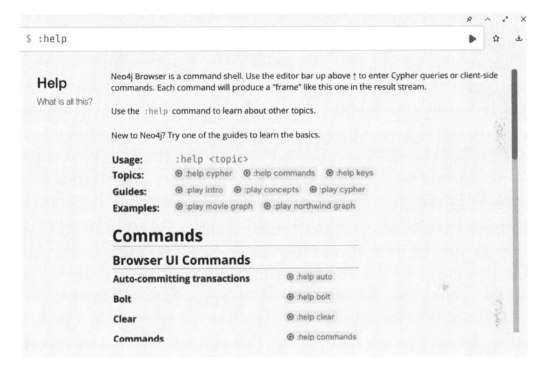

Figure 1.25 – Browser help

If you scroll down, you will see links for various guides for sample graphs to play with. When you click on the link, you get a guided tour of content that the user can follow by clicking along the way. Here are some sample graph concepts and Cypher guides to illustrate how it works:

Figure 1.26 – Graph concepts

The graph concepts guide provides basic concepts for the user to review before working with Cypher. For new graph database users, this would be a very valuable guide to follow to review the basic concepts.

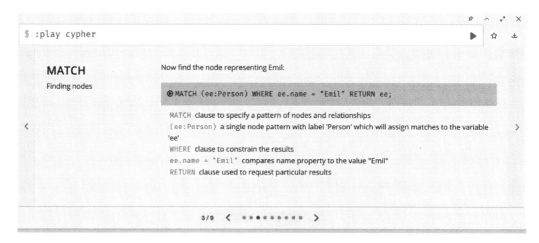

Figure 1.27 – Cypher help

The Cypher help guide introduces keywords and the basic usage of building queries using these keywords. For new users, this provides a good introduction to Cypher in a quick and clean fashion.

Next, we will take a look at the administrative aspect of the local instance.

Working with additional options to manage local DBMS

We will take a look at administrative and filesystem aspects in this section. When you click on the ... icon, it shows a drop-down menu displaying the additional options available, as shown in the following screenshot:

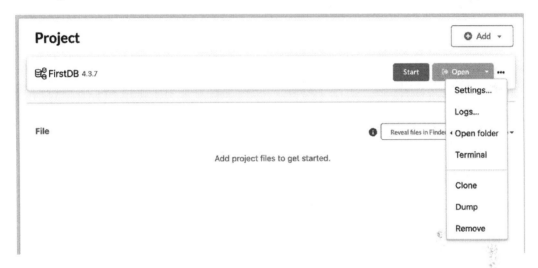

Figure 1.28 – Additional options to manage an instance

As you can see, it provides options to manage the settings, see the logs, look at the folder system where the instance is available, see the terminal, and so on.

Managing settings

When you click on **Settings**, it brings up the settings UI to view and modify the settings for this instance.

Figure 1.29 – Neo4j instance settings

When you modify the settings, the **Apply** button at the bottom will become activated and an **Undo** button will appear. When you click the **Apply** button, it will update the server configuration and restart the instance so that these configurations are applied. The **Undo** button will undo only the latest changes made. When you click on **Reset to defaults**, it will reset all the configuration values to the original defaults and restart the server.

Viewing logs

When you click on **Logs**, you will be faced with the system log window, as shown in the following screenshot:

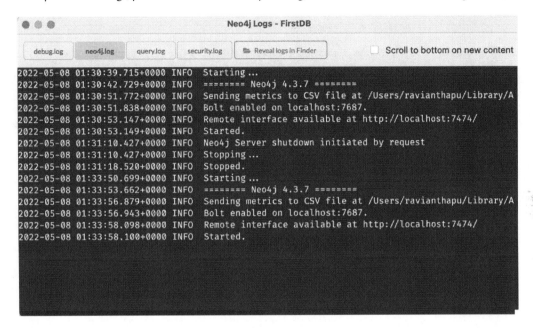

Figure 1.30 – Instance log

There are four different logs are provided by Neo4j, and they are as follows:

1. By default, you get neo4j.log. This is the basic system log. You can click on the filenames at the top to see debug.log, query.log, or security.log.

2. debug.log contains detailed information to help you troubleshoot the server.

3. query.log contains the queries issued against the server.

4. security.log contains the authentication-related logging details.

5. When you click on **Reveal logs in Finder**, it opens up the finder window or file explorer window, so that you can use other text or log reader utilities to read the files.

Opening the Neo4j Desktop terminal

When you click **Terminal** menu item, you get a terminal or command-line window with the directory changed to the location of the DBMS instance.

```
bash-3.2$ pwd
/Users/ravianthapu/Library/Application Support/com.Neo4j.Relate/Data/dbmss/dbms-73eeb
136-3163-4caa-b3d5-9f23dc72c812
bash-3.2$ ▊
```

Neo4j Desktop Terminal - FirstDB

Figure 1.31 – Local DBMS instance terminal window

You can do almost all the things that we've been using the UI to do in the terminal. You can edit a configuration, see logs, and start/stop an instance.

Opening the folder

When you click on **Open Folder** menu item, you'll see a submenu:

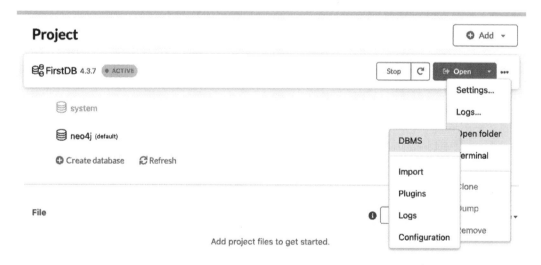

Figure 1.32 – Local DBMS instance file explorer

Depending on which submenu is selected, you will get a finder or file explorer navigated to the root of the installation directory or any of the other sub-directories that are selected. The following screenshot shows the root directory file window:

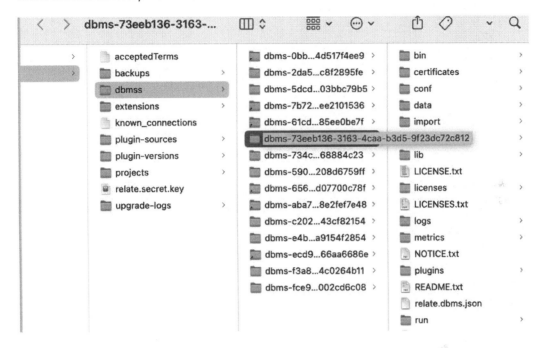

Figure 1.33 – Local DBMS instance root directory

When you select any of the sub-menu items, such as **import**, **plugins** ,**logs**, or **configuration**, it will navigate directly to the **import**, **logs**, **plugins**, or **conf** directory.

Summary

In this chapter, we have covered the process of downloading and installing Neo4j Desktop. We have explored how to activate it by registering with Neo4j, explored the UI in detail, and learned how to create projects and local databases, as well as how to manage a database by changing the configuration or adding/removing plugins. We also explored how to use Neo4j Browser self-help guides to review graph database concepts or to learn Cypher. Finally, we looked at database configuration and log exploration using the command line or file explorer.

We connected to a local instance using Neo4j Browser to start writing queries. With this setup, we should be able to start building Cypher queries to talk to a Neo4j database.

If you would like to learn more about Neo4j Desktop, Neo4j Browser, or available plugins, you can go to `http://neo4j.com/docs` to find more details.

In the next chapter, we will take a detailed look at Cypher fundamentals and keywords to understand how we can use Cypher to work with the instances we create.

2

Components of Cypher

Cypher is a declarative query language that makes it easy to write expressive and efficient queries to traverse, update, and administer a graph database. It provides a powerful way to express even complex graph traversals more simply so that you can concentrate on the domain aspects of your query instead of worrying about syntax.

Cypher expands upon a variety of established practices for querying. For example, the **WHERE**, **ORDER BY**, and **CASE** keywords are inspired by SQL syntax. Some of the list semantics are borrowed from Haskell and Python.

This chapter introduces the Cypher syntax with some examples. We will review the important aspects of the Cypher syntax and semantics in building graph traversal queries. We will discuss important keywords and the role they play in building the queries. We will take a look at the graph data model and how Cypher queries follow the data connections.

In this chapter, we will cover these aspects:

- Graph storage in Neo4j
- Using the Cypher syntax
- Using the nodes syntax
- Using the relationships syntax
- Working with Cypher keywords

Technical requirements

We should have Neo4j Desktop installed and have created a local instance. There are no special technical skills required to follow the concepts discussed in this chapter. Having knowledge of SQL can be useful in understanding Cypher, but is not required.

Graph storage in Neo4j

Before we look into the Cypher syntax to query the data, it is important to understand how the data is persisted as a graph. Data diagram representations give a good idea about how the Cypher queries can be written using the data model. We will take a look at a data diagram and see how it helps us with querying:

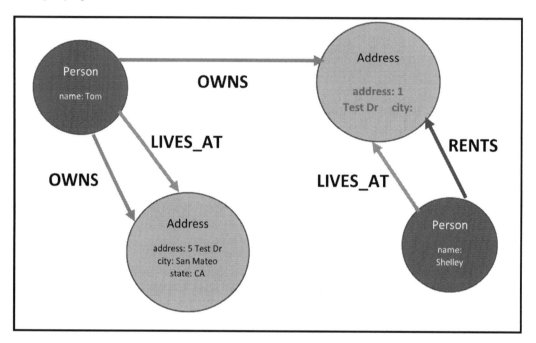

Figure 2.1 – Sample graph data diagram

This diagram shows how the data is stored in the database. Each node represents one entity that knows what relationship entities it is connected to and whether they are incoming or outgoing; each property is an entity that is associated with a node or relationship. Each relationship entity knows what nodes it is connected to and the direction of the relationship.

The preceding diagram tells us that a person named Tom owns two addresses. This person lives at one address and rents the other one. A person named Shelley lives at an address that is rented. If you read this diagram from the address perspective, it can be seen that the **1 Test Dr** address is owned by **Tom** and is rented by **Shelley**, and the **5 Test Dr** address is owned by **Tom** who also lives at that address.

If the preceding data diagram were represented as a graph data model, it would look like this:

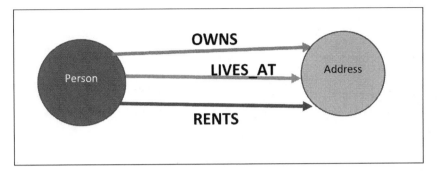

Figure 2.2 – Sample graph data model

This diagram shows what possible relationships can exist between given node types. In real data, these relationships need not exist for all nodes. A graph data model shows how the data can be connected and can provide a starting point for building graph traversals using Cypher queries.

Using the Cypher syntax

Cypher is like **American Standard Code for Information Interchange** (**ASCII**) art. A simple Cypher traversal query can look like this:

```
(A)-[:LIKES]->(B),  (B)-[:LIKES]->(C),  (A)-[:LIKES]->(C)
```

This also can be written as follows:

```
(A)-[:LIKES]->(B)-[:LIKES]->(C)<-[:LIKES]-(A)
```

If you notice the syntax, it reads more like a simple statement. A likes B, who likes C, who is also liked by A. Nouns represent nodes and verbs represent relationships.

Cypher supports various data types, which fall into three different categories.

Property types

The following are the different property types available in Cypher:

- Number:

  - Integer

  - Float

- String
- Boolean
- Spatial:

  - Point

- Temporal:

  - Date
  - Time
  - LocalTime
  - DateTime
  - LocalDateTime
  - Duration

Property types can have the following characteristics.

- Can be a part of data returned by queries
- Can be used as input parameters
- Can be stored as properties on nodes or relationships

Let's move on to the structural types available in Cypher.

Structural types

The following are the different structural types:

- Node
- Relationship
- Path

Let's now move on to the composite types.

Composite types

The following are the different composite types:

- List
- Map

Now that we have reviewed the basic syntax of Cypher queries and property types, let's look at the nodes syntax.

Using the nodes syntax

In Cypher, a node is surrounded by parentheses, `()`, making it resemble a circle in a diagram. Here are some example usages in Cypher:

- `(p)` – This represents a node identified with the p variable/alias. It can be of any type.
- `()` – This represents a node that is not assigned a variable or an alias. This is normally called an anonymous node, as it cannot be referenced later, except as part of a path.
- `(:Person)` – This represents a node with the `Person` label, but is not assigned to a variable or an alias.
- `(p:Person)` – This represents a node with a `Person` label, identified with the p variable/alias.
- `(l:Location:Work)` – This represents a node with multiple labels, `Location` and `Work`, identified with the l variable/alias.

Let's move on to the relationships syntax.

Using the relationships syntax

In Cypher, a relationship can be represented using `-->`, which resembles an arrow on a diagram. Here are some example usages in Cypher:

- `(p)-[:LIVES_AT]->(a)` – This represents that the node identified by p is connected to another node, a, with a `LIVES_AT` relationship type. The direction of the relationship is from p to a.
- `(p)-[r]->(a)` – This represents that the node identified by p is connected to another node, a, with the direction of the relationship going from p to a. They can be connected via any relationship type. The relationship is assigned to the r variable/alias.
- `(p)<-[r]-(a)` – This represents that the node identified by p is connected to another node, a, with the direction of the relationship going from a to p. The nodes can be connected via any relationship type and the relationship is assigned to the r variable/alias.
- `(p)-[r]-(a)` – This represents that the node identified by p is connected to another node, a, with the direction of the relationship going either from p to a or from a to p. The nodes can be connected via any relationship type and the relationship is assigned to the r variable/alias.
- `(p)-->(a)` – This represents that the node identified by p is connected to another node, a, with the direction of the relationship going from p to a. The nodes can be connected via any relationship type. The relationship itself is not associated with any variable or alias. This is called an anonymous relationship.

Now that we have taken a look at the Cypher syntax and data types available, we will take a look at the keywords available in Cypher to build the queries.

Working with Cypher keywords

In this section, we will introduce the Cypher keywords and their syntax. Detailed usage of these keywords will be covered in upcoming sections of the book.

Let us start by using the MATCH and OPTIONAL MATCH keywords.

Using MATCH and OPTIONAL MATCH

The MATCH keyword allows you to specify the graph traversal patterns to find and return the data from Neo4j. It is most often coupled with a WHERE clause to filter out the results, and a RETURN clause to return the results.

- This shows a basic MATCH query that will find all nodes in the database and return them. It will also return all the node properties shown as follows:

```
MATCH (n)
RETURN n
```

- This query finds all the nodes that have the Movie label and returns the title property of that node. If there are no nodes with the Movie label, it does not return any results:

```
MATCH (n:Movie)
RETURN n.title
```

- This query finds any node that has the title property, checks whether its value is My Movie, and if so, returns a property named released. You can see here that there is no label mentioned in the query. This means we are looking at all the nodes that have the title property:

```
MATCH (n {title: 'My Movie' } )
RETURN n.released
```

> **Caution**
>
> This is the most common mistake made in the early phases of learning Cypher. This query can cause a lot of issues to the DB server and should be avoided. We will discuss this more in the later sections.

- The following query will behave the same as the previous one. The only difference here is that the query is using an explicit WHERE condition, whereas the earlier query is using an implicit WHERE condition:

```
MATCH (n)
WHERE n.title = 'My Movie'
RETURN n.released
```

The OPTIONAL MATCH clause works similarly to MATCH with the exception that when there is no data matching the pattern specified, it will not stop the execution and returns null as result. In SQL terms, you can think of it like LEFT JOIN.

Let's go through a few OPTIONAL MATCH clause examples below:

- This query returns data only if the database has nodes with the Movie label:

```
MATCH (n:Movie)
RETURN n.title
```

- This query will return at least a single value. If there are nodes with the Movie label, then the title property of those nodes is returned. If there are no Movie nodes, then a null value is returned:

```
OPTIONAL MATCH (n:Movie)
RETURN n.title
```

The MATCH clause will stop the query execution and returns no results if any of the MATCH segments do not return data. OPTIONAL MATCH will continue the next steps and return the data.

The following queries explain that behavior:

- If the database does not contain nodes with Movie or Person labels, then this query will not return any results. If nodes with these labels are present, then you will see a Cartesian product of those values:

```
MATCH (m:Movie)
MATCH (p:Person)
RETURN m.title, p.name
```

- In this query, if there are no nodes with the Movie label, then no results are returned. If the Movie nodes do exist but there are no nodes with the Person label, then the query would still return the results with p.name as null for each row:

```
MATCH (m:Movie)
OPTIONAL MATCH (p:Person)
RETURN m.title, p.name
```

- In this query, if no nodes with the Movie or Person labels exist, then a single row with null values is returned. If there are nodes with either a Movie or Person label, then the Cartesian product of those node values is returned:

```
OPTIONAL MATCH (m:Movie)
OPTIONAL MATCH (p:Person)
RETURN m.title, p.name
```

- This query shows the syntax of how you can traverse a path and return values of interest. If you notice here, we are accessing the Movie node as an anonymous node as we are not returning its values. We are starting from the Movie node and traversing the incoming ACTED_IN relationship and returning the names of the nodes it is connected to:

```
MATCH (:Movie {title:'Wall Street'})<-[:ACTED_IN]-(actor)
RETURN actor.name
```

Let us continue with creating and deleting data from the graph using the CREATE and DELETE keywords.

Using CREATE and DELETE

The CREATE clause will let you create new nodes and relationships:

- This query creates a node with the Person label and a name property and returns the node:

```
CREATE (p:Person {name: 'Tom'})
RETURN p
```

- This query creates a node without a label but with a property called name, and returns the node:

```
CREATE (p {name: 'Tom'})
RETURN p
```

> **Caution**
>
> This is another common mistake. In Neo4j, labels are optional. By using this query, we create nodes without any labels, and querying for them would be very inefficient.

- This query creates a node with the Person label and a name property with the value of Tom. It has a node with the Address label, and properties of city with the value of New York and country with the value of USA, and a relationship named LIVES_AT between these nodes:

```
CREATE (p:Person {name:'Tom'})
-[:LIVES_AT]->
(:Address {city:'New York', country:'USA'})
```

> **Note**
>
> This query does not have a RETURN clause. For CREATE statements, RETURN is optional.

We will look at the usage of DELETE next:

- The DELETE clause will let you delete nodes and relationships. This query finds a Person node named Tom and deletes it from the database. This can fail if this node has any relationships:

```
MATCH (p:Person {name: 'Tom'})
DELETE p
```

This query finds a Person node with the name Tom and deletes the node and all the relationships this node is attached to from the database.

```
MATCH (p:Person {name:'Tom'})
DETACH DELETE p
```

This query deletes all the relationships with the LIVES_AT type for the Person node with the name Tom, keeping the node as it is.

```
MATCH (:Person {name:'Tom'})-[r:LIVES_AT]->()
DELETE r
```

> **Caution**
>
> If the node is connected to many relationships, this can have a negative impact on the database. We will discuss options to do this safely in the upcoming sections.

This query deletes all the nodes and relationships in the database.

```
MATCH (n)
DETACH DELETE n
```

> **Caution**
>
> Depending on how much data is in the database, this query can cause *Out of Memory* exceptions. We will discuss options for safe bulk deletion in the upcoming sections.

Let us continue with manipulating properties on nodes and relationships using the SET and REMOVE keywords.

SET and REMOVE

The SET clause allows us to set the properties or labels on a node or set the properties on relationships. It can be used in conjunction with the MATCH or CREATE clauses:

- This query finds the Person node named Tom and sets the age to 20:

```
MATCH (n:Person {name:'Tom'})
SET n.age = 20
```

- This query finds the `Person` node named `Tom` and adds the additional label, `Actor`, to it:

```
MATCH (n:Person {name:'Tom'})
SET n:Actor
```

- This query finds the `Person` nodes named `Tom` and `Joe` and copies the properties from Tom to Joe:

```
MATCH (n:Person {name:'Tom'})
MATCH (o:Person {name:'Joe'})
SET o=n
```

The REMOVE clause is used to remove or delete properties from nodes or relationships. It can also remove labels from nodes:

- This query finds a `Person` node that has the `Actor` label and is named `Tom` and removes the `Actor` label from the node:

```
MATCH (n:Person:Actor {name:'Tom'})
REMOVE n:Actor
```

- This query finds the `Person` node named `Tom` and removes the `age` property from the node:

```
MATCH (n:Person {name:'Tom'})
REMOVE n.age
```

Let us continue with filtering data using WHERE and other keywords.

Using WHERE, SKIP, LIMIT, and ORDER BY

The WHERE clause is how we can use filter the data in Cypher. Cypher provides options for both an implicit WHERE qualifier and an explicit WHERE clause:

- This is an implicit WHERE usage in Cypher. This makes our query read more like an English statement. One limitation of this usage is that it can only be used for exact property matches. It cannot be used with range checking or Boolean expressions:

```
MATCH (n:Person {name:'Tom'})
RETURN n.age
```

In explicit WHERE usage, you get a lot more control over the expressions:

- We can see in this query how a complex Boolean expression can be used in the WHERE clause. All the Boolean operators, such as OR, AND, NOT, and XOR, are supported. Also, this query uses alias names for the returned values using the AS keyword:

```
MATCH (n:Person)
WHERE
    n.name = 'Peter'
    XOR (n.age < 30 AND n.name = 'Timothy')
    OR NOT (n.name = 'Timothy' OR n.name = 'Peter')
RETURN
  n.name AS name,
  n.age AS age
```

- This query shows how to filter nodes using a label. It is returning all nodes that are labeled Swedish. The second one shows another way to write the same query:

```
// Explicit WHERE label check
MATCH (n)
WHERE n:Swedish
RETURN n.name, n.age
// Implicit WHERE label check. Most common usage
MATCH (n:Swedish)
RETURN n.name, n.age
```

- The following queries show how to use range values in the WHERE clause. The first query is to find all the Person nodes whose age is less than 50. The second query is to find all the Person nodes whose age is between 30 and 60:

```
// Range query with less than a value
MATCH (n:Person)
WHERE n.age < 50
RETURN n.name, n.age
// Range query with in between values
MATCH (n:Person)
WHERE 30 < n.age < 60
RETURN n.name, n.age
// This query shows how to check for property
// existence. This finds all Person nodes which have
// title property.
```

```
MATCH (n:Person)
WHERE n.title IS NOT NULL
RETURN n.name, n.title
```

- This query shows all the `Person` nodes that do not have the `title` property and returns the names of those nodes:

```
MATCH (n:Person)
WHERE n.title IS NULL
RETURN n.name
```

- You can use a `WHERE` clause on relationships also. The first query shows the explicit usage of a `WHERE` clause. The second query shows the implicit usage of a `WHERE` clause. The usage is the same as with node properties:

```
// Explict WHERE condition
MATCH (n:Person)
    -[k:KNOWS]->(f)
WHERE k.since < 2000
RETURN f.name
// Implicit WHERE condition
MATCH (n:Person)
   -[k:KNOWS {since: 2000}]->(f)
 RETURN f.name
```

- This query shows how to use string operations in the `WHERE` clause. This query finds all `Person` nodes whose name starts with `Tom`. The other available string operators are `ENDS WITH` and `CONTAINS`:

```
MATCH (n:Person)
WHERE n.name STARTS WITH 'Tom'
RETURN n.name, n.age
```

- These queries show the usage of regular expressions in a `WHERE` clause. The second query shows how to escape the patterns in regular expressions:

```
MATCH (n:Person)
WHERE n.email =~ '.*\\.com'
RETURN n.name, n.age, n.email
```

- If you want to have case-insensitive regular expressions, you can prepend the regular expression with `(?i)`. This query can return a `Person` node named `Andy`, and so on:

```
MATCH (n:Person)
WHERE n.name =~ '(?i)ANDY.*'
RETURN n.name, n.age
```

- This query shows how you can use path expressions in the `WHERE` clause. This query finds the `Person` node Tom, and Andy and/or Bob who are connected to Tom; it returns the ages of Andy and/or Bob. This query also shows the usage of the `IN` operator with a list of possible values:

```
MATCH
    (tom:Person {name: 'Tom'}),
    (other:Person)
WHERE
    other.name IN ['Andy', 'Bob']
        AND (other)→(tom)
RETURN other.name, other.age
```

- This query uses a pattern with a `NOT` expression. This query returns the names and ages of all `Person` nodes who are not connected to `Tom` via an outgoing relationship:

```
MATCH
    (person:Person),
    (tom:Person {name: 'Tom'})
WHERE NOT (person)-->(tom)
RETURN person.name, person.age
```

- This query shows how we can use the `WHERE` clause to find all outgoing relationships for Tom that start with C:

```
MATCH (n:Person)-[r]->()
WHERE n.name='Tom' AND type(r) =' 'C.*'
RETURN type( r ), r.since
```

> **Note**
>
> While this is valid syntax, its usage should be limited, as it may lead to non-performant queries. It should be limited to scenarios where you might not know all existing relationship names or relationship names can be dynamic.

In WHERE clauses, you can also use existential subqueries. The syntax of these queries looks like this:

```
EXISTS {
  MATCH [Pattern]
  WHERE [Expression]
}
```

This allows you to specify a subquery as an expression. The WHERE clause in the subquery is optional, shown as follows.

- This query finds all Person nodes that have a HAS_DOG relationship connected to a Dog node:

```
MATCH (person:Person)
WHERE EXISTS {
      MATCH (person)-[:HAS_DOG]->(:Dog)
  }
RETURN person.name AS name
```

- This query returns the names of every Person who has a HAS_DOG relationship connected to a Dog node, further specifying that the person and dog have the same name:

```
MATCH (person:Person)
WHERE EXISTS {
      MATCH (person)-[:HAS_DOG]->(dog:Dog)
      WHERE person.name = dog.name
}
RETURN person.name AS name
```

Existential subqueries can also be nested.

Let us continue manipulating data using the MERGE keyword.

Using MERGE

A MERGE clause is an upsert operation. It will check for the existence of the node or path and if it doesn't exist, it tries to create the node or path as applicable:

- This query creates a Person node if one does not already exist:

```
MERGE (p:Person)
RETURN p
```

> **Note**
>
> Remember this creates only one node. When you run this multiple times, it does not create multiple nodes.
>
> The MERGE operation is not thread-safe. If you run the same query in parallel in multiple threads, it can create multiple nodes. To avoid this, you should use constraints.

MERGE is often used to make sure we do not create duplicate nodes and relationships in the database:

- This query makes sure there is only one Person node that exists in the database named Tom and aged 30. This is the most common usage of the MERGE clause. You should try to use the node primary key values only with the MERGE statement:

```
MERGE (p:Person {name: 'Tom', age: 30})
RETURN p
```

At runtime, a MERGE statement lets us know whether a new node is being created or whether a handle to an existing node is returned. We can identify these scenarios using ON CREATE and ON MATCH clauses in conjunction with a MERGE clause. Both of those clauses are optional:

- If a Person node for Tom did not exist when the query was executed, a created property is set to the current timestamp. If the node did already exist (i.e., was created earlier), the updated property of the node is set to the current timestamp:

```
MERGE (p:Person {name: 'Tom', age: 30})
ON CREATE
SET     p.created = timestamp()
ON MATCH
SET     p.updated = timestamp()
RETURN p
```

- This query does the following:

  - Checks whether the person named Tom exists

  - Checks whether the person named Andy exists

  - Checks whether there is a KNOWS relationship between them

  If any of these conditions is false, it will create a Person node named Tom, a Person node named Andy, and a KNOWS relationship between those nodes. The MERGE clause will try to create the whole path as it is provided. It is immaterial whether a Person node named Tom or Andy already exists. If you had a unique constraint on the name and if any of the nodes already existed, then this query would fail with a constraint error. If all the conditions are `false` or all of them `true`, then there won't be any error:

```
MERGE (tom:Person {name: 'Tom'})
  -[:KNOWS]->
      (andy:Person {name: 'Andy'})
```

- If you had a `name` unique constraint on the `Person` node, then this approach would not raise any errors.

  This query follows these steps:

  - If a person named `Tom` does not exist, it creates a `Person` node

  - If a person named `Andy` does not exist, it creates a `Person` node

  - If there is no `KNOWS` relationship between these `Person` nodes, then it creates one:

```
MERGE (tom:Person {name: 'Tom'})
MERGE (andy:Person {name: 'Andy'})
MERGE (tom)-[:KNOWS]->(andy)
```

For the `MERGE` clause, if you pass a variable as part of the path, it will not try to recreate that node.

> **Note**
>
> You should be very careful with `MERGE` to make sure you do not create multiple nodes and relationships. For that, you should understand `PATH MERGE` as explained previously to make sure you do not get errors with `MERGE` statements or create duplicated nodes. Also, note that the `MERGE` clause cannot be used with an explicit `WHERE` clause.

Let us continue with iterating the lists using the `FOREACH` keyword.

Using FOREACH

A `FOREACH` clause will let you iterate over a list of values and perform write operations using `CREATE`, `MERGE`, `DELETE`, `SET`, or `REMOVE` clauses. You cannot use a `MATCH` clause within a `FOREACH` clause:

- Assuming `nodesList` contains a list of nodes, this query will iterate over each node and set its marked property to `true`:

```
FOREACH (
  n in nodesList |
  SET n.marked = true
)
```

Let us continue with other means of iterating the lists using `UNWIND`.

Using UNWIND

An UNWIND clause converts a list into rows so that each entry can be processed:

- When you run this query, you will get four rows in the response, as shown here:

```
WITH [1,2,3,4] as list
UNWIND list as x
RETURN x
```

Let's visualize the output:

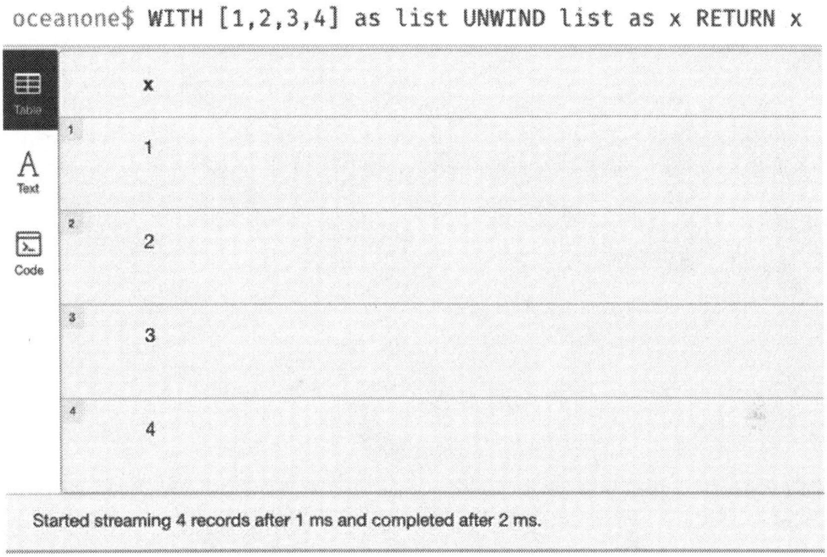

Figure 2.3 – UNWIND usage

Most of the time, an UNWIND clause is used to load batches of data into Neo4j. An example usage of this is shown next.

- This query takes a list of event maps and processes one map at a time to create year and event nodes based on the data in the map. If the list contains 100 records, then the highlighted section is executed once per record – a total of 100 times:

```
UNWIND $events AS event
MERGE (y:Year {year: event.year})
MERGE (y)<-[:IN]-(e:Event {id: event.id})
RETURN e.id AS x ORDER BY x
```

> **Note**
>
> As mentioned, this is the most common pattern used to load data in batches from a client. Also, you can notice here a PATH MERGE operation.

Next, let us take a look at returning data from queries using RETURN and other keywords, such as WITH, RETURN, ORDER BY, SKIP, and LIMIT.

A WITH clause allows queries to be chained together, making sure that the results from one query are piped to the next as starting data points for the next query.

A RETURN clause is the last part of the query.

ORDER BY, SKIP, and LIMIT clauses can be used with either WITH or RETURN clauses:

- In this query, we start with the Person node named Tom and all the Person nodes he knows, filter those nodes using a WITH clause to those whose name starts with An, and return the name and age of those persons ordered by age in descending order:

```
MATCH (tom:Person {name: 'Tom'})
    -[:KNOWS]->(other)
    WITH other
WHERE other.name STARTS WITH 'An'
RETURN other.name as otherName, other.age as age
ORDER BY age DESC
```

- These two queries are the same in terms of results. We are finding all the Person nodes whose name starts with A , skipping the first three results and returning the next three results. You can see some similarities between the WITH and RETURN clauses. In a WITH clause, you have to use an alias when you are referring to properties and so on, but in a RETURN clause, it is not mandatory to use aliases:

```
// Using SKIP and LIMIT along WITH clause
MATCH (p:Person)
WHERE p.name STARTS WITH 'A'
WITH p.name as name
SKIP 3
LIMIT 3
RETURN name
// Using SKIP and LIMIT with RETURN clause
MATCH (p:Person)
```

```
RETURN p.name
SKIP 3
LIMIT 3
```

Next, let us take a look at the usage of the UNION keyword.

Using UNION and UNION ALL

A UNION clause is used to combine the results of two or more queries. Each query must return the same number of values with the same alias names:

- This query returns both Actor names and Movie names as the union of two individual queries. Notice that we use the same alias name in both query fragments. If the Actor name and Movie name are the same, that value is returned only once. UNION will only return distinct values across the query results:

```
MATCH (n:Actor)
RETURN n.name AS name
UNION
MATCH (n:Movie)
RETURN n.title AS name
```

- This query returns both Actor names and Movie names as the union of two individual queries. One difference here is that if the Actor name and Movie name are the same, then that value is repeated twice in the response. Unlike UNION, UNION ALL will return all values without filtering duplicate rows:

```
MATCH (n:Actor)
RETURN n.name AS name
UNION ALL
MATCH (n:Movie)
RETURN n.title AS name
```

Now, let us take a look at how to use indexes and constraints in Cypher.

Using indexes and constraints

Indexes and constraints play a critical role in obtaining optimal performance from the database, along with making sure data integrity is maintained.

The available index options are as follows:

- Single-property index
- Composite property index
- Text index
- Full-text index

The available constraints are as follows:

- Unique node property
- Node property existence
- Node key
- Relationship property existence

Now let us take a look at how to create an index on a single property.

Using a single-property index

Single-property indexes are indexed on a single property name of a node label or relationship.

This is how we can create a single property index on a node. This creates an index on the name property of nodes with the Person label. The highlighted sections are optional. If we don't specify a name, then a generated name will be assigned to the index. The IF NOT EXISTS option will create the index only if an index for this name or combination does not yet exist:

```
CREATE INDEX person_name IF NOT EXISTS
    FOR (n:Person)
    ON (n.name)
```

> **Note**
> Remember the index is associated with a label, and only one label. When you query, you must specify this label in the MATCH query to be able to leverage the index.

This is how we can create a single-property index on a relationship:

```
CREATE INDEX knows_since IF NOT EXISTS
    FOR ()-[r:KNOWS]->()
    ON (r.since)
```

Now that we have seen how to create a single-property index on a node and relationship, let's look at creating composite property indexes.

Using a composite property index

Composite indexes function similarly to single-property indexes but on combinations of two or more properties:

```
CREATE INDEX person_name_age IF NOT EXISTS
    FOR (n:Person)
    ON (n.name, n.age)
```

In most scenarios, a single-property index on each property might be more efficient.

The same approach can be used to create a composite property index on relationships also.

Text index

A text index is the same as a single-property index with the exception that it will only recognize and apply to string values. If there are other types of values assigned to that property, then they are not included in the index.

This creates a TEXT index on the Person name. If you create a TEXT index on a property that does not contain string values, then it is as good as not having an index on that property:

```
CREATE TEXT INDEX person_name_text IF NOT EXISTS
    FOR (n:Person)
    ON (n.name)
```

> **Note**
>
> The TEXT index can only be used as a single-property index.

It is possible to create a TEXT index on a relationship property also.

Now, let us take a look at creating full-text indexes.

Using a full-text index

Full-text indexes are Lucene native indexes. These can support multiple labels and properties to create a single index.

The query creates a full-text index for Movie and Book node labels for the title and description properties:

```
CREATE FULLTEXT INDEX full_text IF NOT EXISTS
    FOR (n:Movie|Book)
    ON EACH (n.title, n.description)
```

We can create a full-text index on relationship properties also.

Now, let us take a look at unique node property constraints.

Using unique node property constraints

We can create unique constraints on node or relationship properties.

This creates a unique constraint on the Person name property:

```
CREATE CONSTRAINT person_name_c IF NOT EXISTS
    FOR (n:Person)
    REQUIRE n.name IS UNIQUE
```

The unique constraint is backed by an index automatically.

Using existence constraints

Existence constraints can make sure a property exists on the node or relationship.

This query enforces that the name property exists when a Person node is created:

```
CREATE CONSTRAINT person_name_e IF NOT EXISTS
    FOR (n:Person)
    REQUIRE n.name IS NOT NULL
```

Existence constraints can be created on relationships as well.

Using node key constraints

Node key constraints are similar to primary keys in the RDBMS world.

Here, we are showing a node key with multiple properties. It can be with a single property also:

```
CREATE CONSTRAINT person_name_age IF NOT EXISTS
    FOR (n:Person)
    REQUIRE (n.name, n.age) IS NODE KEY
```

Let's summarize our understanding of this chapter.

Summary

In this chapter, we have covered these aspects: basic Cypher syntax, nodes syntax, relationships syntax, data types available in Cypher, keywords available in Cypher, working with indexes, working with Constraints, and working with full-text indexes.

By now, you should be aware of the basic Cypher aspects and should be able to build basic Cypher queries.

Certain advanced aspects, such as subqueries and so on, are covered in later chapters, and built-in functions are introduced as we learn more about Cypher.

You can find the latest Cypher documentation in the *Neo4j Cypher Manual* (`https://neo4j.com/docs/cypher-manual/current/`).

You can also find a quick reference guide at `https://neo4j.com/docs/cypher-refcard/current/`.

In the next chapter, we will start building graph models and using Cypher to start loading data. We will be leveraging the concepts learned in this chapter to achieve that.

Part 2: Working with Cypher

This part introduces the Cypher concepts and explores how to use Cypher to load data into a graph database and how to retrieve data using Cypher queries. By the end of this part, you will be able to use Cypher queries to load and retrieve data and you will understand the basics of the Cypher syntax and keywords.

This part comprises the following chapters:

- *Chapter 3, Loading Data with Cypher*
- *Chapter 4, Querying Graph*
- *Chapter 5, Filtering, Sorting, and Aggregations*
- *Chapter 6, List Expressions, UNION, and Subqueries*

3

Loading Data with Cypher

To load data into a graph, we need to understand how to map the source data to a graph model. In this chapter, we will discuss mapping the source data to a graph model, what decisions drive the graph model, and how to load the data into this model. In the last chapter, we looked at Cypher syntax and what queries can be used to create, update, or delete nodes, relationships, and properties. We will use these patterns to map the CSV files to a graph model as we go through each file and build Cypher queries to load this data in a transactional manner.

Neo4j is an ACID-compliant database. To load data into Neo4j, we would need to leverage transactions similar to those in an RDBMS, and Cypher is the query language we use to load the data. There are multiple options to load data into Neo4j using Cypher. They are LOAD CSV, using Neo4j client drivers, and using apoc utilities.

In this chapter, we will cover these topics:

- Before loading the data
- Graph data modeling
- Loading data with LOAD CSV
- Loading data with LOAD CSV using batching
- Loading data using client drivers
- Mapping the source data to graph

We will first take a look at the options available to load the data using Cypher. Once we understand how to load the data, we will look at graph data modeling and take a step-by-step approach to reviewing the data and how the model evolves as we keep adding data to the graph.

Before loading the data

To start loading data with Cypher, we need to build the graph data model first. While Neo4j is a schemaless database, we still need to understand how our data will look in a graph representation and whether it can answer our questions effectively. This process involves understanding the data and seeing what the nodes and relationships would be and what would map to the properties. For example, say we have a list of events with date values in the source data:

- If we are looking for events in the sequence they occurred, then we can have the date as a property on the event node
- If our requirements are to look at the set of events by date, then making the date a node would help us to answer those questions more effectively

We will discuss these aspects in more detail with a sample dataset later in this chapter.

We will introduce the basics of graph data modeling first and the tools available for it before we continue with the data loading discussion.

Graph data modeling

To build a data model, you can use the **Arrows.app** site (`https://arrows.app`). The following screenshot shows an example diagram:

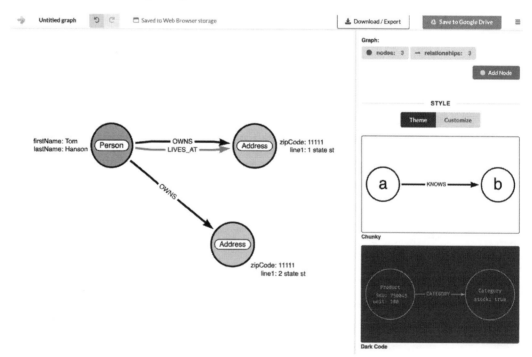

Figure 3.1 – Graph data model

This can be thought of as a data diagram where a set of data is drawn as a graph. It is possible to directly load the data into Neo4j with an assumed data model by skipping this part, but this approach can facilitate larger team collaboration and arrive at a better graph model. One of the aspects of this approach is to represent part of the data as a graph diagram and see how the graph traversal would work to answer our questions.

Say we have a set of questions; we can try to trace the model to see whether we can answer them:

- *How many addresses are OWNED by a person?*

  - Find the person, traverse the OWNS relationship, and count the addresses

- *At which address is a person living?*

  - Find the person and traverse the LIVES_AT relationship to find the required address

- *How many addresses has the person lived at?*

  - We cannot answer this question with this model, as we only know the current address the person lives at. If this is a question that needs to be answered, then we need to update the graph data model.

We will review the options available to load the data into the database first and then continue to loading data for a sample application.

Loading data with LOAD CSV

LOAD CSV can be used to load the data from the following:

- *Local filesystem on a server*: The files have to be in the import directory of the server. LOAD CSV cannot access random locations.

- *From a URL*: It is possible to load the data from any URL that is accessible from the server.

> **Note**
>
> Remember that LOAD CSV is the command issued by the client to the server. If it is a URL, it should be accessible from the server, as the server will try to download the CSV content from the URL and process the next steps.

We will take a look at some LOAD CSV usage examples in this section.

When the server processes the CSV file, each row is converted into a MAP or LIST type depending on how the command is issued.

LOAD CSV without headers

When we use the LOAD CSV command without a header option, then each row is mapped as a list. The screenshot here shows how this would look:

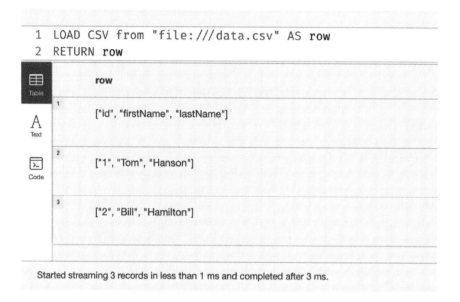

Figure 3.2 – LOAD CSV from the browser

From the picture, we can see the three rows of data. We can also observe that the header is also returned as a row since we did not tell the LOAD CSV command to read with headers.

LOAD CSV with headers

When we use the LOAD CSV command with the header option, then each row of the data gets mapped into a map object (key-value pairs) with each header column being the key and the corresponding value in the row being the value. The screenshot here shows how this would look:

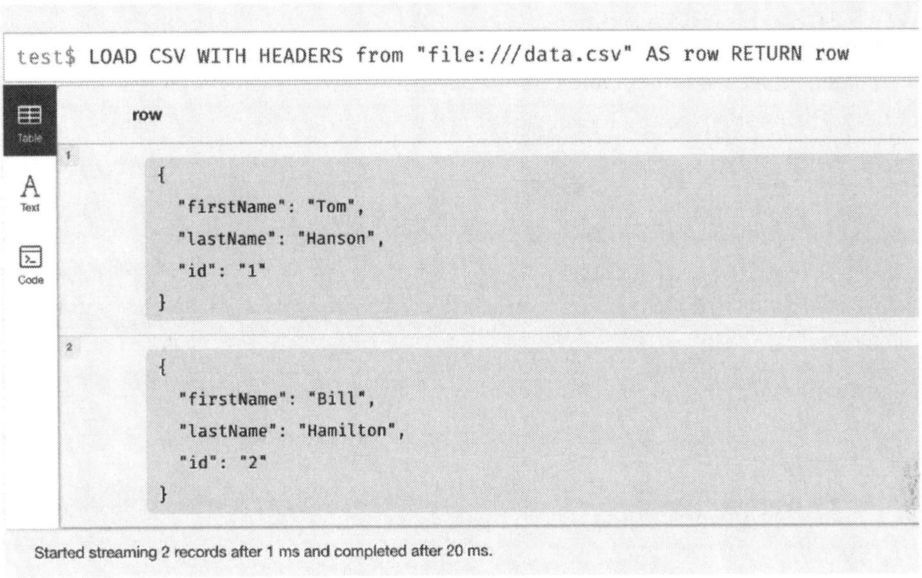

```
test$ LOAD CSV WITH HEADERS from "file:///data.csv" AS row RETURN row
```

row
1
```{   "firstName": "Tom",   "lastName": "Hanson",   "id": "1" }```
2
```{   "firstName": "Bill",   "lastName": "Hamilton",   "id": "2" }```

Started streaming 2 records after 1 ms and completed after 20 ms.

Figure 3.3 – LOAD CSV WITH HEADERS from the browser

We can see here that the data is returned as a map. The server reads the header row and uses the values there as keys for values. This is the most common usage of the LOAD CSV command.

> **Caution**
>
> The LOAD CSV command is executed as part of a single transaction. When you are processing a large dataset or have a small heap, then you should process the data in batches. Otherwise, it could crash the server with an out of memory exception, if no memory guard is set up. If the server has a memory guard, then the query will fail.

Loading data with LOAD CSV using batching

When you have a large amount of data, then you should try to commit the data in batches so that you do not need a large heap to process the data.

There are two options to process the data in batches.

- USING PERIODIC COMMIT
- CALL IN TRANSACTIONS

Let's now go through these two options next.

USING PERIODIC COMMIT

This is an older syntax and is deprecated from Neo4j 4.4 version onward, but if you are using Neo4j software prior to this version, then you must use this option to commit data in batches:

```
:auto USING PERIODIC COMMIT 1
LOAD CSV WITH HEADERS from "file:///data.csv" AS row
WITH row
MERGE (p:Person {id:row.id})
SET p.firstName = row.firstName,
    p.lastName = row.lastName
```

This command will execute a commit after processing one row at a time.

CALL IN TRANSACTIONS

This is the newer syntax and is available from Neo4j 4.4 onward:

```
:auto LOAD CSV WITH HEADERS from "file:///data.csv" AS row
CALL {
    WITH row
    MERGE (p:Person {id:row.id})
    SET p.firstName = row.firstName,
        p.lastName = row.lastName
} IN TRANSACTIONS OF 1 ROWS
```

This command will execute the commit after processing one row at a time.

Loading data using client drivers

When you use LOAD CSV, the server is responsible for downloading the CSV content and executing the Cypher statements to load the data. There is another option to load the data into Neo4j. We can use Neo4j drivers from an application to load the data.

Neo4j documentation - Drivers and APIs (https://neo4j.com/docs/drivers-apis/) contains the documentation on all the options available. In this section, we will discuss using Java and Python drivers to load the data.

Neo4j client applications make use of a driver that, from a data access perspective, will work as the main form of communication within a database. It is through this driver instance that Cypher query execution is carried out. An application should create a driver instance and use it in the application. The driver communicates with the Neo4j server using the Bolt protocol.

Let's take a look at how we can create a driver instance here:

- This shows how a driver instance can be created in Java:

```java
import org.neo4j.driver.AuthTokens;
import org.neo4j.driver.Driver;
import org.neo4j.driver.GraphDatabase;
public class DriverLifecycleExample implements
AutoCloseable {
    private final Driver;
    public DriverLifecycleExample(
      String uri, String user, String password) {
                driver = GraphDatabase.driver(
                uri, AuthTokens.basic(
                    user, password));
        }
    @Override
    public void close() throws Exception {
        driver.close();
    }
}
```

- This shows how a driver instance can be created in JavaScript applications:

```javascript
const driver = neo4j.driver(uri, neo4j.auth.basic(
    user, password))
try {
     await driver.verifyConnectivity()
     console.log('Driver created')
} catch (error) {
    console.log(`connectivity verification failed.
    ${error}`)
}
// ... on application exit:
await driver.close()
```

- This shows how a driver instance can be created in a Python application:

```python
from neo4j import GraphDatabase
class DriverLifecycleExample:
    def __init__(self, uri, auth):
```

```
            self.driver = GraphDatabase.driver(
                uri, auth=auth)
        def close(self):
    self.driver.close()
```

From the code examples, we can see that to create a driver instance, we need the URL for the Neo4j server instance and credentials. The URL should use one of the URI schemes given as follows:

URI scheme	Routing	Description
neo4j	Yes	Unsecured
neo4j+s	Yes	Secured with a fully validated certificate
neo4j+ssc	Yes	Secured with a self-signed certificate
bolt	No	Unsecured
bolt+s	No	Secured with a fully validated certificate
bolt+ssc	No	Secured with a self-signed certificate

Figure 3.4 – URI schemes available

We will take a look at what each of these URI schemes means and how it works next.

URI schemes

This section describes how each URI scheme works and differs from the others and how to choose one to connect to a Neo4j instance.

- neo4j: This is the default URI scheme used by Neo4j from 4.0 onward. When you use this scheme in the URL, then the driver can connect to a single Neo4j instance or a cluster. This scheme is cluster aware. When this scheme is used, the communication with the server is not encrypted.

- neo4j+s: This scheme works exactly how the neo4j scheme works with the exception that all the communication with the server is encrypted.

- neo4j+ssc: This scheme works exactly how the neo4j scheme works with the exception that all the communication with the server is encrypted, but the certificate chain validation is skipped, which is mandatory in the neo4j+s scheme. You will use this option when the neo4j server is configured with a self-signed certificate for encryption purposes.

- bolt: When you use this scheme in the URL, then the driver can only connect to a single neo4j instance. This scheme is not cluster aware. In a cluster environment, if you use this scheme to connect to a FOLLOWER node, then performing write queries will fail.

- bolt+s: This scheme works exactly how the bolt scheme works with the exception that all the communication with the server is encrypted.

- bolt+ssc: This scheme works exactly how the bolt scheme works with the exception that all the communication with the server is encrypted, but the certificate chain validation is skipped, which is mandatory in the neo4j+s scheme. You will use this option when the neo4j server is configured with a self-signed certificate for encryption purposes.

Let's move on to a Neo4j session next.

Neo4j sessions

Once the driver is created to execute the queries you need to create a neo4j session, which provides these options to execute queries:

- run: This is the basic method to execute the queries with or without parameters. This is a WRITE transaction, so in the cluster, all the queries will go to the LEADER instance.

- readTransaction: When you execute a readTransaction method in a clustered environment, the driver will find a FOLLOWER or READ REPLICA instance for the database and will execute the query on that instance. On a single node, there is no change in behavior. When you are building a client application, you should make sure you use this method for read queries. When you use this function, the transaction will be retried automatically when a transaction is cancelled or rolled back with exponential backoff.

- writeTransaction: When you execute a readTransaction method in a clustered environment, the driver will find the LEADER instance for the database and will execute the query on that instance. On a single node, there is no change in behavior. When you are building a client application, you should make sure you use this method for read queries. When you use this function, the transaction will be retried automatically when a transaction is canceled or rolled back with exponential backoff.

Let's take a look at the code examples for each of these methods. We will take a look at the run method usage.

1. First, we will take a look at a Java code snippet:

```
public void addPerson(String name) {
    try (Session = driver.session()) {
        session.run("CREATE (a:Person {name: $name})",
            parameters("name", name));
    }
}
```

2. Now let's look at a Python code snippet:

```python
def add_person(self, name):
    with self.driver.session() as session:
        session.run("CREATE (a:Person {name: $name})",
            name=name)
```

3. Finally, let's take a look at the JavaScript usage of this method:

```javascript
const session = driver.session()
const result = session.run('MATCH (a:Person) RETURN
a.name ORDER BY a.name')
 const collectedNames = []
result.subscribe({
  onNext: record => {
    const name = record.get(0)
    collectedNames.push(name)
  },
  onCompleted: () => {
    session.close().then(() => {
      console.log('Names: ' + collectedNames.join(', '))
    })
  },
  onError: error => {
    console.log(error)
  }
})
```

We will take a look at the writeTransaction usage now:

1. This is the Java code example for this method:

```java
public void addPerson(final String name) {
    try (Session = driver.session()) {
        session.writeTransaction(tx -> {
            tx.run("CREATE (
                    a:Person {name: $name})",
                    parameters("name", name)
                    ).consume();
            return 1;
        });
    }
}
```

2. Now, here's a Python example of this function usage:

```python
def create_person(tx, name):
    return tx.run("CREATE (
        a:Person {name: $name})
    RETURN id(a)", name=name).single().value()
def add_person(driver, name):
    with driver.session() as session:
        return session.write_transaction(
            create_person, name)
```

3. Finally, here's a JavaScript usage of this function:

```javascript
const relationshipsCreated = await session.
writeTransaction(tx =>
    Promise.all(
      names.map(name =>
        tx
          .run(
            'MATCH (e:Person {name: $p_name}) ' +
              'MERGE (c:Company {name: $c_name}) ' +
              'MERGE (e)-[:WORKS_FOR]->(c)',
              { p_name: name, c_name: companyName }
          )
          .then(
            result =>
          result.summary.counters.updates()
            .relationshipsCreated)
          .then(relationshipsCreated =>
            neo4j.int(relationshipsCreated).toInt()
          )
      )
    ).then(values => values.reduce((a, b) => a + b))
  )
  console.log(`Created ${relationshipsCreated} employees
relationship`)
} finally {
```

```
    await session.close()
}
```

We will take a look at `readTransaction` function usage now:

1. This is the Java usage of this function:

```java
public List<String> getPeople() {
    try (Session = driver.session()) {
        return session.readTransaction(tx -> {
            List<String> names = new ArrayList<>();
            Result = tx.run(
"MATCH (a:Person) RETURN a.name ORDER BY a.name");
            while (result.hasNext()) {
                names.add(result.next().get(0).
asString());
            }
            return names;
        });
    }
}
```

The following code segment is the Python usage of the same function:

```python
def match_person_nodes(tx):
    result = tx.run("MATCH (a:Person) RETURN a.name ORDER
BY a.name")
    return [record["a.name"] for record in result]
with driver.session() as session:
    people = session.read_transaction(match_person_nodes)
```

2. Finally, here's the JavaScript usage of the same function:

```javascript
const session = driver.session()
try {
  const names = await session.readTransaction(async tx =>
{
      const result = await tx.run('MATCH (a:Person) RETURN
a.name AS name')
```

```
        return result.records.map(record => record.
    get('name'))
      })
```

Now that we have seen the client aspects, we will take a look at a sample dataset and review the steps to load the data into a graph.

Mapping the source data to graph

When we want to load the data into a graph using Cypher, we need to first map the data to the graph. When we first start mapping the data to the graph, it need not be the final data model. As we understand more and more about the data context and questions, we want to ensure the graph data model can evolve along with it.

In this section, we will work with the Synthea synthetic patient dataset. This site, *Synthea – Synthetic Patient Generation* (synthetichealth.github.io/synthea), provides the outlay of it. This website describes Synthea data like this:

"Synthea™ is an open-source, synthetic patient generator that models the medical history of synthetic patients. Our mission is to provide high-quality, synthetic, realistic but not real, patient data and associated health records covering every aspect of healthcare. The resulting data is free from cost, privacy, and security restrictions, enabling research with Health IT data that is otherwise legally or practically unavailable."

This was built by the MITRE corporation to assist researchers.

A Synthea record (https://github.com/synthetichealth/synthea/wiki/Records) describes the data generated by Synthea. It can generate data in FHIR, JSON, or CSV format. In FHIR and JSON format, a file for each patient is generated. In CSV format, it generates one file per functionality.

After running Synthea, the CSV exporter will create these files. This table is taken from the Synthea documentation site that describes the content available:

File	Description
allergies.csv	Patient allergy data
careplans.csv	Patient care plan data, including goals
claims.csv	Patient claim data
claims_transactions.csv	Transactions per line item per claim
conditions.csv	Patient conditions or diagnoses
devices.csv	Patient-affixed permanent and semi-permanent devices
encounters.csv	Patient encounter data
imaging_studies.csv	Patient imaging metadata

File	Description
`immunizations.csv`	Patient immunization data
`medications.csv`	Patient medication data
`observations.csv`	Patient observations, including vital signs and lab reports
`organizations.csv`	Provider organizations, including hospitals
`patients.csv`	Patient demographic data
`payer_transitions.csv`	Payer transition data (i.e., changes in health insurance)
`payers.csv`	Payer organization data
`procedures.csv`	Patient procedure data, including surgeries
`providers.csv`	Clinicians that provide patient care
`supplies.csv`	Supplies used in the provision of care

Figure 3.5 – CSV data files table

We will be using these CSV files for our graph data model:

- Patients
- Encounters
- Providers
- Organizations
- Medications
- Conditions
- Procedures
- Care plans
- Allergies

We have chosen these aspects to build a patient interaction model. The devices, payers, claims, imaging studies, and so on can be used to enhance the model, but this could be too much information for the exercise we are doing.

Next, we will take a look at the `patients.csv` data and load it into a graph.

Loading the patient data

When we load the data into a graph, we need to understand the source data and see what should be nodes, what should be relationships, and what data should be properties on nodes or relationships.

`patients.csv` (`https://github.com/synthetichealth/synthea/wiki/CSV-File-Data-Dictionary#patients`) contains the patient CSV file data dictionary. We will use `Arrows.app` (`https://arrows.app/#/local/id=zcgBttSPi9_7Bi2yOFuw`) to build the model as we progressively add more data to the graph. The following screenshot shows the data diagram for the `patients.csv` file:

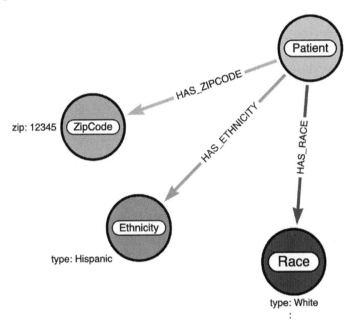

Figure 3.6 – Data diagram with patient data

We can see here that we have chosen to create a **Patient** node. This is as expected. The **Patient** node will have the following properties:

- `Id`
- `marital`
- `ssn`
- `firstName`
- `lastName`
- `suffix`
- `prefix`
- `city`
- `county`

- location (LAT and LON)

- drivers

- birthDate

Most of the properties, such as first name, last name, and so on, are natural properties of the node. The county and city values can be either nodes or properties. It depends on how we would like to query the data. When the city is a property, the value is duplicated on all the nodes with that city value. If we make the city a node, then we will have a single city node, but all the nodes that have this city would be connected via a relationship. We will discuss what option would be better in later sections. The advantage with Neo4j is that say we have something as a property – we can easily convert it into a node or relationship later without having too much impact on the database and client applications.

ZipCode is chosen to be a node by itself. This helps us in providing statistics and seeing aspects of provider and patient interactions in a more performant manner. For the same reason, both **Race** and **Ethnicity** are nodes instead of properties.

First, we need to make sure we define the indexes and constraints before we load the data. This is very important as the data grows – without indexes, the data load performance will start degrading.

The following code segment shows the indexes and constraints that are required before we can load the patient data:

```
CREATE CONSTRAINT patient_id IF NOT EXISTS
FOR (n:Patient)
REQUIRE n.id IS UNIQUE ;
CREATE CONSTRAINT zipcode_id IF NOT EXISTS
FOR (n:ZipCode)
REQUIRE n.zip IS UNIQUE ;
CREATE CONSTRAINT race_id IF NOT EXISTS
FOR (n:Race)
REQUIRE n.type IS UNIQUE ;
CREATE CONSTRAINT eth_id IF NOT EXISTS
FOR (n:Ethnicity)
REQUIRE n.type IS UNIQUE ;
```

In this case, we have created constraints, as we know these values are distinct. This makes sure we don't create multiple nodes with the same values and it also gives the query planner enough details to execute the query efficiently.

Now that we have created indexes and constraints, the following code segment shows the Cypher query to load the data from the browser. We have chosen to use the LOAD CSV option to load the data:

```
:auto LOAD CSV WITH HEADERS from "https://raw.
githubusercontent.com/PacktPublishing/Cypher-Querying/main/
data/csv/patients.csv" as row
CALL {
  WITH row
  MERGE(p:Patient {id: row.Id})
  SET
    p.marital = row.MARITAL,
    p.ssn = row.SSN,
    p.firstName = row.FIRST,
    p.lastName = row.LAST,
    p.suffix = row.SUFFIX,
    p.prefix = row.PREFIX,
    p.city = row.CITY,
    p.county = row.COUNTY,
    p.location = point({latitude:toFloat(row.LAT),
longitude:toFloat(row.LON)}),
    p.drivers=row.DRIVERS,
    p.birthDate=date(row.BIRTHDATE)
  WITH row,p
  MERGE (r:Race {type: row.RACE})
  MERGE (p)-[:HAS_RACE]->(r)
  WITH row,p
  MERGE (e:Ethnicity {type: row.ETHNICITY})
  MERGE (p)-[:HAS_ETHNICITY]->(e)
  WITH row,p
  WHERE row.ZIP IS NOT NULL
  MERGE (z:ZipCode {zip: row.ZIP})
  MERGE (p)-[:HAS_ZIPCODE]->(z)
} IN TRANSACTIONS OF 1000 ROWS
```

The first thing we can notice here is the usage of the :auto keyword. This is not a Cypher keyword. This is a browser helper keyword that tells the browser to create a single transaction to execute the query. This keyword is used only with the browser and cannot be used anywhere else.

The next thing we can notice is that once the row is read from CSV, we are using this Cypher code segment to execute the query:

```
CALL {
    ...
} IN TRANSACTIONS OF 1000 ROWS
```

The preceding code segment shows the new batch processing syntax introduced in 4.4 onward. This optimizes the use of transactions. Before 4.4, you needed to use the apoc.load.csv method to load the data this way. Alternatively, you can also use the USE PERIODIC COMMIT Cypher keyword before 4.4 to load the data in batches:

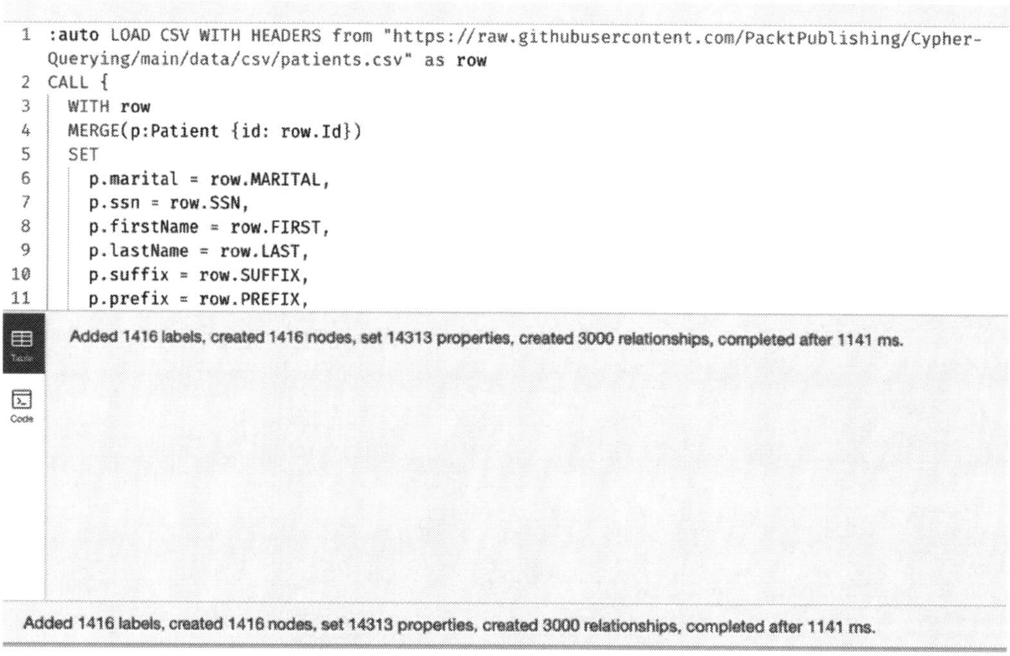

```
 1   :auto LOAD CSV WITH HEADERS from "https://raw.githubusercontent.com/PacktPublishing/Cypher-
     Querying/main/data/csv/patients.csv" as row
 2   CALL {
 3     WITH row
 4     MERGE(p:Patient {id: row.Id})
 5     SET
 6       p.marital = row.MARITAL,
 7       p.ssn = row.SSN,
 8       p.firstName = row.FIRST,
 9       p.lastName = row.LAST,
10       p.suffix = row.SUFFIX,
11       p.prefix = row.PREFIX,
```

Added 1416 labels, created 1416 nodes, set 14313 properties, created 3000 relationships, completed after 1141 ms.

Added 1416 labels, created 1416 nodes, set 14313 properties, created 3000 relationships, completed after 1141 ms.

Figure 3.7 – LOAD CSV for patients.csv

This screenshot shows the results after running the query in the browser. You can see that it shows the total number of nodes, relationships created, and number of properties set.

Next, we will take a look at loading the encounters.csv file.

Loading the encounter data

The encounter data represents patient interactions with the healthcare system, whether a lab encounter, doctor visit, or hospital visit. The data available provides a rich set of information. We will only be ingesting part of the information into a graph.

We will only be ingesting the values for the keys identified here from the CSV file:

- Id
- Start
- Patient
- Organization
- Provider
- EncounterClass
- Code
- Description

We are ignoring the cost details as well as the payer details for this exercise. It might be too overwhelming to review and represent all the data. For that purpose, we are limiting what data we are planning to load to do basic patient analysis.

If we add the encounter data representation to the existing patient data diagram, it could look like this:

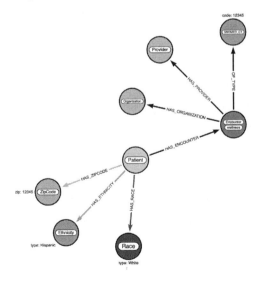

Figure 3.8 – Data diagram enhanced with encounter data

In the diagram, we see an **Encounter** node as expected. We can notice that this node has an extra label, **wellness**, on it. We have chosen to represent the `EncounterClass` value as a label instead of a property. In Neo4j, doing this can make it easier to build performant queries.

Say we want to count all the wellness encounters. When we make it a label, the database can return the count very quickly, as label stores contain statistics related to that node type. The performance remains constant irrespective of how many encounter nodes exist. If we have it as a property and we do not have an index on that property, as the number of encounter nodes grows, the query response time will keep increasing. If we add an index, then we will be using index storage and the performance will be better than not having an index, but still, it has to count using the index store. This topic will be discussed further with examples in later sections.

The **Organization**, **Provider**, and **SNOMED_CT** nodes represent the information this encounter is associated with. We have only the reference IDs for **Organization** and **Provider** in the data, so they should be nodes by themselves, similar to how foreign keys are used in the RDBMS world. We have chosen to make **code** a separate node, as it is industry-standard **SNOMED_CT** code. By making it a node, we might be able to add extra information that can help with data analysis.

The following code segment shows the Cypher code to create the indexes and constraints needed before ingesting the encounter data:

```
CREATE INDEX encounter_id IF NOT EXISTS
FOR (n:Encounter)
 ON n.id
```

We have chosen to use an index here instead of a constraint for encounters. When we are ingesting the other data, the reason for this will become more apparent. We are going to use the following code segment to create the constraints required to load the encounter data:

```
CREATE CONSTRAINT snomed_id IF NOT EXISTS
FOR (n:SNOMED_CT)
 REQUIRE n.code IS UNIQUE ;
CREATE CONSTRAINT provider_id IF NOT EXISTS
FOR (n:Provider)
 REQUIRE n.id IS UNIQUE ;
CREATE CONSTRAINT organization_id IF NOT EXISTS
FOR (n:Organization)
 REQUIRE n.id IS UNIQUE ;
```

The following Cypher snippet loads the encounter data into a graph:

```
:auto LOAD CSV WITH HEADERS from "https://raw.
githubusercontent.com/PacktPublishing/Cypher-Querying/main/
data/csv/encounters.csv" as row
CALL {
  WITH row
  MERGE(e:Encounter {id: row.Id})
  SET
    e.date=datetime(row.START),
    e.description=row.DESCRIPTION,
    e.isEnd = false
  FOREACH (ignore in CASE WHEN row.STOP IS NOT NULL AND row.
STOP <> '' THEN [1] ELSE [] END |
        SET e.end=datetime(row.STOP)
  )
  FOREACH (ignore in CASE WHEN row.CODE IS NOT NULL AND row.
CODE <> '' THEN [1] ELSE [] END |
    MERGE(s:SNOMED_CT {code:row.CODE})
    MERGE(e)-[:OF_TYPE]->(s)
  )
  WITH row,e
  CALL apoc.create.setLabels( e, [ 'Encounter', row.
ENCOUNTERCLASS ] ) YIELD node
  WITH row,e
  MERGE(p:Patient {id: row.PATIENT})
  MERGE (p)-[:HAS_ENCOUNTER]->(e)
  WITH row,e
  MERGE (provider:Provider {id:row.PROVIDER})
  MERGE(e)-[:HAS_PROVIDER]->(provider)
  FOREACH (ignore in CASE WHEN row.ORGANIZATION IS NOT NULL
AND row.ORGANIZATION <> '' THEN [1] ELSE [] END |
    MERGE (o:Organization {id: row.ORGANIZATION})
    MERGE (e)-[:HAS_ORGANIZATION]->(o))
} IN TRANSACTIONS OF 1000 ROWS
```

In this code, you can see there is a new pattern in which FOREACH is introduced. FOREACH is normally used to iterate a list and add or update the data in a graph.

Let's take a step-by-step look at one of these statements used in the preceding code block that uses a FOREACH clause to simulate an IF condition, which does not exist in Cypher. The code block that we are exploring is shown here:

```
FOREACH (
    ignore in
    CASE
        WHEN row.CODE IS NOT NULL AND row.CODE <> ''
        THEN
            [1]
        ELSE
            []
    END |
        MERGE(s:SNOMED_CT {code:row.CODE})
        MERGE(e)-[:OF_TYPE]->(s)
)
```

The execution flow of the preceding code segment can be described with these steps:

1. First, we are using a CASE statement to check for a condition.
2. The WHEN clause is checking for the condition.
3. If the condition is true, the THEN clause will activate and return a list with one value, [1].
4. If the condition is false, the ELSE clause will activate and return an empty list, [].
5. We are iterating the list returned and assigning it to a variable, ignore.
6. If the list is not empty, then the ignore variable will be assigned to the value in the list, which contains one element, 1 and will process the set of statements after the | separator. We are calling this variable ignore as we don't need to know what value this holds. We want to execute what's after the | separator exactly once if the condition is true.

This is how we can simulate the IF condition in Cypher. If you want IF and ELSE conditional execution, then you have to use apoc procedures.

Also, we are using the apoc procedure to add EncounterClass to an encounter node. Since we are trying to add labels dynamically, we have to use the apoc option:

```
CALL apoc.create.setLabels( e, [ 'Encounter',
    row.ENCOUNTERCLASS ] ) YIELD node
```

In Cypher, it is not possible to set the label with a dynamic value.

Next, we will take a look at ingesting provider data.

Loading provider data

The provider data represents the physicians that participate in the healthcare system. We will be using all the data provided except the utilization value.

After adding the provider data details, our data diagram will look like this:

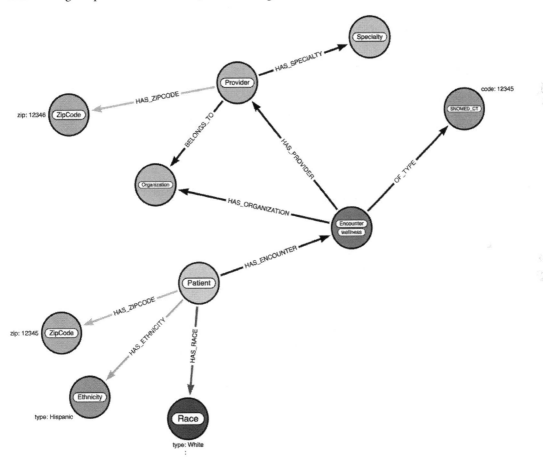

Figure 3.9 – Data diagram enhanced with provider data

We have a new **Specialty** node added. We have new relationships added between the **Provider**, **Organization**, and **ZipCode** nodes. By making **Speciality** a node, it can make it easier to group **Provider** nodes in queries.

Since we introduced a new label type, we need to add an index or a constraint for this. The code segment here shows the Cypher code for this:

```
CREATE CONSTRAINT specialty_id IF NOT EXISTS
FOR (n:Specialty)
REQUIRE n.name IS UNIQUE
```

The following Cypher code loads the provider data into a graph:

```
:auto LOAD CSV WITH HEADERS from "https://raw.
githubusercontent.com/PacktPublishing/Cypher-Querying/main/
data/csv/providers.csv" as row
CALL {
  WITH row
  MERGE (p:Provider {id: row.Id})
  SET p.name=row.NAME,
      p.gender=row.GENDER,
      p.address = row.ADDRESS,
      p.state = row.STATE,
      p.location = point({latitude:toFloat(row.LAT),
longitude:toFloat(row.LON)})
  WITH row,p
  MERGE (o:Organization {id: row.ORGANIZATION})
  MERGE (p)-[:BELONGS_TO]->(o)
  WITH row,p
  MERGE (s:Specialty {name: row.SPECIALITY})
  MERGE (p)-[:HAS_SPECIALTY]->(s)
  WITH row,p
  WHERE row.ZIP IS NOT NULL
  MERGE (z:ZipCode {zip: row.ZIP})
  MERGE (p)-[:HAS_ZIPCODE]->(z)
} IN TRANSACTIONS OF 1000 ROWS
```

Here, we are using a different approach to conditional execution. For providers, the ZIP code value is optional and since we are processing the ZIP code, in the end, we can use a WHERE clause alongside a WITH clause:

```
WITH row,p
WHERE row.ZIP IS NOT NULL
```

When we use this approach, the query execution continues only when the ZIP value is not `null`. This can only work when the conditional check is the last one. If we do this in between, all the logic below this will not get executed if the ZIP value is null.

Next, we will load the organization data.

Loading organization data

The organization data represent the hospitals or labs. We will be loading all the values except the `Revenue` and `Utilization` values into the graph.

After adding the organization data details, our data diagram will look like this:

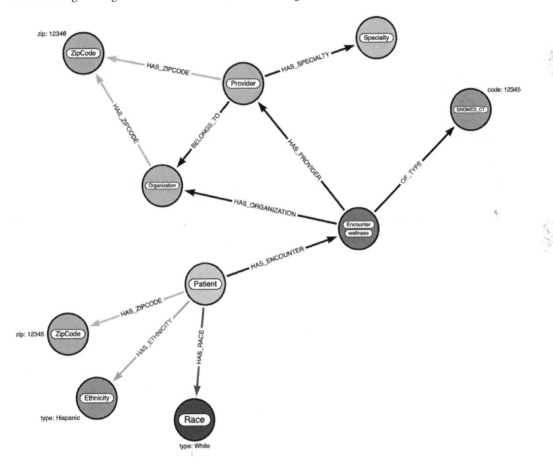

Figure 3.10 – Data diagram enhanced with organization data

Here, we did not introduce any new node types. The only change to the diagram is the presence of a new relationship between **Organization** and **ZipCode**.

The following Cypher code loads the organization data into a graph:

```
:auto LOAD CSV WITH HEADERS from "https://raw.
githubusercontent.com/PacktPublishing/Cypher-Querying/main/
data/csv/organizations.csv" as row
CALL {
  WITH row
  MERGE (o:Organization {id: row.Id})
  SET o.name=row.NAME,
      o.address = row.ADDRESS,
      o.state = row.STATE,
      o.location = point({latitude:toFloat(row.LAT),
longitude:toFloat(row.LON)})
  WITH row,o
  WHERE row.ZIP IS NOT NULL
  MERGE (z:ZipCode {zip: row.ZIP})
  MERGE (o)-[:HAS_ZIPCODE]->(z)
} IN TRANSACTIONS OF 1000 ROWS
```

This is pretty much similar to the provider data load. We are creating or updating organization data and connecting it to a ZIP code when it is available.

Next, we will take a look at loading medication data.

Loading medication data

The medication data represents the drugs prescribed to the patient. From medication data, we will be using these values:

- Patient
- START
- STOP
- Encounter
- CODE
- DESCRIPTION
- REASONCODE
- REASONDESCRIPTION

As you can see here, we want to represent the START and STOP values of medication in the graph. If we just make them properties on the node, then we will lose the timing context of the patient encounters. To make sure we preserve the timing context, we might create a new **Encounter** node with the same Encounter ID and STOP time as the distinct values. If you remember, only for the **Encounter** node did we add an index on id, whereas for almost all the other entities, we created a constraint. This makes START and STOP distinct entities in the graph and can help in analyzing the data.

After adding the organization data details, our data diagram will look like this:

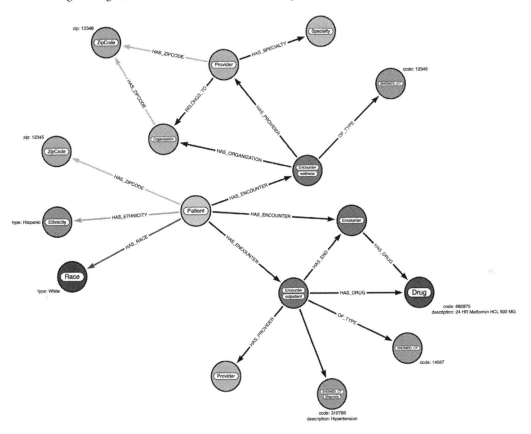

Figure 3.11 – Data diagram enhanced with medication data

From the data diagram, we can see the model getting more complex as more and more context is ingested into the graph. Especially the addition of a new **Encounter** node and the **HAS_END** relationship are a bit different from how we approach the data in the RDBMS world. This can assist us in analyzing how a drug being used could have an effect on patient health.

The following Cypher code loads the medication data into a graph:

```
:auto LOAD CSV WITH HEADERS from "https://raw.
githubusercontent.com/PacktPublishing/Cypher-Querying/main/
data/csv/medications.csv" as row
CALL {
  WITH row
  MERGE (p:Patient {id:row.PATIENT})
  MERGE (d:Drug {code:row.CODE})
    SET d.description=row.DESCRIPTION
  MERGE (ps:Encounter {id:row.ENCOUNTER, isEnd: false})
  MERGE (ps)-[:HAS_DRUG]->(d)
  MERGE (p)-[:HAS_ENCOUNTER]->(ps)
  FOREACH( ignore in CASE WHEN row.REASONCODE IS NOT NULL AND
row.REASONCODE <> '' THEN [1] ELSE [] END |
    MERGE(s:SNOMED_CT {code:row.CODE})
      SET s:Diagnosis, s.description = row.REASONDESCRIPTION
    MERGE (ps)-[:HAS_DIAGNOSIS]->(s)
  )
  WITH row,ps,p
  WHERE row.STOP IS NOT NULL and row.STOP <> ''
  CREATE (pe:Encounter {id:row.ENCOUNTER, date:datetime(row.
STOP)})
    SET pe.isEnd=true
  CREATE (p)-[:HAS_ENCOUNTER]->(pe)
  CREATE (pe)-[:HAS_DRUG]->(d)
  CREATE (ps)-[:HAS_END]->(pe)
} IN TRANSACTIONS OF 1000 ROWS
```

Here, we can see that when there is an underlying condition for the drug prescribed, we are creating a SNOMED_CT node, but adding the Diagnosis label on it. This is the same approach we had used with Encounter class values.

In the code, to create the new Encounter node to represent the Stop value, we are using the CREATE clause. This can be very performant, but the negative effect is that when we process this data again, say by mistake, we are going to create duplicate nodes. We are going to look at using MERGE with a Stop timestamp in the next data file processing. You would need to decide which approach would suit your data ingestion needs better.

Next, we will look at loading condition, procedure, and allergy data.

Loading condition, procedure, and allergy data

The data loading is pretty similar to the medication data. Even the data diagram won't alter much. The pattern would be pretty similar to the drug data.

After adding these data details, our data diagram will look like this:

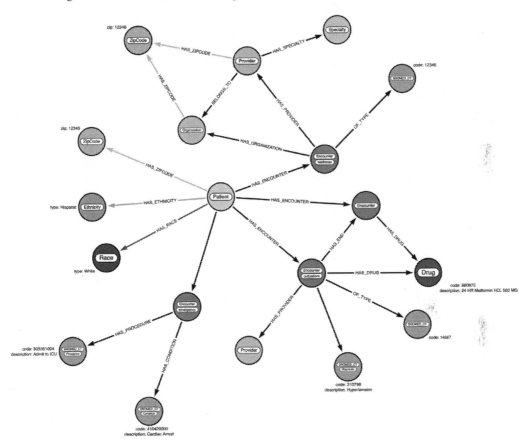

Figure 3.12 – Data diagram enhanced with condition, procedure, and allergy data

We will add two more relationships, HAS_CONDITION and HAS_PROCEDURE. We have not represented the HAS_END relationship here:

- The following Cypher code loads the condition data into a graph:

```
:auto LOAD CSV WITH HEADERS from "https://raw.
githubusercontent.com/PacktPublishing/Cypher-Querying/
main/data/csv/conditions.csv" as row
CALL {
```

```
    WITH row
    MATCH (p:Patient {id:row.PATIENT})
    MERGE (c:SNOMED_CT {code:row.CODE})
    SET c.description=row.DESCRIPTION, c:Condition
    MERGE (cs:Encounter {id:row.ENCOUNTER, isEnd: false})
    ON CREATE
      SET cs.date=datetime(row.START)
    MERGE (p)-[:HAS_ENCOUNTER]->(cs)
    MERGE (cs)-[:HAS_CONDITION]->(c)
    WITH p,c,cs,row
    WHERE row.STOP IS NOT NULL and row.STOP <> ''
    MERGE (ce:Encounter {id:row.ENCOUNTER,
  date:datetime(row.STOP)})
    SET ce.isEnd=true
    MERGE (p)-[:HAS_ENCOUNTER]->(ce)
    MERGE (ce)-[:HAS_CONDITION]->(c)
    MERGE (cs)-[:HAS_END]->(ce)
  } IN TRANSACTIONS OF 1000 ROWS
```

In this code, we can see that for a condition, we are also adding a SNOMED_CT node with a Condition label added to it. We also have a MERGE clause here to add to the Encounter node to represent the STOP condition.

- The following Cypher code loads the procedure data into a graph:

```
:auto LOAD CSV WITH HEADERS from "https://raw.
githubusercontent.com/PacktPublishing/Cypher-Querying/
main/data/csv/procedures.csv" as row
CALL {
  WITH row
  MATCH (p:Patient {id:row.PATIENT})
  MERGE (c:SNOMED_CT {code:row.CODE})
  SET c.description=row.DESCRIPTION, c:Procedure
  MERGE (cs:Encounter {id:row.ENCOUNTER, isEnd: false})
  ON CREATE
    SET cs.date=datetime(row.START)
  MERGE (p)-[:HAS_ENCOUNTER]->(cs)
  MERGE (cs)-[:HAS_PROCEDURE]->(c)
} IN TRANSACTIONS OF 1000 ROWS
```

We can see the ingestion of data is simple.

- The following Cypher code loads the allergy data into a graph:

```
:auto LOAD CSV WITH HEADERS from "https://raw.
githubusercontent.com/PacktPublishing/Cypher-Querying/
main/data/csv/allergies.csv" as row
CALL {
  WITH row
  MATCH (p:Patient {id:row.PATIENT})
  MERGE (c:SNOMED_CT {code:row.CODE})
  SET c.description=row.DESCRIPTION, c:Allergy
  MERGE (cs:Encounter {id:row.ENCOUNTER, isEnd: false})
  ON CREATE
    SET cs.date=datetime(row.START)
  MERGE (p)-[:HAS_ENCOUNTER]->(cs)
  MERGE (cs)-[:ALLERGY_STARTED]->(c)
  WITH p,c,cs,row
  WHERE row.STOP IS NOT NULL. and row.STOP <> ''
  MERGE (ce:Encounter {id:row.ENCOUNTER,
date:datetime(row.STOP)})
  SET ce.isEnd=true
  MERGE (p)-[:HAS_ENCOUNTER]->(ce)
  MERGE (ce)-[:ALLERGY_ENDED]->(c)
  MERGE (cs)-[:HAS_END]->(ce)
} IN TRANSACTIONS OF 1000 ROWS
```

We can see we are following the exact same pattern as with conditions. Here, we are capturing the STOP aspect, as it might be useful for analysis purposes.

Next, we will take a look at loading care plan data.

Loading care plan data

Care plan data contains the care schedule associated with a patient. It follows the same pattern as the medication or condition data loading process.

After adding these data details, our data diagram will look like this:

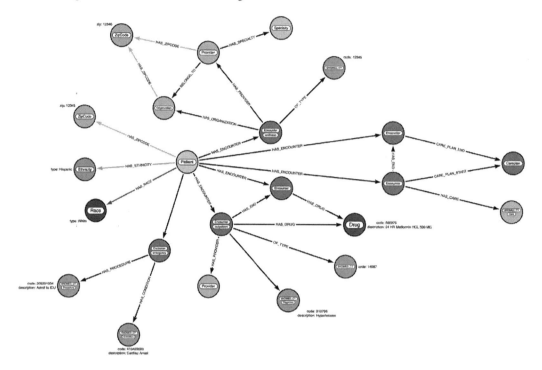

Figure 3.13 – Data diagram enhanced with care plan data

We can see that we are seeing more nodes, but the pattern those nodes follow is similar. Our graph data model is not too complex. We will take a look at how Neo4j interprets the graph data model in the next section.

The following Cypher code loads the procedure data into a graph:

```
:auto LOAD CSV WITH HEADERS from "https://raw.
githubusercontent.com/PacktPublishing/Cypher-Querying/main/
data/csv/careplans.csv" as row
CALL {
  WITH row
  MATCH (p:Patient {id:row.PATIENT})
  MERGE (cp:CarePlan {code:row.Id})
  MERGE (c:SNOMED_CT {code:row.CODE})
  SET c.description=row.DESCRIPTION, c:Care
  SET c.description=row.DESCRIPTION
  MERGE (cp)-[:HAS_CARE_TYPE]->(c)
```

```
  MERGE (cs:Encounter {id:row.ENCOUNTER, isEnd: false})
  ON CREATE
    SET cs.date=datetime(row.START)
  MERGE (cs)-[:HAS_CARE_TYPE]->(c)
  MERGE (p)-[:HAS_ENCOUNTER]->(cs)
  MERGE (cs)-[:CARE_PLAN_START]->(cp)
  WITH p,cp,cs,row
  WHERE row.STOP IS NOT NULL and row.STOP <> ''
    CREATE (ce:Encounter {id:row.ENCOUNTER, date:datetime(row.
STOP)})
    SET ce.code=row.CODE, ce.isEnd=true
    MERGE (p)-[:HAS_ENCOUNTER]->(ce)
    MERGE (ce)-[:CARE_PLAN_END]->(cp)
    MERGE (cs)-[:HAS_END]->(ce)
  } IN TRANSACTIONS OF 1000 ROWS
```

We can see from the Cypher code that it follows the same pattern as medication data and others.

Now that we have seen the whole data loaded using LOAD CSV, next, we will take a brief look at how we can do the same thing using the client driver.

Using client drivers

While LOAD CSV is convenient, it is not recommended for production usage, so when you have data that needs to be loaded at regular intervals or as a stream, you will need to leverage the client drivers to be able to load the data.

Here, we will take a look at a simple Python client that can load the data into Neo4j using Python drivers. The utility is called **pyingest** (https://github.com/neo4j-field/pyingest/tree/parquet). This utility can load CSV, JSON, or Parquet data from a local filesystem, from a URL, or an S3 bucket. The whole loading process is controlled by a configuration file, which is in YML format.

The following parameters can be configured in the configuration YML file:

- server_uri: Address of the Neo4j driver (required).

- admin_user: Username of the Neo4j user (required).

- admin_pass: Password for the Neo4j user (required).

- pre_ingest: List of Cypher statements to be run before the file ingests.

- `post_ingest`: List of Cypher statements to be run after the file ingests.
- `files`: Describes the ingestion of a file – one stanza for each file. If a file needs to be processed more than once, just use it again in a separate stanza. We will discuss parameters for files now.

File-related configuration options are as follows:

- `url`: Path to the file (required).
- `cql`: Cypher statement to be run (required).
- `chunk_size`: Number of records to batch together for ingest (default: 1,000).
- `type`: Type of file being ingested (either CSV or JSON). This parameter is not required. If missing, the script will guess based on the file extension, defaulting to CSV.
- `field_separator`: The character separating values in a line of CSV (the default is ,)
- `compression`: The type of compression used on a file (either `gzip`, `zip`, or `none` – the default is `none`)
- `skip_file`: If `true`, do not process this file (either `true` or `false` – the default is `false`)
- `skip_records`: Skips a specified number of records while ingesting the file (the default is 0)

Here, we are including the YML configuration file (`https://github.com/PacktPublishing/Cypher-Querying/blob/main/data/config.yml`) so that you can try it out yourself.

Once you download the file, you can run the following command to load the data:

```
Python3 ingest.py config.yml
```

We can see how having a script like this to load the data can simplify our data load process instead of running LOAD CSV commands one by one from the browser.

Summary

In this chapter, we have seen how we can map the data to graph model using `Arrows.app` (`https://arrows.app/#/local/id=jAGBmsu828g36qjzMAG4`), along with working with the browser to load the data using LOAD CSV commands. Along the way, we looked at when to make a value a property or a node or use it an extra label that makes understanding our data much easier in a graph format.

We also discussed various commands for conditional data loading, such as using FOREACH to simulate an IF condition. We also looked at conditional data loading by combining a WHERE clause with a WITH clause.

Along the way, we discussed how the graph data model evolves as we keep considering more data being added to the database. This is made possible since Neo4j is a schemaless database. In a schema-strict database such as an RDBMS, we have to think through all the aspects of the data model before we can attempt to ingest the data. This makes data modeling iterations simpler and gives us the opportunity to tune the model as we understand the data nuances more.

At the end of this chapter, we discussed loading the data using a Python client in a more automated way, rather than the step-by-step approach we have used with LOAD CSV.

In the next chapter, we will look at the graph model that is inferred by Neo4j and will try a few queries to understand how we can query the graph and retrieve it efficiently.

4

Querying Graph

In the previous chapter, we loaded the data into Graph. Now, it's time to look into how we can query the graph using Cypher. We will take a look at the graph data model and how to leverage it to build effective queries and understand what works and what doesn't work. By the end of the chapter, you will have learned how to build Cypher queries and understand what is required to build performant queries.

In this chapter, we will cover the following topics:

- Exploring the data in Graph
- Querying the nodes
- Querying the paths

Before we start with queries, let's explore the graph first.

Exploring the data in Graph

Once we load the data into the graph, as we learned about in the previous chapter, when we go to the database in the browser, it shows basic details such as the node labels in the database, the relationship types available, the total node count, and the total count of relationships, along with the property names that exist in the database.

The following screenshot shows these details:

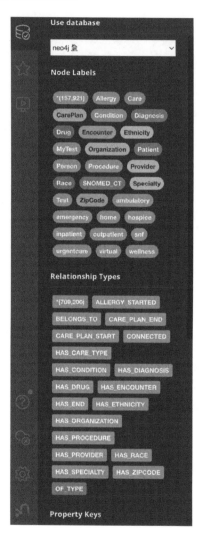

Figure 4.1 – Graph data counts in the database

We can see the node-related details on the top left-hand side of the screen, and below it, we can see the relationship details. All of these are selectable items and when you click on them, a Cypher query runs against the database to show a sample related to the name you clicked. For instance, if you click on the node label, 25 nodes of those types are shown. The same applies to the relationship types shown.

We can get the database statistics by executing the Cypher query:

```
CALL apoc.meta.stats()
```

The following screenshot shows the database statistics:

Figure 4.2 – Database statistics

We can see from the screenshot the number of label types, relationship types, and property types. The fourth column shows the total number of nodes in the database. The next column shows the total number of relationships in the database. The next column shows the node counts by label. The next column shows the relationship count based on start or end label types.

For example, "()-[:HAS_ENCOUNTER]->(:wellness)": 22019 tells us that there are 22,019 HAS_ENCOUNTER relationships that have the wellness node label as the end node.

The next column shows the frequencies of different relationships in the graph. The last column is the JSON representation of all the previous column data. This provides a wealth of information on how the graph is connected.

Now that we have seen how the data is distributed, let us see how the data is connected in graph format next. We can get the graph schema by running this Cypher query:

```
CALL db.schema.visualization()
```

We can see the graph visualization in the following screenshot:

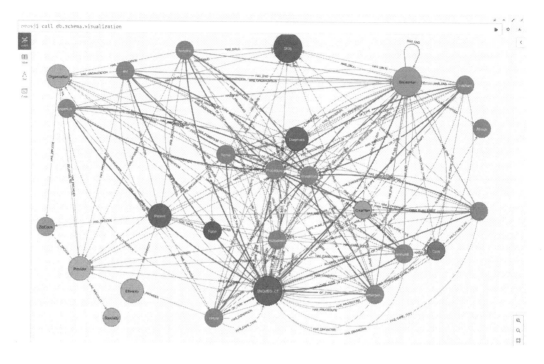

Figure 4.3 – Database graph schema visualization

Our schema looks very busy here. This is because we have used a lot of secondary labels for Encounter nodes and SNOMED_CT nodes. Once we remove them, the schema will look cleaner. The following image represents the clean schema visualization:

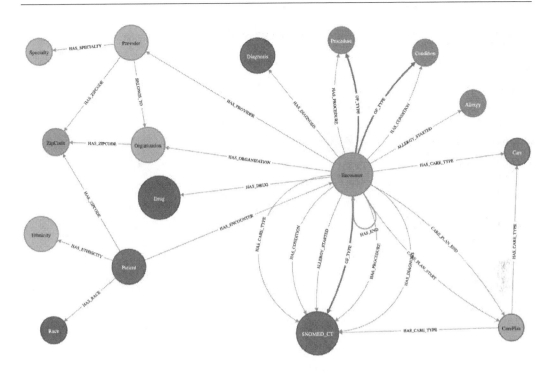

Figure 4.4 – Database graph schema visualization – clean version

Now, this looks like the data diagram we started building using *Arrows App* (https://arrows.app) in the previous chapter. One difference we see here is that the Encounter node is connected to the SNOMED_CT node via multiple relationship types. This is because the SNOMED_CT node can have secondary labels and these relationship types map to those secondary labels.

Now, let us look at one of the pieces of patient node data in the graph that we have loaded, to see how it matches the data diagram we built in the last chapter to assist us with data loading. The following picture shows the Neo4j-Browser visualization:

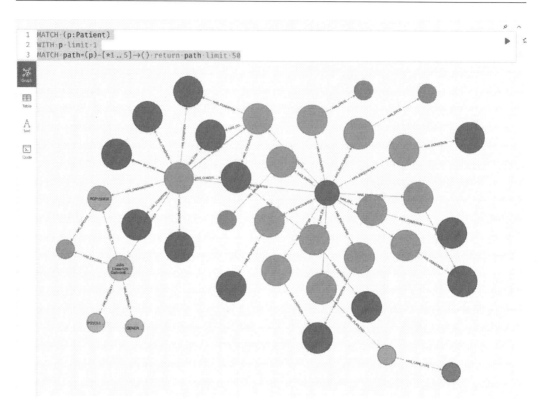

```
1  MATCH (p:Patient)
2  WITH p limit 1
3  MATCH path=(p)-[*1..5]→() return path limit 50
```

Figure 4.5 – Patient data visualization in Neo4j Browser

This seems somewhat closer to what we built. Since we cannot control how the browser renders the visualization, it is difficult to tell how similar it is. Let us view it in the Neo4j Bloom visualization that comes along with Neo4j Desktop:

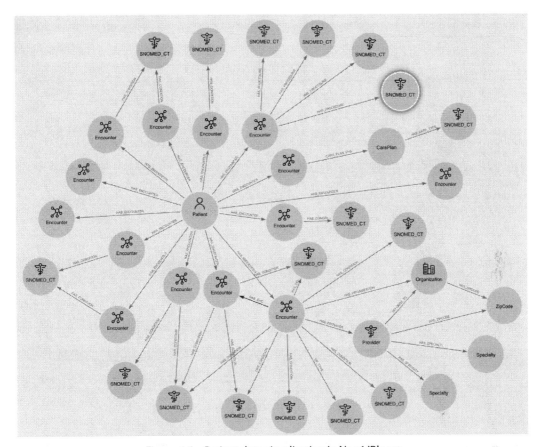

Figure 4.6 – Patient data visualization in Neo4 jBloom

This looks closer to what we built as a data diagram. We have a `Patient` node in the middle and the `Encounter` nodes around it, which are connected to `Diagnosis (SNOMED-CT)` nodes, `Provider` nodes, `Organization` nodes, and so on.

Now that we have explored the data in a graph, let us get into querying the graph using Cypher. We will start by querying for the nodes first.

Querying the nodes

We have the patient data set along with the encounters with the healthcare system. We will look at a question and how we can represent it in Cypher. To find the total number of patients in the system, type the following into the console:

```
MATCH (p:Patient) RETURN count(p)
```

This Cypher query returns the total number of patients in the system. This screenshot shows the response in the browser:

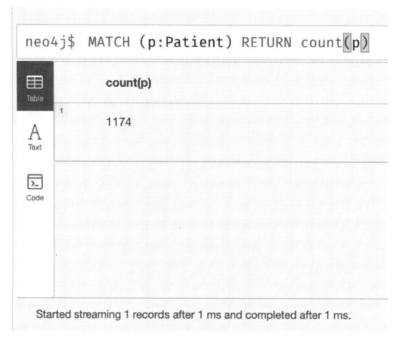

Figure 4.7 – Patient count query

You can see that it is instantaneous. Neo4j maintains the count stores for labels, so when we ask for counts in this way, Neo4j uses the count stores to return the response. The response time is consistent when we have one node or one million nodes of this label.

The `Patient` node only had one label. We know the `Encounter` node has multiple labels. Let us write a query to find label distribution. The Cypher query looks as follows:

```
MATCH (e:Encounter)
RETURN labels(e) as labels, count(e) as counts
```

This query returns all the `Encounter` label combinations available, along with the count of the nodes per label combination:

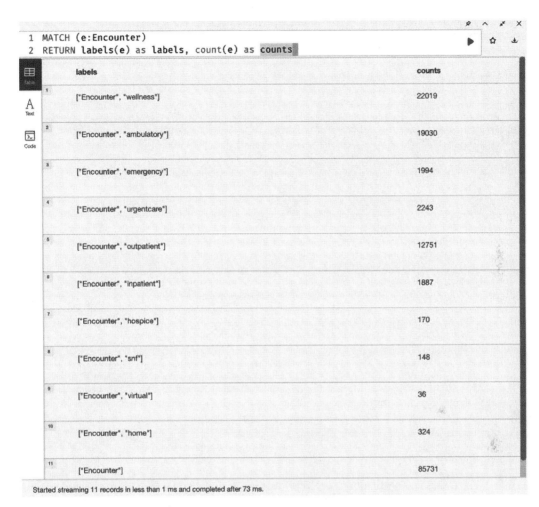

Figure 4.8 – Encounter label distribution count query

We can see that basic `Encounter` nodes, which also contain the `Stop` representation, are the majority here. After that, the `wellness` nodes are the majority. We can also see that this query takes more time, as it cannot leverage the count stores. Now, let us find a patient by ID:

```
MATCH (p:Patient
      {id:'7361ce15-cf67-ae76-88e6-bcbdca19ce0b'})
RETURN p
```

This query should return a single patient node identified by the ID value provided.

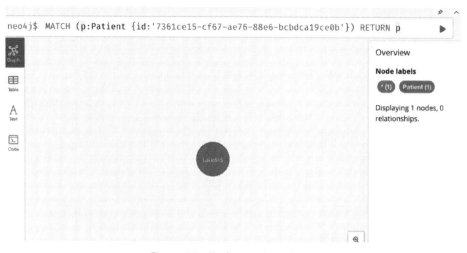

neo4j$ MATCH (p:Patient {id:'7361ce15-cf67-ae76-88e6-bcbdca19ce0b'}) RETURN p

Overview

Node labels

* (1)   Patient (1)

Displaying 1 nodes, 0
relationships.

Lakin515

Figure 4.9 – Finding patients by ID

This is straightforward and we can see the node is shown here. If we select the **Table** view, the data is shown as follows:

neo4j$ MATCH (p:Patient {id:'7361ce15-cf67-ae76-88e6-bcbdca19ce0b'}) RETURN p

p

{
    "identity": 35,
    "labels": [
      "Patient"
    ],
    "properties": {
"lastName": "Lakin515",
"firstName": "Jason347",
"marital": "S",
"city": "Ashland",
"prefix": "Mr.",
"county": "Middlesex County",
"location": point({srid:4326, x:-71.46554360447165, y:42.21791230406913}),
"id": "7361ce15-cf67-ae76-88e6-bcbdca19ce0b",
"drivers": "S99917028",
"birthDate": "1972-05-26",

Started streaming 1 records in less than 1 ms and completed after 1 ms.

Figure 4.10 – Finding patients by ID – Table view

We can see the JSON representation of the node data shown here in the **Table** mode. Since we are leveraging the index here, the response is quick. Now, let us get patients using their first names. The Cypher query would look as follows:

```
MATCH (p:Patient {firstName:'Jason347'}) return p
```

In this query, we are trying to find all the patents whose first name is Jason347:

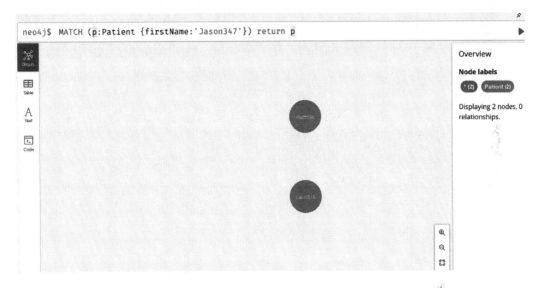

Figure 4.11 – Finding patients by firstName

We can see that two nodes are returned. Since our dataset is smaller, the response can be quick. Let us check how the database executed the query. The quickest option is to use the EXPLAIN clause. Let us run the explain query. It would look as follows:

```
EXPLAIN MATCH (p:Patient {firstName:'Jason347'}) return p
```

Here, we are trying to see how the database will try to execute this query.

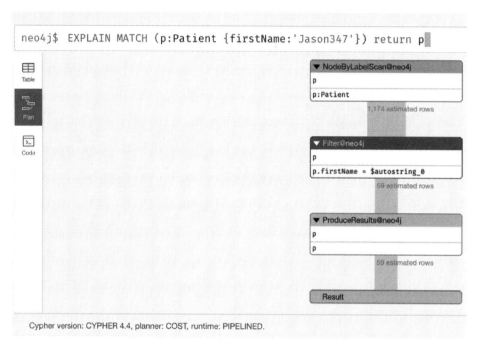

Figure 4.12 – Finding patients by firstName – EXPLAIN MATCH

From the picture, we can see the database did a `NodeByLabelScan`. This is similar to a table scan in RDBMS terms. Since there was no index on the `firstName`, the database finds all the nodes identified by the label `Patient` and checks if it has a `firstName` property with specified value. To understand the true cost, we can try `PROFILE` clause. The Cypher query will look like this.

```
PROFILE MATCH (p:Patient {firstName:'Jason347'}) return p
```

Here, we are trying to **PROFILE** the query to retrieve the patient using the `firstName` property.

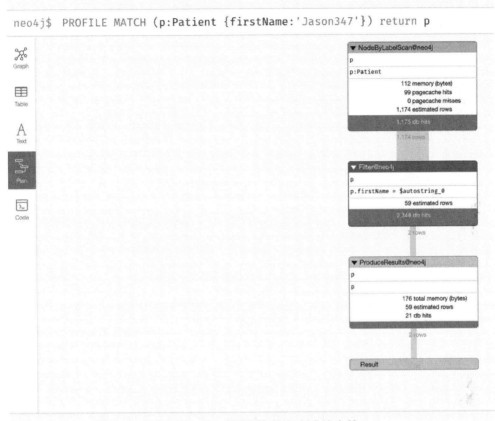

```
neo4j$  PROFILE MATCH (p:Patient {firstName:'Jason347'}) return p
```

Figure 4.13 – Finding patients by firstName – PROFILE plan

We can see that there are 3,544 DB hits to execute the query. Each DB hit means a unit of work done by the database. The higher the DB hits, higher the amount of work the database is doing and can have an impact on query SLAs.

Since we don't have a point of reference yet, let us see what the number of DB hits would be if we execute a query with an index. For this, we can execute the query with patient ID. The Cypher would look like this:

```
PROFILE
MATCH (p:Patient
        {id:'7361ce15-cf67-ae76-88e6-bcbdca19ce0b'})
RETURN p
```

Here, we are trying to **PROFILE** the query that retrieves the patient using the id property.

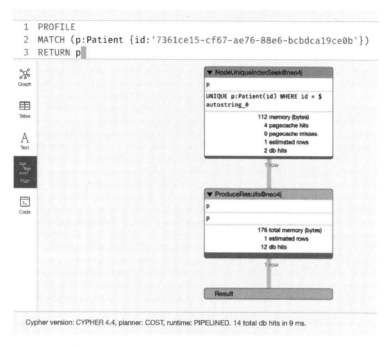

```
1  PROFILE
2  MATCH (p:Patient {id:'7361ce15-cf67-ae76-88e6-bcbdca19ce0b'})
3  RETURN p
```

Figure 4.14 – Finding patients by ID – PROFILE plan

From the profile, we can see that it took 14 DB hits, out of which 12 DB hits were to return all the properties of the Patient node. We can see how big a difference an index can make when we are executing queries. We will touch upon this subject more in the later chapters.

Now, let us add an index for the firstName property, to make sure we are not seeing this behavior by chance:

```
CREATE INDEX p_firstName IF NOT EXISTS
FOR (n:Patient)
ON n.firstName
```

Execute this query in the browser first.

Now, let's profile the query again and compare the results.

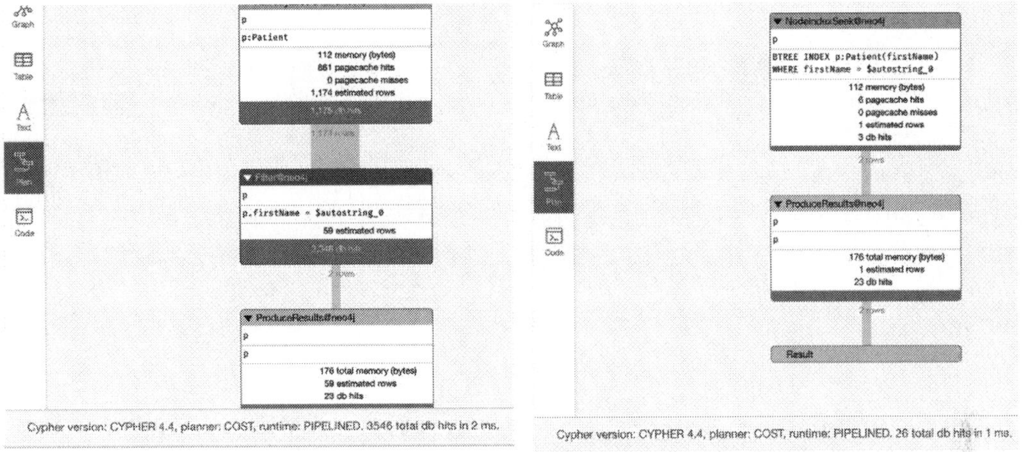

Figure 4.15 – Finding patients by name – PROFILE with and without index

We can see after adding an index that DB hits reduced from 3,546 to 26, which is more than 100 times better. Not all queries see this kind of improvement, but having an index can make queries orders of magnitude better.

In Cypher, we can use STARTS WITH or ENDS WITH clauses for string properties. Let us find all the patients whose ID starts with 73. The Cypher query looks as follows:

```
MATCH (p:Patient) WHERE p.id STARTS WITH '73' RETURN p
```

This query is trying to retrieve all the patient nodes whose ID property starts with 73:

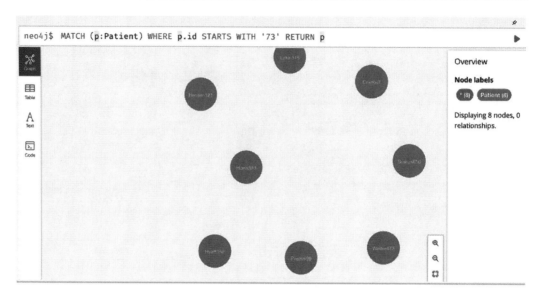

Figure 4.16 – Finding patients by ID – STARTS WITH

We can see there are eight nodes matching that pattern. We are also using the WHERE clause here. We can use the { } query pattern only when we are looking for exact values. Also, when you have multiple values in that pattern, it acts like an AND condition. If we are looking for range or using other clauses, then we need to use a WHERE clause to build our queries. Before now, we only got nodes as a response. Say we want CSV values as our response, such as a patient's first name and last name to be returned. The query would look as follows:

```
MATCH (p:Patient) WHERE p.id STARTS WITH '73'
RETURN p.firstName as firstName, p.lastName as lastName
```

This query is trying to retrieve the firstName and lastName values for patients whose ID starts with 73:

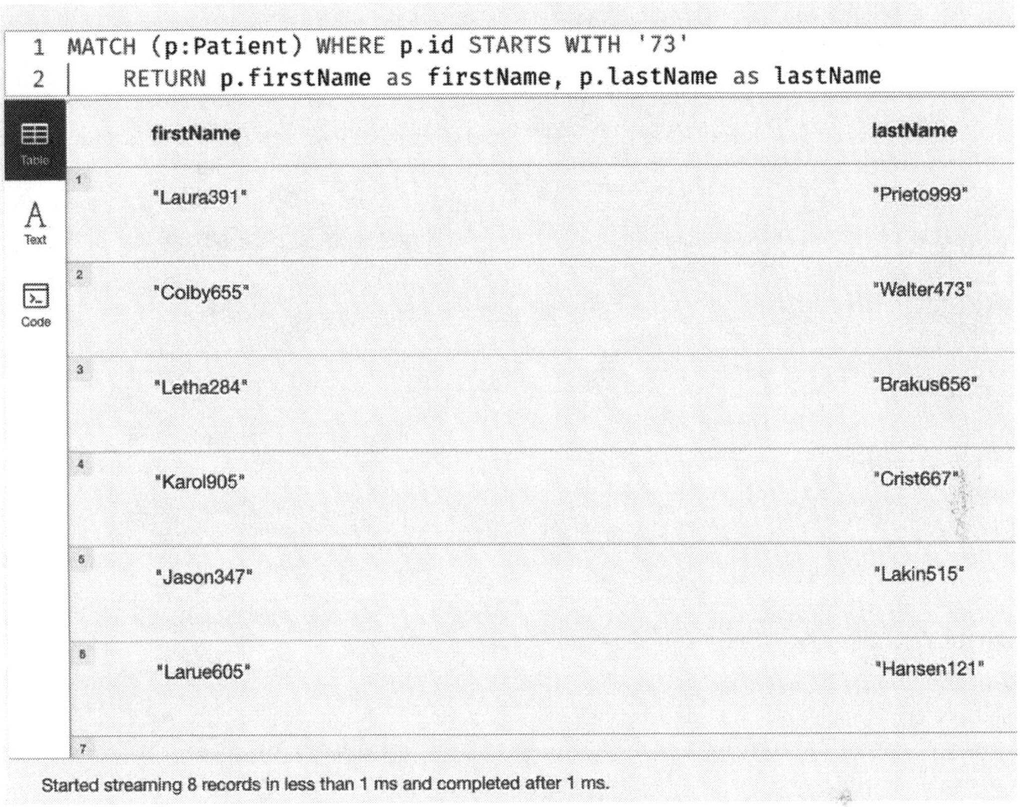

```
1  MATCH (p:Patient) WHERE p.id STARTS WITH '73'
2      RETURN p.firstName as firstName, p.lastName as lastName
```

	firstName	lastName
1	"Laura391"	"Prieto999"
2	"Colby655"	"Walter473"
3	"Letha284"	"Brakus656"
4	"Karol905"	"Crist667"
5	"Jason347"	"Lakin515"
6	"Larue605"	"Hansen121"
7		

Started streaming 8 records in less than 1 ms and completed after 1 ms.

Figure 4.17 – Finding patients by ID – STARTS WITH – CSV response

When we return individual properties, then the data is returned in CSV format. For visualizations or other processing, we can return the data as nodes and relationships; to consume the data in a tabular format, we can return the data in CSV format as shown here.

Let us do a profile on this query to see whether we are using indexes or not using this query:

```
PROFILE MATCH (p:Patient) WHERE p.id STARTS WITH '73'
RETURN p.firstName as firstName, p.lastName as lastName
```

This is telling the database to execute the query (excluding the PROFILE keyword) and tell us exactly the amount of work that the database did:

```
1   PROFILE MATCH (p:Patient) WHERE p.id STARTS WITH '73'
2   RETURN p.firstName as firstName, p.lastName as lastName
3
```

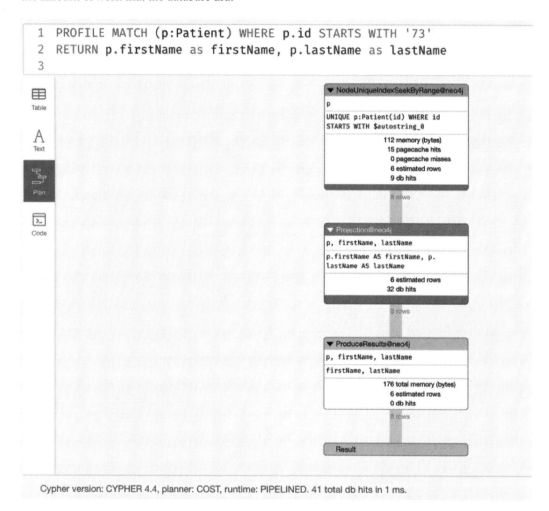

Cypher version: CYPHER 4.4, planner: COST, runtime: PIPELINED. 41 total db hits in 1 ms.

Figure 4.18 – Finding patients by ID – STARTS WITH – CSV response – PROFILE

We can see that for string properties when we have an index for the STARTS WITH clause, the index is leveraged. It is very important to understand this aspect. The WHERE clause works pretty similarly to all the other types except the Spatial Point type. For a Point type, we need to use spatial functions in the WHERE clause. Since we already have a location attribute on the Patient node, which is of the Point type, let us see how we can build a Cypher query on it.

Say we have a point of reference, {longitude: -71.46554, latitude: 42.217916}, in mind. We want to find all the patients within 5 kilometers of this point. Please remember that the majority of the time, the distance calculated by the spatial functions is in meters.

To achieve this, the Cypher query looks as follows:

```
WITH point({longitude: -71.46554, latitude: 42.217916}) as
refPoint
MATCH (p:Patient)
WITH p, point.distance(refPoint, p.location) as distance
WITH p, distance
WHERE distance < 5000
RETURN p.firstName as firstName, p.lastName as lastName,
distance
```

This query is using the `point` capabilities of the graph database to do a geolocation search.

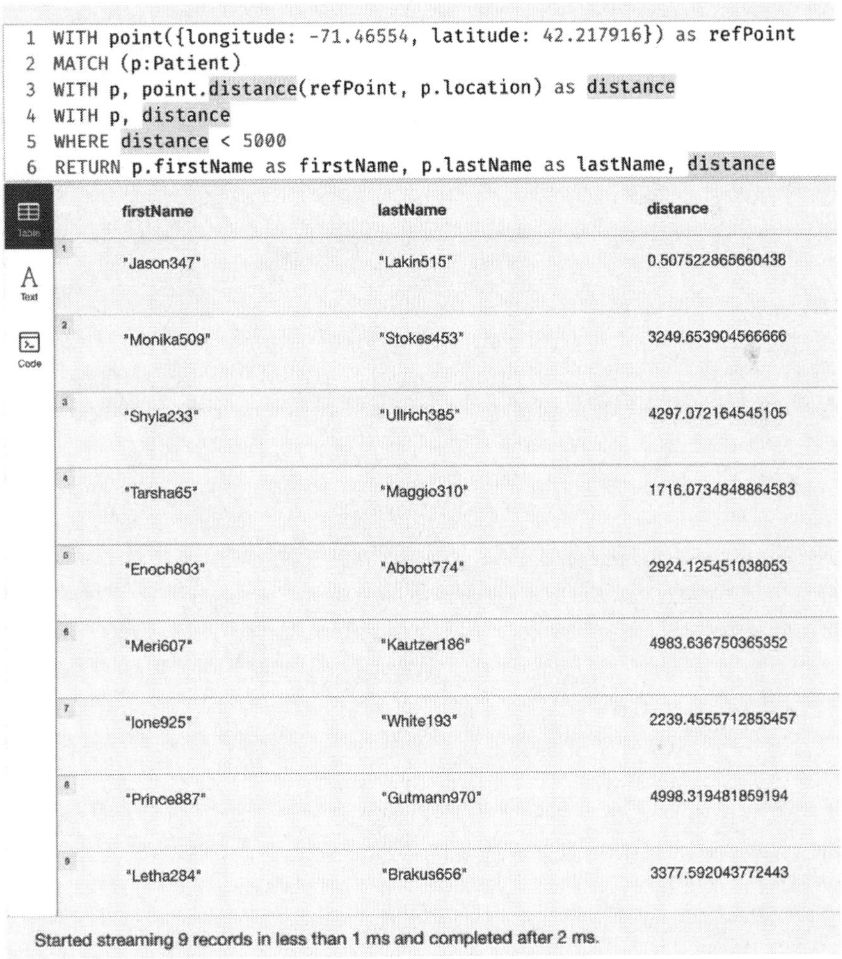

Figure 4.19 – Finding patients within a certain distance of a point

We can see we have 9 results, which are within 5 km of the reference point.

Now that we have worked with querying nodes, let us look at querying for the paths.

Querying the paths

A path here consists of an anchor node or starting node and traverses one or more hops in any direction from it. In the earlier section, we worked with the `Patient` node to showcase how to query nodes. Here, let us start from the `Patient` node and what it is connected to at one hop.

Our Cypher query can look as follows:

```
MATCH path=
    (:Patient {id:'7361ce15-cf67-ae76-88e6-bcbdca19ce0b'})-->()
RETURN path
```

This returns all the paths in one hop in the outgoing direction from the `Patient` node:

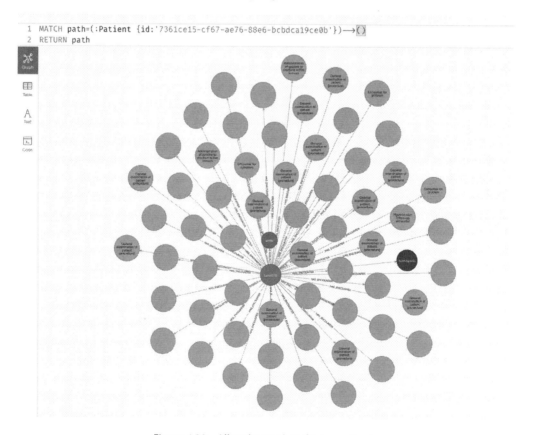

Figure 4.20 – All paths one hop from a patient

Here, we can see one `Race` node, one `Ethnicity` node, and 60 `Encounter` nodes. Say that we want to find out the race demographics of our patients where we can use paths to get these values. The Cypher query for it will look as follows:

```
MATCH (r:Race)
RETURN r.type as type, size((r)<-[:HAS_RACE]-()) as count
```

This query retrieves all the `Race` nodes and returns the `type` property and the number of nodes connected to it:

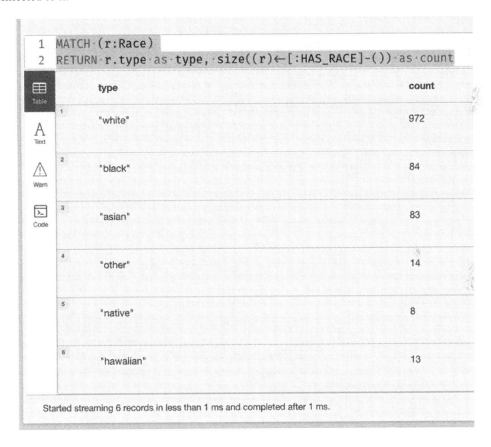

Figure 4.21 – Patient count by race

The approach we have taken here is to use path comprehension to find the values. This approach will also leverage the count stores to give a response quickly. We can get the same results using this query:

```
MATCH (r:Race)<-[:HAS_RACE]-(p)
RETURN r.type as type, count(p) as count
```

Let's profile each query to see which one is performing better.

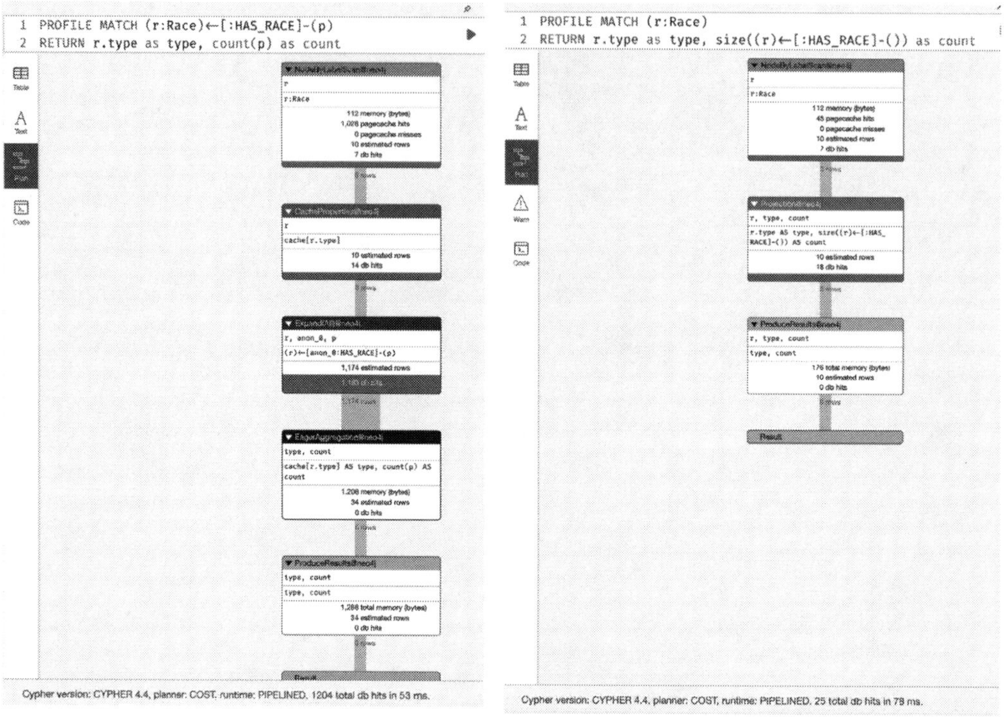

Figure 4.22 – Patient count by Race – PROFILE of different queries

We can see from the profile that the path comprehension way of getting counts is way cheaper (25 DB hits) than traversing the relationship and counting the nodes (1,204 DB hits). This is the advantage of leveraging the count stores to return the counts. This was possible here because only `Patient` was connected to the `Race` node. Let us take the `ZipCode` node, to which both the `Patient` and `Provider` nodes are connected via the same relationship, `HAS_ZIPCODE`. Let us see how the query is being processed by the database when we use a similar approach. First, the Cypher queries look like this.

Here's the first version of the query:

```
MATCH (z:ZipCode)<-[:HAS_ZIPCODE]-(p:Patient)
RETURN z.zip as zip, count(p) as count
```

Here's the second version of the query:

```
MATCH (z:ZipCode)
RETURN z.zip as zip, size((z)<-[:HAS_ZIPCODE]-(:Patient)) as
count
```

You can see one difference between the queries, but we had to give the `Patient` label explicitly in both of the queries.

Let us look at the profile of each of these queries:

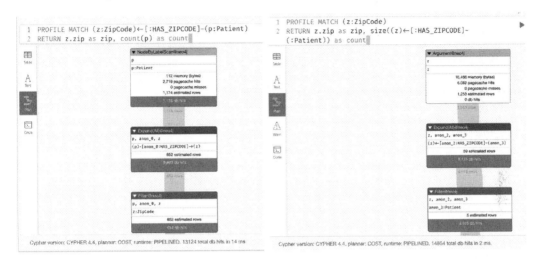

Figure 4.23 – Patient count by ZIP code – PROFILE of different queries

We can see here that using path comprehension does not benefit us at all. In fact, that is a costlier query due to the way the database has to traverse and apply the label check. So, if there is a requirement to provide counts such as these more often, say a dashboard that refreshes every 30 seconds, then having distinct relationships can make a huge difference not only in terms of that query performance but also in terms of overall database resource consumption. This is where tuning the data model as our requirements grow and making changes are required. Neo4j being schema-less is great for this.

Now, let us look at some functional questions. Let us build a query for how many patients visited the providers within the same ZIP code. We know that `Patient` and `Provider` are not connected directly. They are only connected via the `Encounter` nodes. The Cypher query for it looks as follows:

```
MATCH (p:Patient)-[:HAS_ZIPCODE]->(zip)
WITH p, zip
MATCH (p)-[:HAS_ENCOUNTER]->()-[:HAS_PROVIDER]->
      (prov)-[:HAS_ZIPCODE]->(zip)
WITH DISTINCT p,prov, zip
RETURN p.firstName as patientFirst,
       p.lastName as patientLast,
       prov.name as provider,
       zip.zip as zipcode
```

We are starting with patients who have a ZIP code, then we are traversing via the Encounter node to Provider to the ZIP code that any given Patient is connected to. This screenshot shows the results:

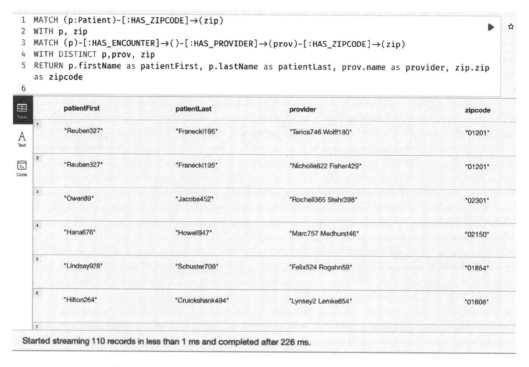

Figure 4.24 – Patients who visited providers in the same zip code

Also, in the query, we are using the WITH clause after we get patient and zip. The WITH clause will separate the previous section of the query from the next section. The data from the first section of the query is streamed to the next section of the query and processed in that order. This avoids the Cartesian product.

Now, let us take a look at a slightly more complex query: once a condition is identified, what a patient's activity from the previous 60 days has been.

The Cypher query for this can look as follows:

```
MATCH (c:Condition {code:'160903007'})
    <-[:HAS_CONDITION]-(encounter)
WITH encounter LIMIT 1
MATCH (encounter)<-[:HAS_ENCOUNTER]-(patient)
WITH patient, encounter
MATCH (patient)-[:HAS_ENCOUNTER]->(e)
```

```
WHERE ( encounter.date - duration('P60D') )  <= e.date <
(encounter.date)
WITH e ORDER BY e.date
MATCH (e)-[:HAS_DRUG|:HAS_PROCEDURE]->(x)
RETURN labels(x)[0] AS eventType, x.description AS name,    e.
date AS startDate
```

We can see from the query that, we find a patient with a given `Condition`, and within the previous 60 days, we are looking for any related DRUG or PROCEDURE delivered.

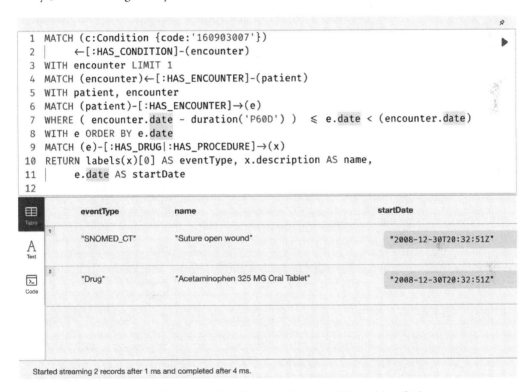

Figure 4.25 – Activity for 60 days before a condition is identified

We can see that one procedure has been performed and one drug prescribed 60 days before the condition has been identified.

Let us try one more query. For each drug, let us see how many patients it has been prescribed to. To be able to do this, we need to start from the `Drug` node first and via `Encounter` node, we can reach the `Patient` node.

Cypher looks as follows for the query:

```
MATCH (d:Drug)<-[:HAS_DRUG]-()<-[:HAS_ENCOUNTER]-(p)
WITH DISTINCT d, p
RETURN d.description as drug, count(p) as patients
```

This query is trying to retrieve all the drugs in the system, along with how many patients they have been prescribed to.

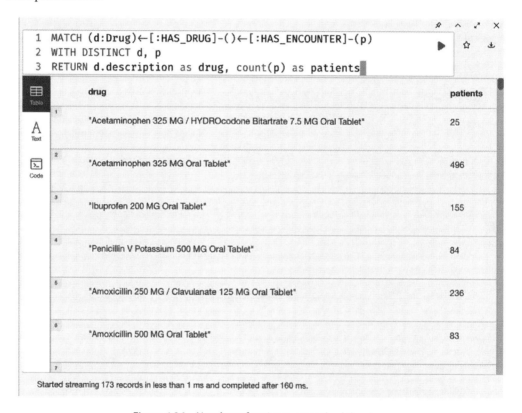

Figure 4.26 – Number of patients prescribed the drug

We can see it is simple to traverse and collect the details as needed.

All this time, we have been using hardcoded values to execute the query. This is fine for validating and tuning queries occasionally. The negative side of hardcoding values is that there would be query planning involved each time we executed the query. This is not going to be a small amount of time. Depending on what the query is like, the query plan time may be much longer than the actual execution. When the application is executing a large number of queries against the database, using parameterized queries to reduce or eliminate the query planning time can have a huge impact on system performance.

Now, we will look at how to use parameterized queries in Neo4j Browser.

The first step is to define the parameters. For this, we will use the `:Param` keyword in Browser.

We need to execute this query to set a parameter in the Browser session:

```
:param id => '7361ce15-cf67-ae76-88e6-bcbdca19ce0b'
```

Please remember that this is Browser-specific usage only. For applications, you need to use the driver API.

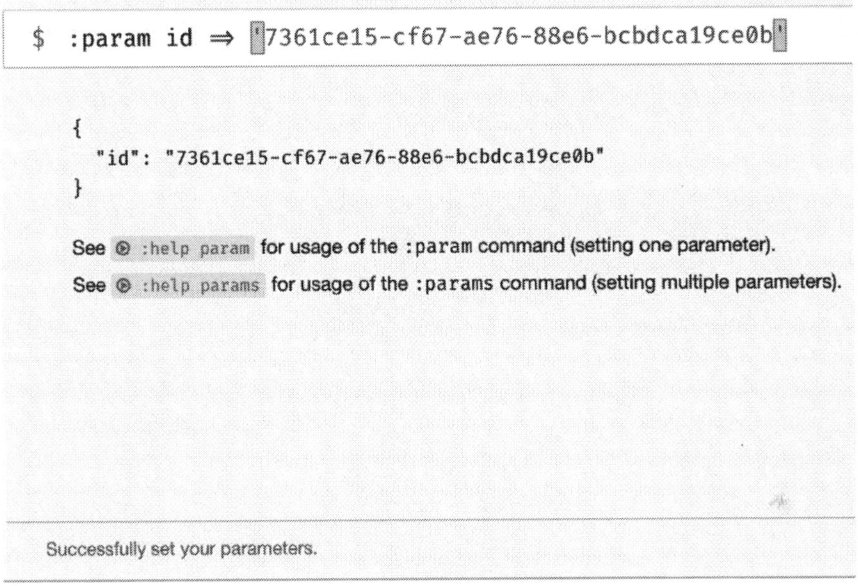

```
$ :param id ⇒ 7361ce15-cf67-ae76-88e6-bcbdca19ce0b

{
  "id": "7361ce15-cf67-ae76-88e6-bcbdca19ce0b"
}

See ⊗ :help param for usage of the :param command (setting one parameter).
See ⊗ :help params for usage of the :params command (setting multiple parameters).

Successfully set your parameters.
```

Figure 4.27 – Defining a parameter

The screenshot shows that we are able to successfully define a new parameter called `id` in a Browser query context.

Now that we have defined the parameter, let us use it in a query:

```
MATCH (p:Patient {id:$id}) RETURN p
```

We refer to the parameter using the $ symbol in the query. We can define one or many parameters and all of them can be referenced in the query using the $ symbol. The following screenshot shows the query execution in Browser and the results.

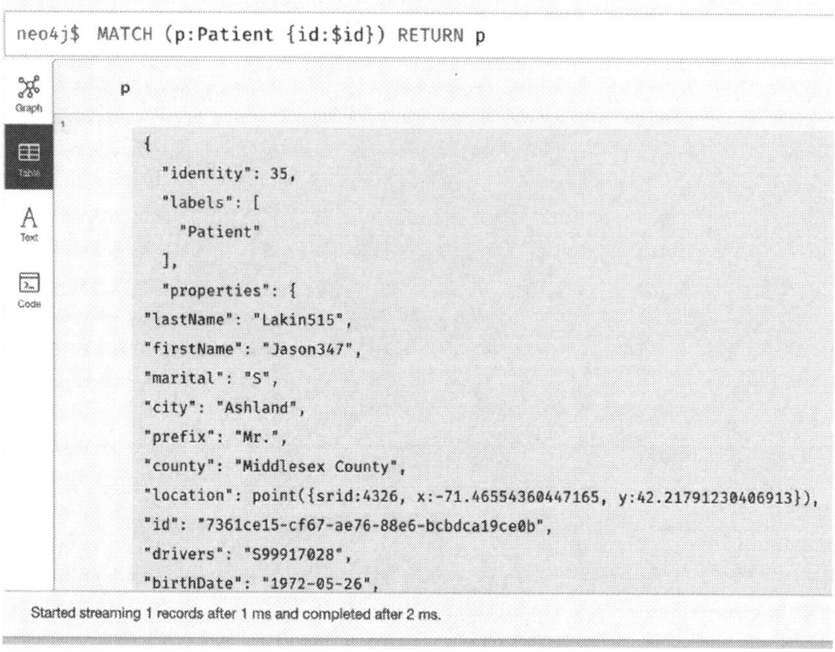

```
neo4j$ MATCH (p:Patient {id:$id}) RETURN p
```

Figure 4.28 – Executing a parameterized query

There are some limitations to using parameters. We cannot use parameters in place of labels or relationship types. This is because Cypher does not allow variable substitution for node labels or relationship types. Otherwise, anywhere we can have a variable, we can use parameterized values.

Let's look at a slightly more complex parameter definition. Say we want to define a map as a single parameter. We can achieve this using this query:

```
:param test => { RETURN 123 as type, "test" as name}
```

This defines a map with `name` and `type` keys and assigns the value to a parameter named `test`. One difference here is that the map is wrapped into a list.

First, let's execute the query.

```
$ :param test ⇒ { RETURN 123 as type, "test" as name}

{
  "test": [
    {
      "type": 123,
      "name": "test"
    }
  ]
}

See ⊕ :help param for usage of the :param command (setting one parameter).
See ⊕ :help params for usage of the :params command (setting multiple parameters).
```

Successfully set your parameters.

Figure 4.29 – Defining a complex parameter in Browser

We can see the test key is associated with a list and the first element in the list is the map with the values we have defined.

Let's write a Cypher query to use this parameter:

```
WITH $test[0] as data
RETURN data.name as name, data.type as type
```

We can see from the query that we are taking the first element of the input parameter and returning name and type values from it.

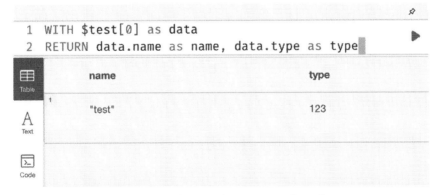

Figure 4.30 – Using the complex parameter from the query

From the screenshot, we can see that we can retrieve the individual values from the map the way we defined them.

Now, let us look at what we have learned so far.

Summary

In this chapter, we have taken a look at the graph data model and explored the graph using database statistics and schema visualization.

In this chapter, we learned about how to find nodes by leveraging indexes or without using indexes; compared the performance of different queries to understand the importance of using indexes for querying; used PROFILE to understand performance issues in the queries; learned about using the STARTS WITH clause, which leverages an index; worked with point properties to leverage the geospatial capabilities of Graph; traversed the graph efficiently; leveraged count stores; and built complex queries using the WITH clause.

In the next chapter, we will continue our graph exploration by performing more complex queries, which will involve filtering, sorting, and aggregation.

5

Filtering, Sorting, and Aggregations

In the last chapter, we looked at basic querying using Cypher. In this chapter, we will take it a step further by discussing adding filtering, sorting, and aggregations to the querying. We will cover these aspects in this chapter:

- Filtering with node labels and relationship types
- Filtering with WHERE and WITH clauses
- Sorting data using the ORDER BY clause
- Working with aggregations

We will start by filtering the data in queries.

Filtering with node labels and relationship types

In Cypher, filtering starts with the usage of node labels and relationship types. Let us take a look at a query where we do not apply any filters in Cypher:

```
MATCH p=()--() RETURN p
```

This query returns all paths where any nodes are connected. In this query, there is no filtering. This query is shown to illustrate the fact that filtering is a bit different from SQL queries. Now, let us take a look at this query:

```
MATCH p=()-->() RETURN p
```

In this query, we are not using any node labels or relationship types, but we are filtering on relationships by outgoing direction:

```
MATCH p=(:Patient)-->() RETURN p
```

When we look at this query, we are looking for `Patient` nodes first and traversing all the outgoing relationships to find the paths. This showcases how node labels are leveraged for filtering:

```
MATCH p=(:Patient)-[:HAS_ZIPCODE]->() RETURN p
```

This query applies one more filter to the previous query. Now, we are only looking at outgoing HAS_ZIPCODE relationship types from `Patient` nodes and only returning those paths.

We will take a look at one of the queries we built in the previous chapter and see how adding labels and relationships to the path impacts the performance of the query. The query we are picking is the one where we look at the number of patients to which a drug has been prescribed:

```
MATCH (d:Drug)<-[:HAS_DRUG]-()<-[:HAS_ENCOUNTER]-(p)
WITH DISTINCT d, p
RETURN d.description as drug, count(p) as patients
```

In this query, we are starting from the `Drug` node and traversing an incoming HAS_DRUG relationship, ignoring the node label, traversing the HAS_ENCOUNTER relationship, and ignoring the label of the node coming next. Let us profile this query and see the performance of the query. The DISTINCT clause also acts as a filter in this query. If we have more than one prescription of the same drug for a patient, we want to count that as only one, so using DISTINCT here eliminates duplicates.

```
1  PROFILE MATCH (d:Drug)←[:HAS_DRUG]-()←[:HAS_ENCOUNTER]-(p)
2  WITH DISTINCT d, p
3  RETURN d.description as drug, count(p) as patients
```

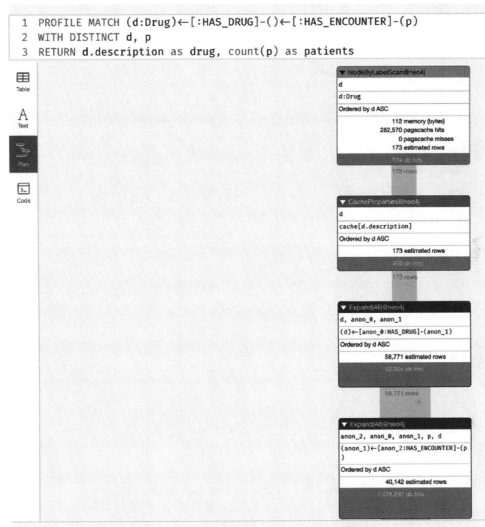

Figure 5.1 – Profile of drug-patient interactions – iteration 1

We can see that it generates 1,137,930 db hits.

Now, let us look at the same query – most developers are going to write it as follows:

```
MATCH (d:Drug)<-[:HAS_DRUG]-(e:Encounter)<-[:HAS_ENCOUNTER]-
(p:Patient)
WITH DISTINCT d, p
RETURN d.description as drug, count(p) as patients
```

One difference we see in the query here is that we have added labels and variables for intermediate nodes where we used to ignore the labels. Let us look at this query's performance:

```
1  PROFILE MATCH (d:Drug)←[:HAS_DRUG]-(e:Encounter)←[:HAS_ENCOUNTER]-(p:Patient)
2  WITH DISTINCT d, p
3  RETURN d.description as drug, count(p) as patients
```

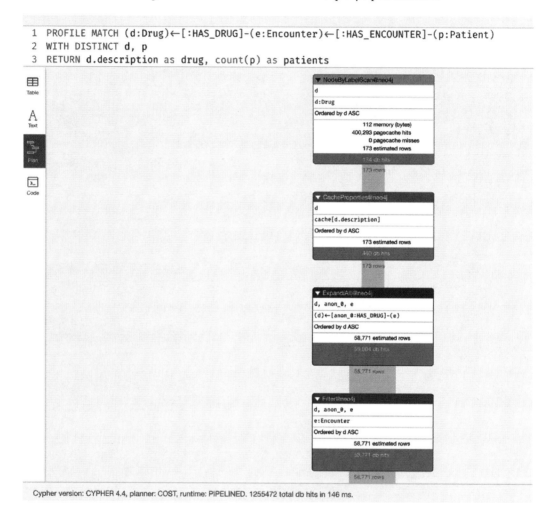

Cypher version: CYPHER 4.4, planner: COST, runtime: PIPELINED. 1255472 total db hits in 146 ms.

Figure 5.2 – Profile of drug-patient interactions – iteration 2

We can see that this query generates 1,255,472 db hits, which is 11% more than the previous iteration, where we didn't specify labels for more strict filtering. This is a bit counterintuitive for SQL developers. This is because of the way Neo4j processes the query. Neo4j optimizes the traversal patterns. When we add a label to a node in the traversal, then Neo4j must stop there and check whether the node in the path has that label. This is one extra db hit. This is why this query requires more database work to complete the query while making the most sense from a filtering perspective.

Here's another iteration of the same query that most SQL developers would write when migrating to graph databases:

```
MATCH (d:Drug)<--(e:Encounter)<--(p:Patient)
WITH DISTINCT d, p
RETURN d.description as drug, count(p) as patients
```

In this query, we can see the developer relying on node labels that are connected to others ignoring the relationship types. Let us look at the performance of this query:

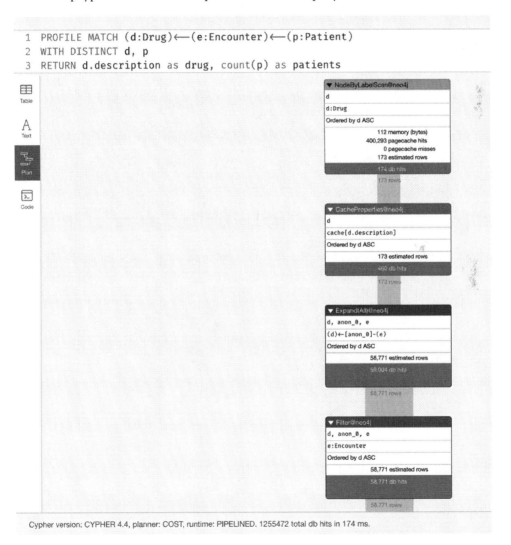

```
1  PROFILE MATCH (d:Drug)←(e:Encounter)←(p:Patient)
2  WITH DISTINCT d, p
3  RETURN d.description as drug, count(p) as patients
```

Table

Text

Plan

Code

▼ NodeByLabelScan@neo4j

d

d:Drug

Ordered by d ASC

112 memory (bytes)
400,293 pagecache hits
0 pagecache misses
173 estimated rows

174 db hits

173 rows

▼ CacheProperties@neo4j

d

cache[d.description]

Ordered by d ASC

173 estimated rows

460 db hits

173 rows

▼ Expand(All)@neo4j

d, anon_0, e

(d)←[anon_0]-(e)

Ordered by d ASC

58,771 estimated rows

59,004 db hits

58,771 rows

▼ Filter@neo4j

d, anon_0, e

e:Encounter

Ordered by d ASC

58,771 estimated rows

58,771 db hits

58,771 rows

Cypher version: CYPHER 4.4, planner: COST, runtime: PIPELINED. 1255472 total db hits in 174 ms.

Figure 5.3 – Profile of drug-patient interactions – iteration 3

We can see this version of the query generates 1,255,472 db hits. This is the same as the previous revision of the query. This is because both `Drug` and `Encounter` nodes only have one type of incoming relationship. So, in this case, there is no difference in the performance whether we specify the relationship type or not.

Now, let us take a look at another version of the same query that most SQL developers would write:

```
MATCH (d:Drug)--(e:Encounter)--(p:Patient)
WITH DISTINCT d, p
RETURN d.description as drug, count(p) as patients
```

The difference in the query here is that the direction of the relationship is taken out. This is one of the most common query patterns that new developers would attempt to write. Let us look at the performance of this query:

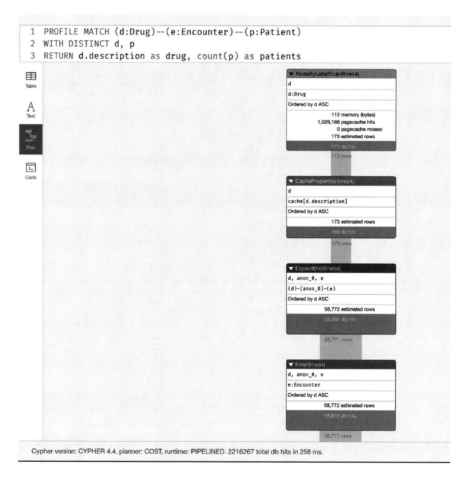

Figure 5.4 – Profile of drug-patient interactions – iteration 4

We can see this query is taking 2,216,267 db hits. This is 80% more db hits than the last version and almost double the number of db hits when compared to the original version of the query.

From these queries, we can see that node labels and relationship types can act as filters in the query, unlike in SQL, where only the WHERE clause is used for filtering or JOINS. Another aspect we can notice here is that using relationship types and the direction of the relationship in the query is more performant than using node labels.

> **Tip**
>
> When a relationship type uniquely identifies the start or end node types, then not providing labels in the traversal can improve the query performance. The only place we should use a label is when we are using a WHERE condition and want to leverage indexes or a relationship type is not enough.

Now, let us look at filtering the data using WHERE and WITH clauses.

Filtering with WHERE and WITH clauses

Now, let us build on the previous query and say we only want to return drugs that have more than 100 patients associated with them. This is the scenario in which the WHERE clause would come into the picture.

The Cypher query looks like this:

```
MATCH (d:Drug)<-[:HAS_DRUG]-()<-[:HAS_ENCOUNTER]-(p)
WITH DISTINCT d, p
WITH d.description as drug, count(p) as patients
WHERE patients > 100
RETURN drug, patients
```

To achieve what we want, we changed the query as shown in the highlighted section. We have to use the WITH clause first to collect the data and then apply a filter using the WHERE clause to prevent the data from being returned:

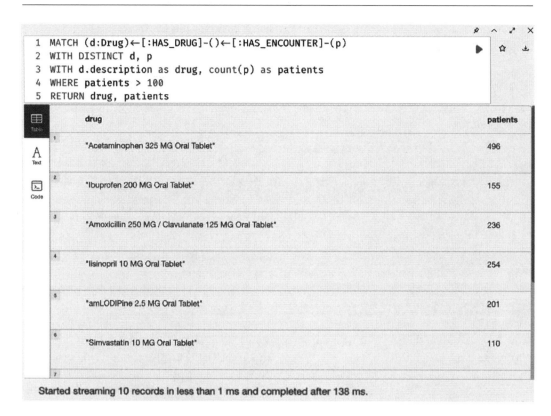

```
1  MATCH (d:Drug)←[:HAS_DRUG]-()←[:HAS_ENCOUNTER]-(p)
2  WITH DISTINCT d, p
3  WITH d.description as drug, count(p) as patients
4  WHERE patients > 100
5  RETURN drug, patients
```

drug	patients
"Acetaminophen 325 MG Oral Tablet"	496
"Ibuprofen 200 MG Oral Tablet"	155
"Amoxicillin 250 MG / Clavulanate 125 MG Oral Tablet"	236
"lisinopril 10 MG Oral Tablet"	254
"amLODIPine 2.5 MG Oral Tablet"	201
"Simvastatin 10 MG Oral Tablet"	110

Started streaming 10 records in less than 1 ms and completed after 138 ms.

Figure 5.5 – Drugs with more than 100 patients associated with them

The preceding screenshot shows the response. We can see there are only 10 drugs that have more than 100 patients who have a prescription for them.

We can also use SKIP and LIMIT to filter the data being returned. Say we only wanted to return 20 records from the drug prescriptions query – it would look like this:

```
MATCH (d:Drug)<-[:HAS_DRUG]-()<-[:HAS_ENCOUNTER]-(p)
WITH DISTINCT d, p
RETURN d.description as drug, count(p) as patients
LIMIT 20
```

This is the same as the original drug interaction query. The only change we have made is to add a LIMIT clause to the end to limit the number of results.

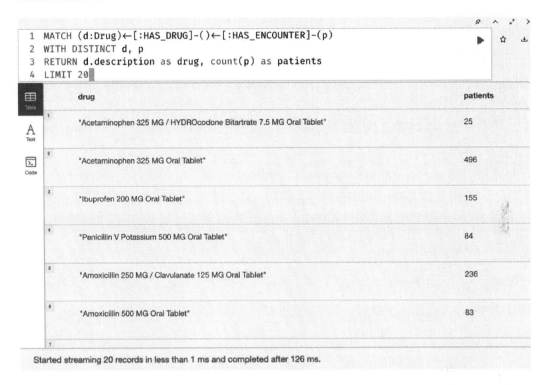

```
1  MATCH (d:Drug)←[:HAS_DRUG]-()←[:HAS_ENCOUNTER]-(p)
2  WITH DISTINCT d, p
3  RETURN d.description as drug, count(p) as patients
4  LIMIT 20
```

drug	patients
"Acetaminophen 325 MG / HYDROcodone Bitartrate 7.5 MG Oral Tablet"	25
"Acetaminophen 325 MG Oral Tablet"	496
"Ibuprofen 200 MG Oral Tablet"	155
"Penicillin V Potassium 500 MG Oral Tablet"	84
"Amoxicillin 250 MG / Clavulanate 125 MG Oral Tablet"	236
"Amoxicillin 500 MG Oral Tablet"	83

Started streaming 20 records in less than 1 ms and completed after 126 ms.

Figure 5.6 – First 20 records of drugs with the patients associated with them

We can see in the response that we got exactly 20 records. If the response data has less than 20 records, then all the records would be returned.

Similarly, we can use the SKIP clause to skip the initial records. Let us take a look at the query to skip the first 20 records and return the remaining data:

```
MATCH (d:Drug)<-[:HAS_DRUG]-()<-[:HAS_ENCOUNTER]-(p)
WITH DISTINCT d, p
RETURN d.description as drug, count(p) as patients
SKIP 20
```

This query will skip the first 20 records and return the remaining data:

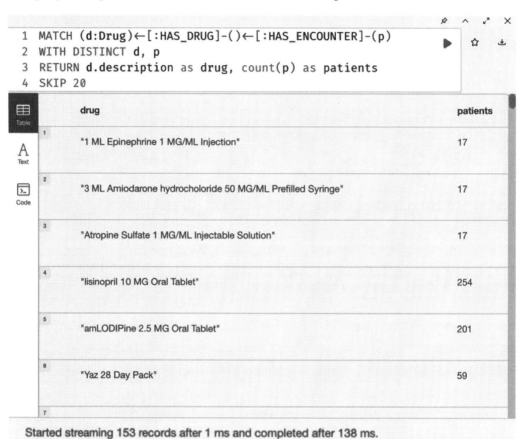

Figure 5.7 – Skipping the first 20 records of drugs and the patients associated with them

We can see we have 153 more records of data that are returned after skipping the first 20 records. If the original data set had less than 20 records, then no data would be returned.

We can also combine SKIP and LIMIT to skip the first few records and then limit the next set of records.

In this case, the query looks like this:

```
MATCH (d:Drug)<-[:HAS_DRUG]-()<-[:HAS_ENCOUNTER]-(p)
WITH DISTINCT d, p
RETURN d.description as drug, count(p) as patients
SKIP 20
LIMIT 20
```

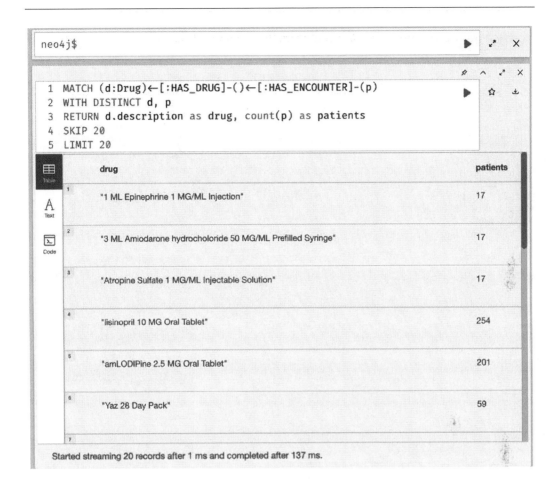

```
neo4j$
```

```
1  MATCH (d:Drug)←[:HAS_DRUG]-()←[:HAS_ENCOUNTER]-(p)
2  WITH DISTINCT d, p
3  RETURN d.description as drug, count(p) as patients
4  SKIP 20
5  LIMIT 20
```

drug	patients
"1 ML Epinephrine 1 MG/ML Injection"	17
"3 ML Amiodarone hydrocholoride 50 MG/ML Prefilled Syringe"	17
"Atropine Sulfate 1 MG/ML Injectable Solution"	17
"lisinopril 10 MG Oral Tablet"	254
"amLODIPine 2.5 MG Oral Tablet"	201
"Yaz 28 Day Pack"	59

Started streaming 20 records after 1 ms and completed after 137 ms.

Figure 5.8 – Skipping the first 20 records and returning the next 20
records of drugs with the patients associated with them

We can see here that 20 of the 153 records are returned from the previous query. It is possible to use SKIP and LIMIT to paginate the response. One thing we need to understand here is that the query execution time may not differ much from the full query and should be used with care. Let us look at the profile of this query to understand the db hits:

```
1  PROFILE MATCH (d:Drug)←[:HAS_DRUG]-()←[:HAS_ENCOUNTER]-(p)
2  WITH DISTINCT d, p
3  RETURN d.description as drug, count(p) as patients
4  SKIP 20
5  LIMIT 20
```

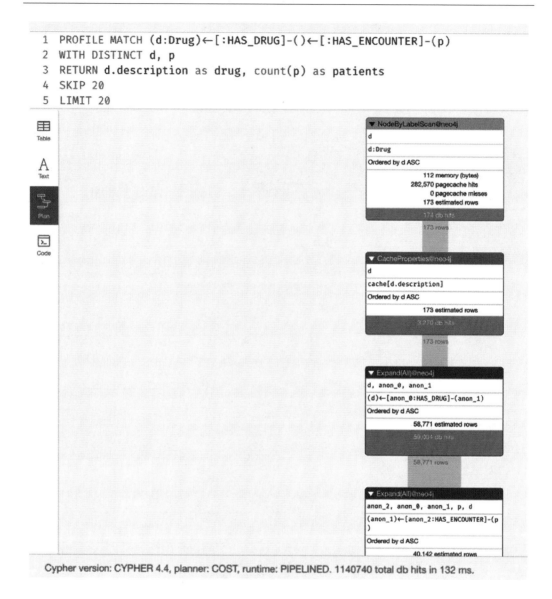

Cypher version: CYPHER 4.4, planner: COST, runtime: PIPELINED. 1140740 total db hits in 132 ms.

Figure 5.9 – Query profile with SKIP and LIMIT

We can see that the query generates 1,140,740 db hits, which is slightly higher than the db hits for the original query. It seems the LIMIT clause is adding a few extra db hits in terms of performance. This is why when we are thinking of pagination using SKIP and LIMIT, we need to take a holistic approach to the overall performance of the system rather than forcing pagination at the database level.

For filtering, along with the WHERE clause, we can also use an EXISTS or NOT EXISTS clause to filter data. We can use an EXISTS clause to check whether a pattern exists or a property exists for a node or a relationship. Let us count the encounter nodes that do have an end date property.

The Cypher code for this looks like this:

```
MATCH (e:Encounter)
WHERE EXISTS(e.end)
RETURN count(e)
```

This returns the number of encounters that have the end property:

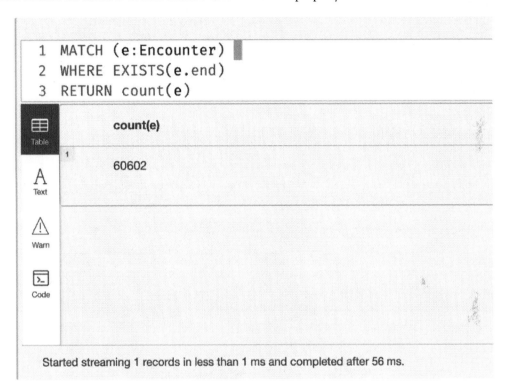

Figure 5.10 – Query using the EXISTS property

When we try this in the browser, it gives a warning that the use of EXISTS is deprecated for property checking. The supported way of doing this in Cypher is shown here:

```
MATCH (e:Encounter)
WHERE e.end IS NOT NULL
RETURN count(e)
```

This is the supported usage of checking whether a property exists in future versions of Cypher.

Let us see the usage of NOT EXISTS with a pattern check. Let us find patients that do not have a ZIP code associated with them. The Cypher code for this looks like this:

```
MATCH (p:Patient)
WHERE NOT EXISTS ((p)-[:HAS_ZIPCODE]->())
RETURN p
LIMIT 5
```

We can see in this query that we are checking for the absence of the ((p)-[:HAS_ZIPCODE]->()) pattern and returning the five patients that match this condition:

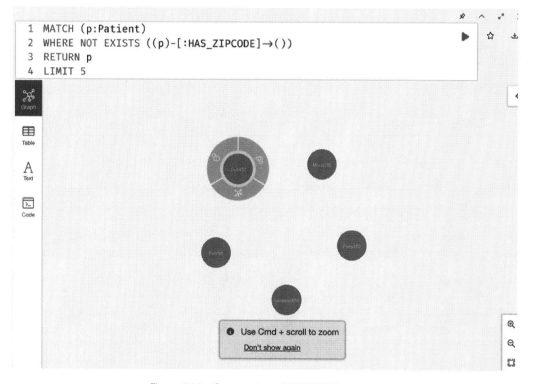

Figure 5.11 – Query using a NOT EXISTS pattern

We can see from the results that we are seeing patients who do not have ZIP codes associated with them. We can also use regular expressions in the WHERE clause to find data. Let's find patients whose first name starts with Jas using a regular expression. The Cypher query for this looks like this:

```
MATCH (p:Patient)
WHERE p.firstName =~'Jas.*'
RETURN p.firstName
```

This query finds all the patients whose first name starts with `Jas` and returns those first names.

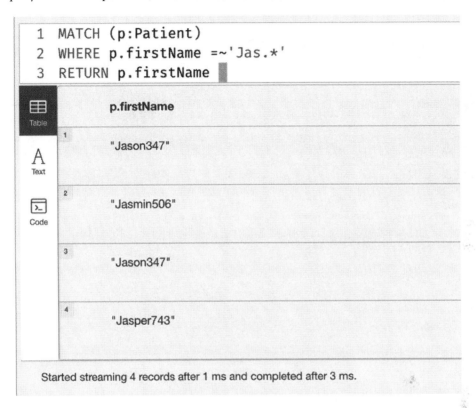

Figure 5.12 – Query using a regular expression

From the screenshot, we can see the response that matches the regular expression.

Now, let us look at sorting the results after filtering.

Sorting data using the ORDER BY clause

We can sort the results using the ORDER BY clause. Let us take the drug prescription query and apply sorting to it. First, let us take a look at the query that sorts results by the number of patients to which they are prescribed:

```
MATCH (d:Drug)<-[:HAS_DRUG]-()<-[:HAS_ENCOUNTER]-(p)
WITH DISTINCT d, p
RETURN d.description as drug, count(p) as patients
ORDER BY patients
```

This query returns the drug prescriptions in ascending order based on the number of patients they are prescribed to.

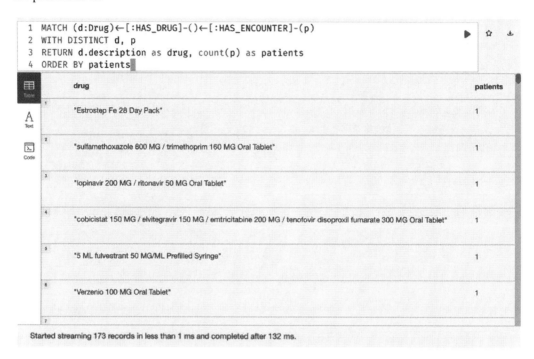

Figure 5.13 – Drug prescriptions ordered by the number of patients they are prescribed to

We can see the data in ascending order based on the number of patients the drugs are prescribed to. Now, let us look at the query where the data is in descending order:

```
MATCH (d:Drug)<-[:HAS_DRUG]-()<-[:HAS_ENCOUNTER]-(p)
WITH DISTINCT d, p
RETURN d.description as drug, count(p) as patients
ORDER BY patients DESC
```

Let us take a screenshot of the query results:

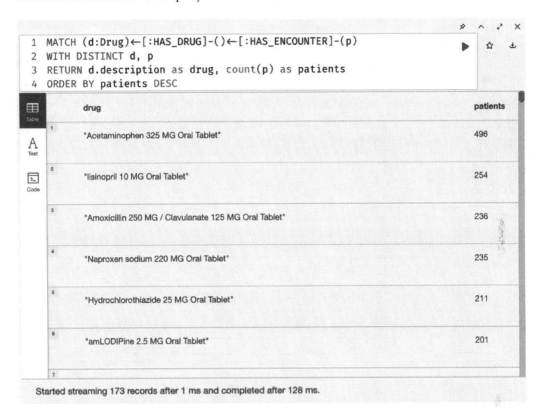

```
1  MATCH (d:Drug)←[:HAS_DRUG]-()←[:HAS_ENCOUNTER]-(p)
2  WITH DISTINCT d, p
3  RETURN d.description as drug, count(p) as patients
4  ORDER BY patients DESC
```

drug	patients
"Acetaminophen 325 MG Oral Tablet"	496
"lisinopril 10 MG Oral Tablet"	254
"Amoxicillin 250 MG / Clavulanate 125 MG Oral Tablet"	236
"Naproxen sodium 220 MG Oral Tablet"	235
"Hydrochlorothiazide 25 MG Oral Tablet"	211
"amLODIPine 2.5 MG Oral Tablet"	201

Started streaming 173 records after 1 ms and completed after 128 ms.

Figure 5.14 – Drug prescriptions in descending order by the number of patients they are prescribed to

We can see from the screenshot that the data is in descending order based on the number of patients the drug is prescribed to.

Now, let us take a look at another query. We will write a query to retrieve the top 10 drugs prescribed based on the number of patients they are prescribed to. The Cypher code looks like this:

```
MATCH (d:Drug)<-[:HAS_DRUG]-()<-[:HAS_ENCOUNTER]-(p)
WITH DISTINCT d, p
RETURN d.description as drug, count(p) as patients
ORDER BY patients DESC
LIMIT 10
```

This query returns the top 10 drugs prescribed.

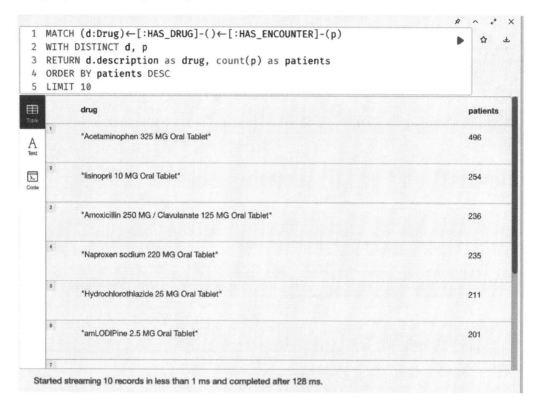

Figure 5.15 – Top 10 drugs prescribed

The screenshot shows the top 10 drugs prescribed. Now, let us add a filter to sort queries. Let us get the first 10 drugs prescribed that have been prescribed to at least 50 patients and order them by the number of patients.

The Cypher query looks like this:

```
MATCH (d:Drug)<-[:HAS_DRUG]-()<-[:HAS_ENCOUNTER]-(p)
WITH DISTINCT d, p
WITH d.description as drug, count(p) as patients
WHERE patients > 50
RETURN drug, patients
ORDER BY patients
LIMIT 10
```

We can see in the query that the `patients` count filter is added before returning the data sorted in ascending order.

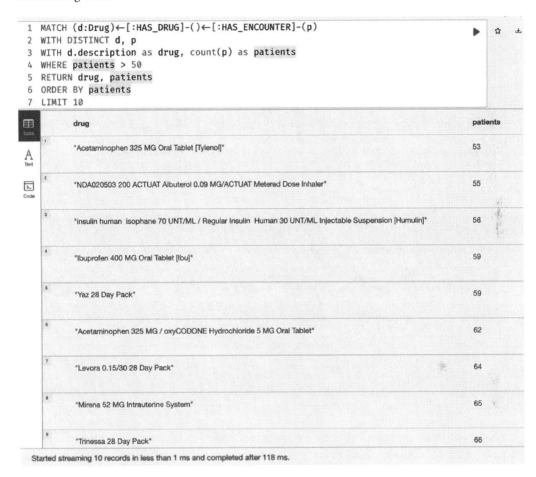

```
1  MATCH (d:Drug)←[:HAS_DRUG]-()←[:HAS_ENCOUNTER]-(p)
2  WITH DISTINCT d, p
3  WITH d.description as drug, count(p) as patients
4  WHERE patients > 50
5  RETURN drug, patients
6  ORDER BY patients
7  LIMIT 10
```

drug	patients
"Acetaminophen 325 MG Oral Tablet [Tylenol]"	53
"NDA020503 200 ACTUAT Albuterol 0.09 MG/ACTUAT Metered Dose Inhaler"	55
"insulin human isophane 70 UNT/ML / Regular Insulin Human 30 UNT/ML Injectable Suspension [Humulin]"	58
"Ibuprofen 400 MG Oral Tablet [Ibu]"	59
"Yaz 28 Day Pack"	59
"Acetaminophen 325 MG / oxyCODONE Hydrochloride 5 MG Oral Tablet"	62
"Levora 0.15/30 28 Day Pack"	64
"Mirena 52 MG Intrauterine System"	65
"Trinessa 28 Day Pack"	66

Started streaming 10 records in less than 1 ms and completed after 118 ms.

Figure 5.16 – Bottom 10 drugs prescribed with at least 50 patients

We can see from the result set that we are getting drugs that have more than 50 patients associated with them.

We can apply the ORDER BY clause first before applying the filter. The Cypher query looks like this:

```
MATCH (d:Drug)<-[:HAS_DRUG]-()<-[:HAS_ENCOUNTER]-(p)
WITH DISTINCT d, p
WITH d.description as drug, count(p) as patients
ORDER BY patients
WITH drug, patients
WHERE patients > 50
```

```
RETURN drug, patients
LIMIT 10
```

We can see from the query that we are applying the ORDER BY clause first and then applying the patients > 50 filter after that.

Let us take a look at the results to see whether they are the same:

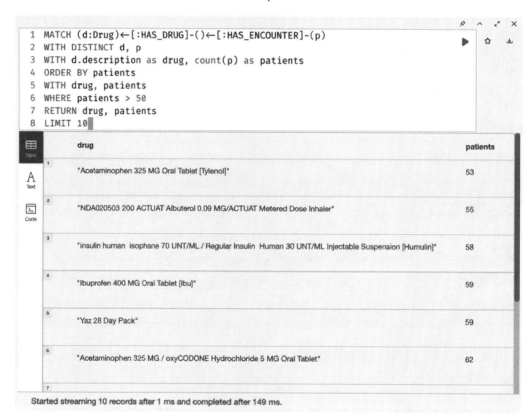

Figure 5.17 – Bottom 10 drugs prescribed with at least 50 patients – ORDER BY first

We can see that the response is the same in both cases. We have seen ORDER BY with one property. Let us try the query with multiple properties in the ORDER BY clause. Let us sort the data by the drug name and patient count first. The Cypher query looks like this:

```
MATCH (d:Drug)<-[:HAS_DRUG]-()<-[:HAS_ENCOUNTER]-(p)
WITH DISTINCT d, p
WITH d.description as drug, count(p) as patients
WHERE patients > 100
RETURN drug, patients
```

```
ORDER BY   drug, patients
LIMIT 10
```

In this query, we are using the drug name as the primary sorting point and the patient count as the secondary sorting point.

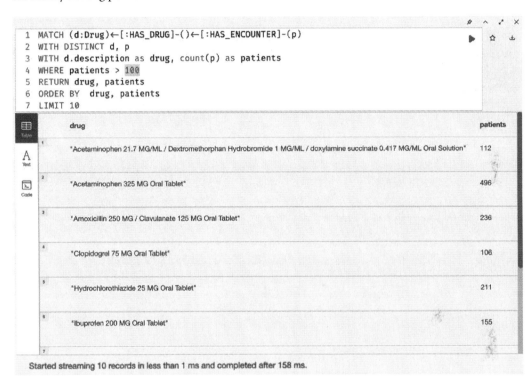

```
1  MATCH (d:Drug)←[:HAS_DRUG]-()←[:HAS_ENCOUNTER]-(p)
2  WITH DISTINCT d, p
3  WITH d.description as drug, count(p) as patients
4  WHERE patients > 100
5  RETURN drug, patients
6  ORDER BY  drug, patients
7  LIMIT 10
```

drug	patients
"Acetaminophen 21.7 MG/ML / Dextromethorphan Hydrobromide 1 MG/ML / doxylamine succinate 0.417 MG/ML Oral Solution"	112
"Acetaminophen 325 MG Oral Tablet"	496
"Amoxicillin 250 MG / Clavulanate 125 MG Oral Tablet"	236
"Clopidogrel 75 MG Oral Tablet"	106
"Hydrochlorothiazide 25 MG Oral Tablet"	211
"Ibuprofen 200 MG Oral Tablet"	155

Started streaming 10 records in less than 1 ms and completed after 158 ms.

Figure 5.18 – Bottom 10 drugs prescribed – ordered by drug name and patient count

We can see here both the drug name and patient count are used for sorting. Let us change the primary and secondary sorting points to the patient count and drug name.

The Cypher query for this looks like this:

```
MATCH (d:Drug)<-[:HAS_DRUG]-()<-[:HAS_ENCOUNTER]-(p)
WITH DISTINCT d, p
WITH d.description as drug, count(p) as patients
WHERE patients > 100
RETURN drug, patients
ORDER BY patients, drug
LIMIT 10
```

In this query, we are using the patient count as the primary sorting point and the drug name as the secondary sorting point.

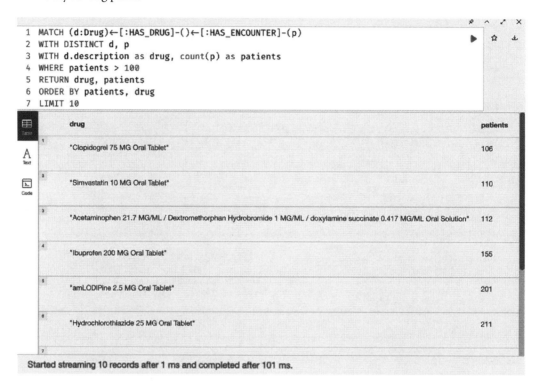

```
1  MATCH (d:Drug)←[:HAS_DRUG]-()←[:HAS_ENCOUNTER]-(p)
2  WITH DISTINCT d, p
3  WITH d.description as drug, count(p) as patients
4  WHERE patients > 100
5  RETURN drug, patients
6  ORDER BY patients, drug
7  LIMIT 10
```

drug	patients
"Clopidogrel 75 MG Oral Tablet"	106
"Simvastatin 10 MG Oral Tablet"	110
"Acetaminophen 21.7 MG/ML / Dextromethorphan Hydrobromide 1 MG/ML / doxylamine succinate 0.417 MG/ML Oral Solution"	112
"Ibuprofen 200 MG Oral Tablet"	155
"amLODIPine 2.5 MG Oral Tablet"	201
"Hydrochlorothiazide 25 MG Oral Tablet"	211

Started streaming 10 records after 1 ms and completed after 101 ms.

Figure 5.19 – Bottom 10 drugs prescribed – ordered by patient count and drug name

We can see the sorted results changed from the previous query. When we have multiple properties, we can change the order of sorting per field. Let us take a look at the drug name descending as the primary sorting point and the patient count ascending as the secondary point.

The Cypher query in this case looks like this:

```
MATCH (d:Drug)<-[:HAS_DRUG]-()<-[:HAS_ENCOUNTER]-(p)
WITH DISTINCT d, p
WITH d.description as drug, count(p) as patients
WHERE patients > 100
RETURN drug, patients
ORDER BY  drug DESC, patients
LIMIT 10
```

Here, we are using drug names descending as the primary sorting point and patient counts ascending as a secondary sorting point:

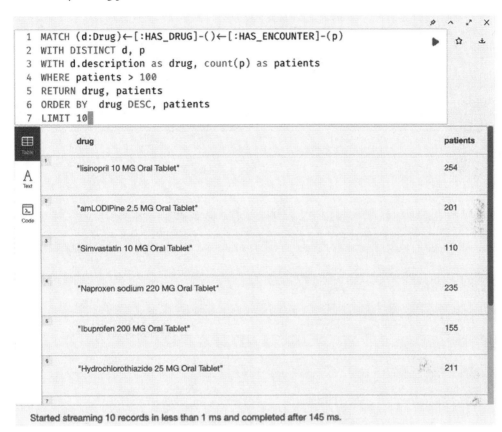

```
1  MATCH (d:Drug)←[:HAS_DRUG]-()←[:HAS_ENCOUNTER]-(p)
2  WITH DISTINCT d, p
3  WITH d.description as drug, count(p) as patients
4  WHERE patients > 100
5  RETURN drug, patients
6  ORDER BY  drug DESC, patients
7  LIMIT 10
```

drug	patients
"lisinopril 10 MG Oral Tablet"	254
"amLODIPine 2.5 MG Oral Tablet"	201
"Simvastatin 10 MG Oral Tablet"	110
"Naproxen sodium 220 MG Oral Tablet"	235
"Ibuprofen 200 MG Oral Tablet"	155
"Hydrochlorothiazide 25 MG Oral Tablet"	211

Started streaming 10 records in less than 1 ms and completed after 145 ms.

Figure 5.20 – Drug prescriptions – ordered by drug names in
descending order and patient counts in ascending order

We can see from the screenshot that the drug names are in descending order and the patient counts are in ascending order. Let us add descending order for both properties:

```
MATCH (d:Drug)<-[:HAS_DRUG]-()<-[:HAS_ENCOUNTER]-(p)
WITH DISTINCT d, p
WITH d.description as drug, count(p) as patients
WHERE patients > 100
RETURN drug, patients
ORDER BY  drug DESC, patients DESC
LIMIT 10
```

In this query, we are sorting data by both sorting points in descending order.

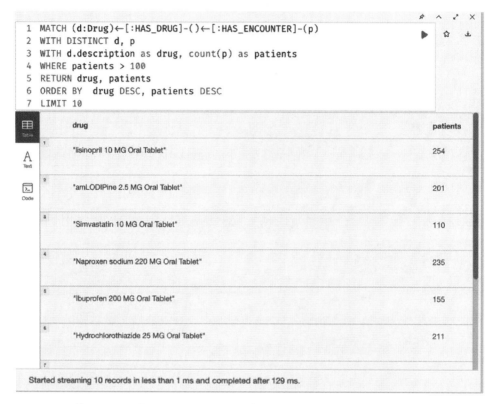

```
1 MATCH (d:Drug)←[:HAS_DRUG]-()←[:HAS_ENCOUNTER]-(p)
2 WITH DISTINCT d, p
3 WITH d.description as drug, count(p) as patients
4 WHERE patients > 100
5 RETURN drug, patients
6 ORDER BY  drug DESC, patients DESC
7 LIMIT 10
```

drug	patients
"lisinopril 10 MG Oral Tablet"	254
"amLODIPine 2.5 MG Oral Tablet"	201
"Simvastatin 10 MG Oral Tablet"	110
"Naproxen sodium 220 MG Oral Tablet"	235
"Ibuprofen 200 MG Oral Tablet"	155
"Hydrochlorothiazide 25 MG Oral Tablet"	211

Started streaming 10 records in less than 1 ms and completed after 129 ms.

Figure 5.21 – Drug prescriptions – ordered by drug names in descending
order and patient counts in descending order

The data seems the same as the query before because of the way the data is distributed. The drug name order causes the response to be similar to the other query.

Now that we have worked with filtering and sorting data, let us take a look at working with aggregations.

Working with aggregations

In Cypher, aggregations are supported using the COUNT, SUM, AVG, MIN, MAX, COLLECT, PERCENTILE, and STDEV functions. Except for the COLLECT function, all the other functions are standard mathematical functions. COLLECT functions create a list of entities similar to data pivoting by converting a list of rows into a column value.

We have seen the usage of the COUNT function numerous times in this chapter. We can combine COUNT and COLLECT to count the entities as well as collect the values as a list. Let us take a look at the drug prescription query where we were returning patient counts. We will also return the first names of those patients along with the count.

For this, the Cypher query looks like this:

```
MATCH (d:Drug)<-[:HAS_DRUG]-()<-[:HAS_ENCOUNTER]-(p)
WITH DISTINCT d, p
WITH d.description as drug,
     COUNT(p) as patients,
     COLLECT(p.firstName) as firstNames
WHERE patients > 10
RETURN drug, patients, firstNames
ORDER BY patients
LIMIT 10
```

In this query, we are returning the drug name and patient count where the patient count is more than 10 along with the first names of those patients. We can see here we are combining the COUNT and COLLECT functions together. In Cypher, when we are doing aggregations, the group-by functionality is automatic, unlike SQL. It will group by all the values that are not part of COUNT or COLLECT:

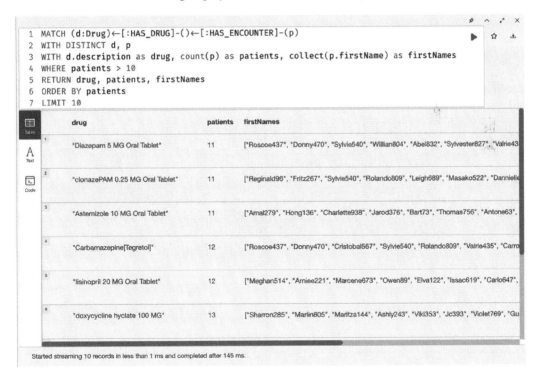

Figure 5.22 – Drug prescriptions – COUNT and COLLECT usage

We can see in the screenshot we are seeing the patient count as well as the patients' first names. Since lists are first-class citizens in Cypher, it is easier to pivot the data from rows into columns.

Now, let us take a look at the same drug interaction query, with patient MIN, MAX, and AVG ages instead of first names.

The Cypher query for this looks like this:

```
MATCH (d:Drug)<-[:HAS_DRUG]-()<-[:HAS_ENCOUNTER]-(p)
WHERE p.birthDate IS NOT NULL
WITH DISTINCT d, p
WITH d, p, duration.between(p.birthDate, date()).years as age
WITH d.description as drug,
     count(p) as patients,
     min(age) as minAge,
     max(age) as maxAge,
     avg(age) as avgAge
WHERE patients > 25
RETURN drug, patients, minAge, maxAge, avgAge
ORDER BY patients
LIMIT 20
```

First, this query only selects the patients for whom we have a birth date. Once we have found the patients, we use the `duration` function to calculate the age of the patient. Once have we calculated the age, while counting the number of patients for that group of patients, we calculate the minimum, maximum, and average age using aggregation functions. For more documentation on the usage of `duration`, please visit the *Durations* documentation: `https://neo4j.com/docs/cypher-manual/current/syntax/temporal/#cypher-temporal-durations`.

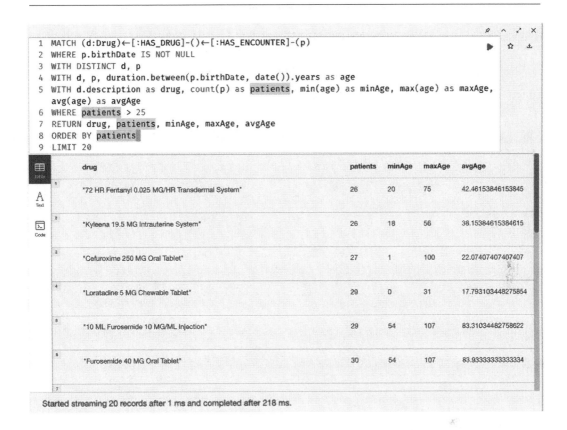

Figure 5.23 – Drug prescriptions – MIN, MAX, and AVG usage

We can see from the screenshot we get the minimum, maximum, and average ages of the patients associated with the drug.

Summary

In this chapter, we looked at building queries while applying filters. We have taken a look at filtering the data using node labels and relationship types, using relationship directions, the performance impact of using node labels when compared to relationship types for traversal, using WHERE clauses, WITH clauses, SKIP clauses, LIMIT clauses, and EXISTS clauses, and using regular expressions.

We looked at sorting the data using the ORDER BY clause with one value or multiple values in ascending order or in descending order and combining the ORDER BY clause with the WITH clause.

Finally, we looked at aggregating results using the COUNT, COLLECT, MIN, MAX, and AVG functions. Along with this, we also looked at combining the COUNT and COLLECT functions to perform some complex aggregations.

In the next chapter, we will take a look at using LIST expressions, working with the UNION clause. We will also take a look at using sub-queries using the CALL clause.

6

List Expressions, UNION, and Subqueries

We have looked at filtering and sorting in Cypher queries in earlier chapters. In this chapter, we will take a look at more advanced options for querying.

We will cover the following topics:

- Working with list expressions
- Working with UNION in Cypher
- Working with subqueries

List expressions provide a powerful paradigm to manipulate list results in Cypher. UNION queries provide the means to combine the results of distinct queries and return data. Subqueries provide a powerful option for executing a query inside another query and using the results in the main query.

Now, let us take a look at list expressions.

Working with list expressions

Cypher provides native support for lists. This means that not only are they treated as first-class entities, such as integers or strings, but all the functions that can create, manipulate, or process the lists are built into Cypher. Let us look at the following functions, all of which are available to process lists:

- `range`
- `head`
- `tail`
- `last`
- `size`

- `reverse`

- `reduce`

As well as these functions, we can also use list comprehensions. First, we will take a look at the preceding functions, and then we will explore list comprehensions in greater depth.

Let us look at the `range` function.

Working with the range function

The `range` function provides a way to create a list with numbers. It takes a `start` value and an `end` value with an optional `step` parameter and returns a list of all integer values bound by `start` and `end`. The syntax of the `range` function is as follows:

```
range(start, end [, step])
```

The `step` value is optional as seen by the syntax. When the `step` value is not provided it defaults to `1`. If you provide a *negative* `step` value, this function returns an empty list. Let us look at a few examples:

```
RETURN range(1,10)
```

This query is preparing a list of integers starting with a value of `1` and ending with a value of `10`, in increments of `1`. We can see this aspect in the following figure:

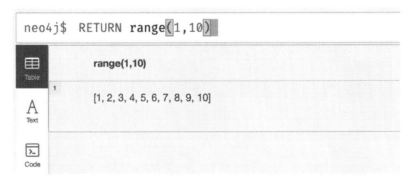

Figure 6.1 – Basic range function usage

In the screenshot, we can see the response when we execute this function. We can see that this function returns a list with values from `1` to `10`. Let us look at an example where the `step` parameter has a value of `3`:

```
RETURN range(5,35,3)
```

This query is preparing a list of integers starting with a value of 5 and ending with a value of 35 in increments of 3. We can see this in the following figure:

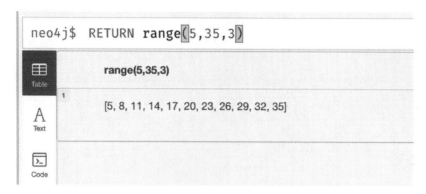

Figure 6.2 – range function usage with a step parameter

In the screenshot, we can see that when we use a `step` parameter, we get a list of values starting from the `start` value, with increments of the `step` value, until we reach the `end` value.

Now let us look at the `head` function.

Working with the head function

The `head` function returns the first element of a list.

Let us look at the usage of the `head` function:

```
WITH [1,2,3,4] as list
RETURN head(list)
```

This query is returning the head (first) element of the list, as shown in the following figure:

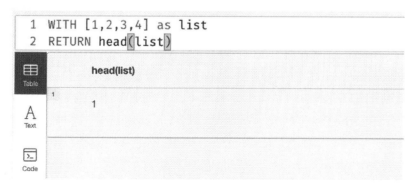

Figure 6.3 – Usage of the head function

This screenshot shows the usage of the head function. We can see that this function returns the first element of the list.

Next, we will look at the tail function.

Working with the tail function

The tail function returns all the elements except for the first element of a list.

Let us look at the usage of the tail function:

```
WITH [1,2,3,4] as list
RETURN tail(list)
```

This query returns the tail part of a list, which is the list without the first element, as shown in the following figure:

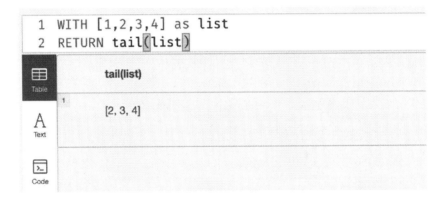

Figure 6.4 – Usage of the tail function

This screenshot shows the usage of the tail function. We can see that the tail function returns a list without the first element of the input list provided.

Next, we will look at the last function.

Working with the last function

The last function returns the last element in a list.

Let us look at the usage of the last function:

```
WITH [1,2,3,4] as list
RETURN last(list)
```

This query returns the last element of a list, as shown in the following figure:

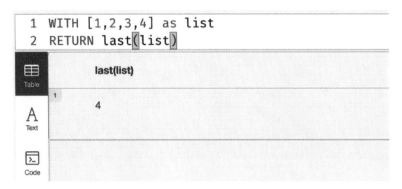

Figure 6.5 – Usage of the last function

This screenshot shows the usage of the `last` function. We can see that this function returns the last element in a list.

Next, we will look at the `size` function.

Working with the size function

The `size` function returns the last element in a list.

Let us look at the usage of the `size` function:

```
WITH [1,2,3,4,10,15] as list
RETURN size(list)
```

This query returns the size of a list, as shown in the following figure:

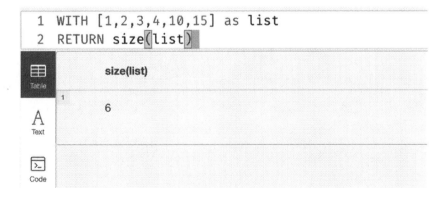

Figure 6.6 – Usage of the size function

This screenshot shows the usage of the `size` function. We can see this function returns the size of a list.

Next, we will look at the `reverse` function.

Working with the reverse function

The `reverse` function returns the elements of a list in reverse order.

Let us look at the usage of the `reverse` function:

```
WITH [1,2,3,4,10,15] as list
RETURN reverse(list)
```

This query returns a list in reverse order, as shown in the following figure:

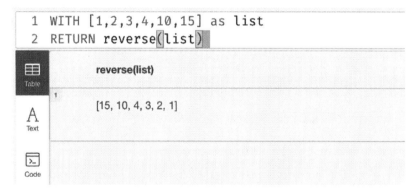

Figure 6.7 – Usage of the reverse function

This screenshot shows the usage of the `reverse` function. We can see it returns a list with values in reverse order.

Next, we will look at the `reduce` function.

Working with the reduce function

The `reduce` function is used to aggregate a result by traversing the list. This function will iterate through each of the elements in the given list, run the expression on element e, while taking into account the current partial result, and store the new partial result in the accumulator value:

```
The syntax of this function looks like this. reduce(accumulator
= initial, variable IN list | expression)
```

The following table explains the arguments of the reduce function:

Name	Description
accumulator	A variable that will hold the result, and the partial results, as we iterate through the list.
initial	Expression to assign an initial value to the accumulator.
list	An expression that returns a list.
variable	The variable is used to assign the element while we iterate through the list.
expression	The expression will run once for each value in the list, and produce the result value.

Figure 6.8 – Arguments of the function

Let us look at the usage of this function:

```
WITH [1,2,3,4,10,15] as list
RETURN reduce(sum=0, x in list | sum + x) as total
```

This query returns the sum of all the values in the list, as shown in the following figure:

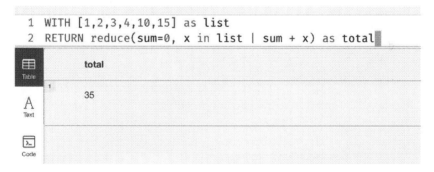

Figure 6.9 – Usage of the reduce function

From the screenshot, we can see the reduce function here is used to calculate the sum of the values in the list.

Let us take a look at another example to calculate the sum of squares:

```
1  WITH [1,2,3,4,10,15] as list
2  RETURN reduce(sum=0, x in list | sum + (x*x)) as total
```

	total
1	355

Figure 6.10 – Usage of the reduce function – 2

From the screenshot, we can see that we got the sum of squares of the list values as the final result.

Next, we will look at list comprehensions.

Working with list comprehensions

List comprehensions are a means to create lists from other lists, based on expression evaluation of the elements of the original list. They are similar to set comprehensions.

Let us look at an example where we get a list of the squares of even values in the list:

```
WITH [1,2,3,4,10,15] as list
RETURN [x in list WHERE x % 2 = 0  | x*x ] as squareList
```

This query returns a list with the square values of only the even numbers in the list, as shown in the following figure:

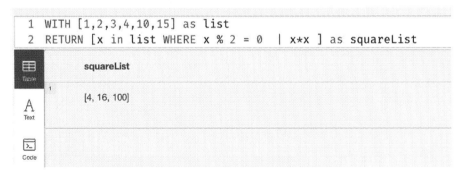

```
1  WITH [1,2,3,4,10,15] as list
2  RETURN [x in list WHERE x % 2 = 0  | x*x ] as squareList
```

	squareList
1	[4, 16, 100]

Figure 6.11 – Usage of list comprehensions

From the screenshot, we can see that list comprehension returns a list of squares of values, which are even in the original list.

We can see from our earlier usage of the `reduce` function that we cannot use a conditional traversal of a list. In list comprehensions, we cannot iterate through a list and create a single value out of it. However, we can combine both of these to do some complex operations. Say we want to calculate the sum of squares but only when the value is even; we can combine both to achieve that. Let us see the query that can help us accomplish this:

```
WITH [1,2,3,4,10,15] as list
RETURN reduce(
        total = 0 ,
        y in
            [x in list WHERE x % 2 = 0  | x ]
        | total+y*y)
as sumOfSquares
```

Let us see the result of the execution of this query

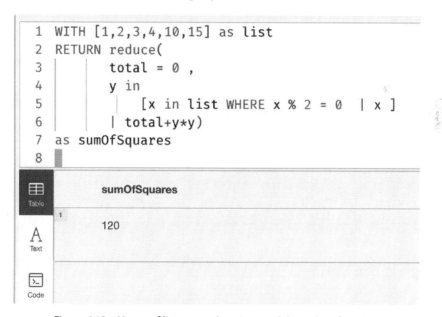

Figure 6.12 – Usage of list comprehensions and the reduce function

We can see from the result that we can get a single by filtering the list for even numbers from the original list and using the `reduce` function to calculate the sum of squares.

We will take a look at using UNION cypher queries in the next section.

Working with UNION in Cypher

The UNION clause combines the results of two or more queries and returns the results. It works pretty similarly to how it works in SQL queries. Normally, we use the UNION clause when we want to combine the results of multiple, disparate queries returning similar datasets.

Let's look at an example usage of the UNION clause:

```
MATCH (p:Patient)-[:HAS_ENCOUNTER]->()-[:HAS_DIAGNOSIS]->(d)
WHERE p.id='f237e253-9052-a038-7c9e-dbd9a1d7da32'
RETURN d.code as drug
UNION
MATCH (p:Patient)-[:HAS_ENCOUNTER]->()-[:HAS_DIAGNOSIS]->(d)
WHERE p.id='ffa580de-08e5-9a47-b12a-db312ad6825b'
RETURN d.code as drug
```

This query returns the diagnosis codes used among two patients, as shown in the following figure:

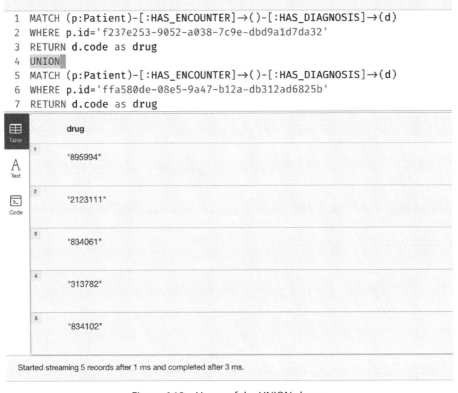

Figure 6.13 – Usage of the UNION clause

We can see there are five records returned. The UNION clause eliminates duplicate records in the results if there are any.

We could have written the same query without using the UNION clause. Let's take a look at that query and see if there are any differences in the response:

```
MATCH (p:Patient)-[:HAS_ENCOUNTER]->()-[:HAS_DIAGNOSIS]->(d)
WHERE p.id='f237e253-9052-a038-7c9e-dbd9a1d7da32' OR
p.id='ffa580de-08e5-9a47-b12a-db312ad6825b'
RETURN d.code as drug
```

This query returns the diagnosis codes used among two patients, as shown in the following figure:

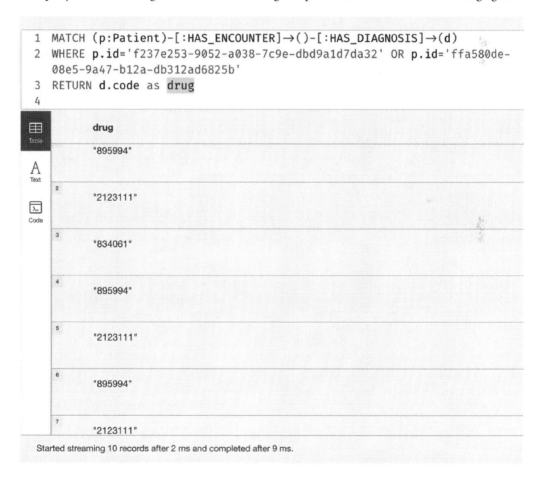

Figure 6.14 – Query without the UNION clause for comparison

We can see from the screenshot that this query returns 10 records in total. We can also see that there are duplicate records. This explains the difference between this query and the UNION query. The UNION query removed duplicates and returned the distinct values.

Say we don't want to eliminate duplicates in the response; then, we need to use the UNION ALL clause, as shown here:

```
MATCH (p:Patient)-[:HAS_ENCOUNTER]->()-[:HAS_DIAGNOSIS]->(d)
WHERE p.id='f237e253-9052-a038-7c9e-dbd9a1d7da32'
RETURN d.code as drug
UNION ALL
MATCH (p:Patient)-[:HAS_ENCOUNTER]->()-[:HAS_DIAGNOSIS]->(d)
WHERE p.id='ffa580de-08e5-9a47-b12a-db312ad6825b'
RETURN d.code as drug
```

Let us look at the response to this query:

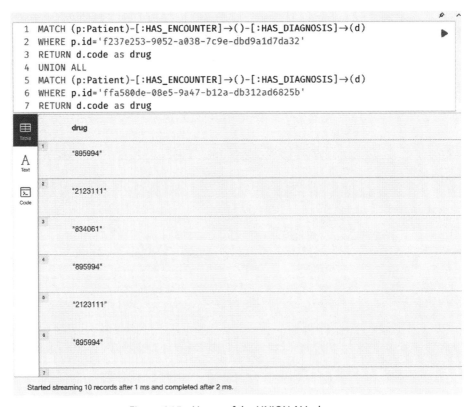

Figure 6.15 – Usage of the UNION ALL clause

From the screenshot, we can see that the UNION ALL query returns 10 records, some of which are duplicates. This matches what we are expecting from the response.

While the example we have used for the UNION query could have been built using a single query, it showcases its capabilities.

Next, we will take a look at working with subqueries in Cypher.

Working with subqueries

Cypher allows you to write subqueries using the CALL clause. There are two types of subqueries available:

- Returning subqueries
- Unit subqueries

The subqueries are evaluated for each incoming row that is provided by the parent query.

Let us work with returning subqueries first.

Working with returning subqueries

Subqueries that end with a RETURN statement are called **returning subqueries**. Every row from a returning subquery is combined with the input row to prepare the result of the query. This means the final output of the outer query can be impacted by the subquery returned values.

> **Note**
>
> If a subquery does not return any rows, then there will not be any rows returned by the outer query.

Returning subqueries are very useful when we want to apply sorting and extra filtering to UNION queries. When we use the UNION clause, it is not possible to apply any sorting. Let us take a look at a UNION query with sorting using a subquery:

```
CALL {
    MATCH (p:Patient)-[:HAS_ENCOUNTER]->()-[:HAS_DIAGNOSIS]->(d)
     WHERE p.id='f237e253-9052-a038-7c9e-dbd9a1d7da32'
     RETURN d.code as drug
     UNION
     MATCH (p:Patient)-[:HAS_ENCOUNTER]->()-[:HAS_DIAGNOSIS]-
>(d)
     WHERE p.id='ffa580de-08e5-9a47-b12a-db312ad6825b'
     RETURN d.code as drug
}
```

```
RETURN drug
ORDER BY drug DESC
```

This query should return the drugs in descending order. Let's execute the query and check:

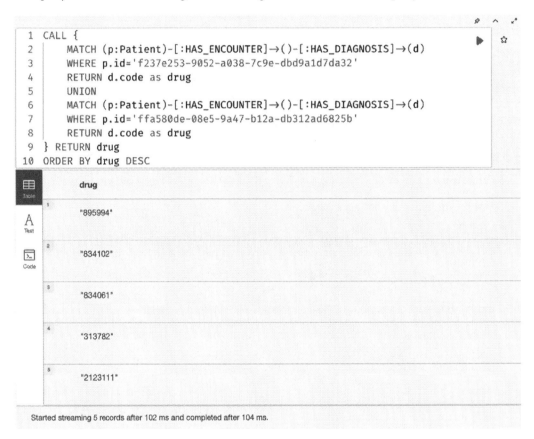

```
 1  CALL {
 2      MATCH (p:Patient)-[:HAS_ENCOUNTER]→()-[:HAS_DIAGNOSIS]→(d)
 3      WHERE p.id='f237e253-9052-a038-7c9e-dbd9a1d7da32'
 4      RETURN d.code as drug
 5      UNION
 6      MATCH (p:Patient)-[:HAS_ENCOUNTER]→()-[:HAS_DIAGNOSIS]→(d)
 7      WHERE p.id='ffa580de-08e5-9a47-b12a-db312ad6825b'
 8      RETURN d.code as drug
 9  } RETURN drug
10  ORDER BY drug DESC
```

drug
"895994"
"834102"
"834061"
"313782"
"2123111"

Started streaming 5 records after 102 ms and completed after 104 ms.

Figure 6.16 – Usage of a subquery to sort UNION results

We can see from the screenshot that the drug codes are returned in descending order. It is also possible to apply extra filtering or use this data to execute another set of queries.

Let us modify the query to get the drug names after getting the codes:

```
CALL {
    MATCH (p:Patient)-[:HAS_ENCOUNTER]->()-[:HAS_DIAGNOSIS]-
>(d)
    WHERE p.id='f237e253-9052-a038-7c9e-dbd9a1d7da32'
    RETURN d as drug
```

```
    UNION
    MATCH (p:Patient)-[:HAS_ENCOUNTER]->()-[:HAS_DIAGNOSIS]-
>(d)
    WHERE p.id='ffa580de-08e5-9a47-b12a-db312ad6825b'
    RETURN d as drug
}
WITH drug
RETURN drug.code as code, drug.description as name
```

In this query, after the subquery returns the drug node and we get the drug code and drug name.

Let's execute the query and check the results:

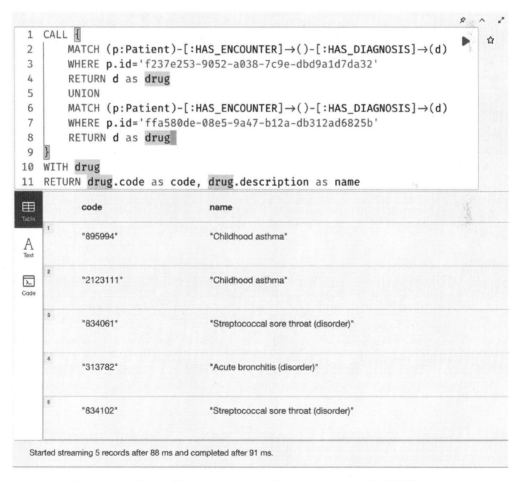

Figure 6.17 – Usage of the subquery to perform extra logic on the UNION results

We can see from the screenshot that we can take the results from a UNION subquery and perform extra logic on the results.

> **Note**
>
> This is where subqueries differ from SQL subqueries. SQL subqueries are limited to joining aspects. In Cypher, after a subquery, we can perform extra logic.

In the preceding query, we started with a subquery and processed the results later. If we have some data before we go into the subquery, then we have to use the WITH clause to pass the data to the subquery.

Let's look at an example of this:

```
UNWIND [1, 2, 3] AS x
CALL {
  WITH x
  RETURN x * x AS y
}
RETURN x, y
```

This query processes the list in the outer query and assigns each element to a variable named x. To pass this variable to the subquery, which calculates the square of that value, we have to use the WITH clause.

Let's execute the query and check the results:

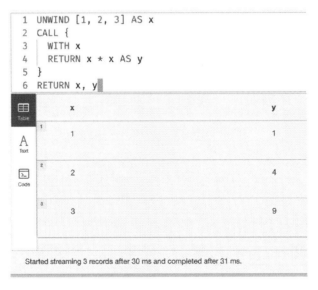

Figure 6.18 – Passing data to the subquery

We can see the results of this query in the screenshot. If we do not use the WITH clause in the query, it throws an error that looks as follows:

```
Variable `x` not defined (line 3, column 10 (offset: 38))
```

It is also possible to combine the results from the outer query and subquery. Let's look at an example of this:

```
MATCH (p:Patient {id:'f237e253-9052-a038-7c9e-dbd9a1d7da32'})
CALL {
    WITH p
    MATCH (p)-[:HAS_ENCOUNTER]->()-[:HAS_DIAGNOSIS]->(d)
    RETURN d as drug
}
WITH DISTINCT p, drug
RETURN
    p.firstName as firstName,
    drug.code as code,
    drug.description as drug
```

In this query, we find a patient and can use a subquery to get all the drugs that were prescribed to him and return the patient's first name, drug code, and drug name. We are also using the DISTINCT clause here to make sure that even if a drug is prescribed more than once, we are only returning the code and name once.

Let's look at this query execution.

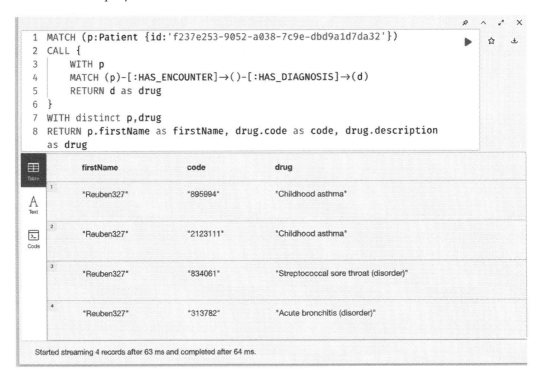

Figure 6.19 – Combing data from an outer query and a subquery

We can see from the screenshot that we can combine the data from an outer query and a subquery and return the results. Now, let's take a look at unit subqueries.

Working with unit subqueries

Unit subqueries do not use the RETURN clause. This means we can only perform data updates when we use this pattern. Since there is no RETURN clause in the subquery, the number of rows returned by the enclosing query is not affected by what the subquery does.

Let's look at an example of a unit subquery:

```
UNWIND range (1, 5) AS index
CALL {
    WITH index
    CREATE (t:Test {id:index})
```

```
}
RETURN index
```

In this query, the subquery creates a node and does not return any data. Let's see the execution results of this query:

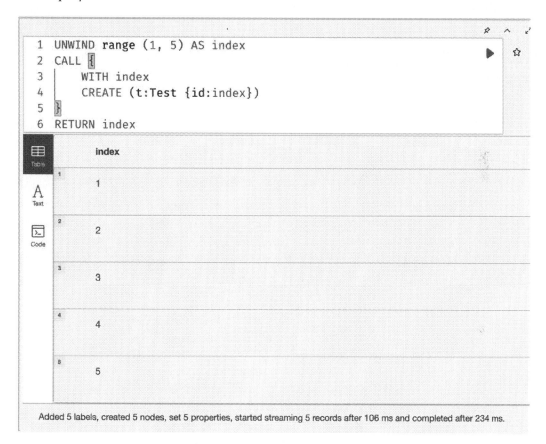

```
1  UNWIND range (1, 5) AS index
2  CALL {
3      WITH index
4      CREATE (t:Test {id:index})
5  }
6  RETURN index
```

index
1
2
3
4
5

Added 5 labels, created 5 nodes, set 5 properties, started streaming 5 records after 106 ms and completed after 234 ms.

Figure 6.20 – Example usage of the unit subquery

From the screenshot, we can see that this query returns the index. Also, we can see from the status that we have created five nodes. Unit subqueries can be used to perform batch commits in a single query. In this case, each subquery executes in a separate transaction. The syntax for this looks as follows:

```
CALL {
    sub query …
} IN TRANSACTIONS
```

Let's try an example. We can delete the `Test` nodes we created in the earlier query using batch mode, with two nodes deleted per batch. The query looks like this:

```
MATCH (n:Test)
 CALL {
   WITH n
   DETACH DELETE n
 } IN TRANSACTIONS OF 2 ROWS
```

Let's run this query in the browser and see what happens:

Figure 6.21 – Example usage of a unit subquery in batch mode – error

You can see from the screenshot that it fails to run with an error. This is because when we use the `IN TRANSACTIONS` clause, the outer query must run in its own transaction. It cannot be part of an explicit transaction. Let's fix it and run the query again:

```
:auto MATCH (n:Test)
 CALL {
   WITH n
   DETACH DELETE n
 } IN TRANSACTIONS OF 2 ROWS
```

Let's see whether the query succeeds now:

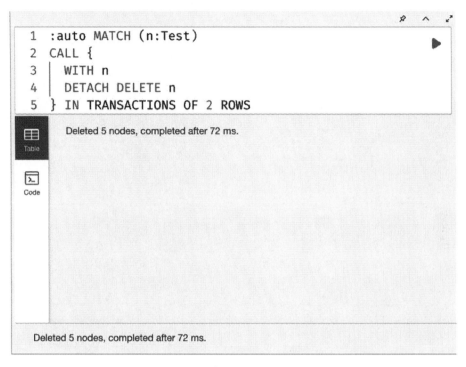

```
1  :auto MATCH (n:Test)
2  CALL {
3    WITH n
4    DETACH DELETE n
5  } IN TRANSACTIONS OF 2 ROWS
```

Deleted 5 nodes, completed after 72 ms.

Deleted 5 nodes, completed after 72 ms.

Figure 6.22 – Example usage of a unit subquery in batch mode – fixed

We can see that the query is successful now and five nodes were deleted. If we were to run this query from an application, such as a Java driver, then we should not use the : auto prefix. This is browser-specific command usage.

Summary

In this chapter, we have learned about using list expressions, UNION queries, and subqueries. We worked with multiple functions to process lists, using the reduce function to calculate a single value by iterating through a list, using list comprehensions to manipulate lists, combining list comprehensions and the reduce function with filter expressions to calculate a single value, using UNION to combine the results of multiple queries, using UNION ALL to keep the duplicates from multiple queries, using subqueries to apply to filters and for sorting UNION queries, using subqueries to perform isolated updates, and finally using the IN TRANSACTIONS clause, along with subqueries, to perform batch updates in separate transactions.

In the next chapter, we will take a deeper look at how lists and maps form the core of Cypher data types, and how these data types can make working with data much easier.

Part 3:
Advanced Cypher Concepts

This part introduces the more advanced concepts of Cypher querying. It explains how to work with lists and maps in Cypher as input as well as output along with processing them using Cypher. It also introduces the concept of querying for data that may not always exist and how to handle those scenarios. Later, it introduces APOC functions and procedures to be able to perform operations that may not be possible with core Cypher. At the end of this part, you will be able to leverage lists and maps in theory queries and also understand how to tune queries for performance.

This part comprises the following chapters:

- *Chapter 7, Working with Lists and Maps*
- *Chapter 8, Advanced Query Patterns*
- *Chapter 9, Query Tuning*
- *Chapter 10, Using APOC Utilities*
- *Chapter 11, Cypher Ecosystem*
- *Chapter 12, Tips and Tricks*

7

Working with Lists and Maps

We have worked with lists and maps in earlier chapters in various queries. But we have not discussed how lists and maps can make Cypher queries more powerful. They are first-class types in Cypher, like string and integer, and can make it easy to build complex queries. This chapter discusses how we can handle both lists and maps as input and output. We will discuss how we can prepare lists from data, iterate lists to process data, handle nested maps, and return map projections.

The following aspects will be covered in this chapter:

- Working with lists
- Working with maps

We will be covering lists first. We will discuss in detail how lists work in Cypher and explore various ways we can manipulate and work with lists, both as input and output. We will also look at different types of lists and the functions available to work with them.

Let's get onto working with lists.

Working with lists

Lists are the core data type in Cypher and because of this, there is extensive support for lists in Cypher. Lists hold elements in a sequence so that we can iterate the list in any order. They can hold any type of value. All of the elements in a list can be of the same type: whether integer, string, map, or list. It is also possible to mix and match different types in the same list.

We will take a look at different aspects of lists, such as using them as input and building lists for output or intermediate processing, along with using various built-in functions to process lists in this section.

Working with basic list capabilities

Cypher lists can be used to hold any type of data, including integers, strings, and so on. They hold the data in sequence like an array but are not limited to a single type. We can use indexing to access content or leverage built-in functions from Cypher to access data.

Let's take a look at an example:

```
WITH [1,2,3,4] as intList, ['test1', 'test2', 'test3'] as
strList
RETURN intList[0] as intValue, strList[0] as strValue
```

This code snippet shows how a list can hold different types of data objects:

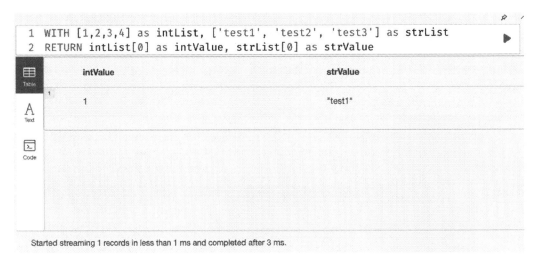

Figure 7.1 – Basic list usage

From the screenshot, we can see the usage of an integer list and a string list. When we access the values from the list, we get the appropriately typed value returned.

It is also possible for a list to contain multiple types of data objects. Let's take a look at an example:

```
WITH [1,2,3,4] as intList, ['test1', 'test2', 'test3'] as
strList
RETURN intList+strList as final
```

In this code snippet, we are attempting to combine an integer list and a string list.

```
1  WITH [1,2,3,4] as intList, ['test1', 'test2', 'test3'] as strList
2  RETURN intList+strList as final
```

	final
Table	
A Text	[1, 2, 3, 4, "test1", "test2", "test3"]
Code	

Started streaming 1 records in less than 1 ms and completed after 1 ms.

Figure 7.2 – Combining lists with different data types

From the previous screenshot, we can see that when we combine an integer list and a string list, we get a single list with both types of data objects.

It is also possible to have lists as elements in a list. Let's look at an example:

```
WITH [1,2,[10,11],3,4] as list
RETURN list[0] as e1, list[2] as e2
```

We can see in the previous code snippet that we have a list embedded in another list.

Let's run this in the browser to see what the response looks like:

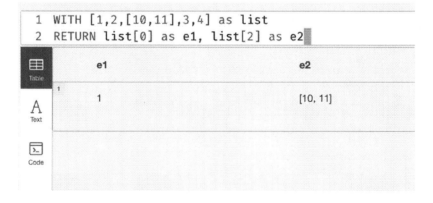

Figure 7.3 – A list embedded in another list

From the screenshot, we can see when we refer to element 0, we get an integer value, and element 2 returns the embedded list.

Next, let's take a look at list operators.

Working with list operators

In this section, we will discuss list operators along with their usage.

First, let's take a look at the + operator. This operator concatenates one or more lists:

```
WITH [1,2,3,4] as list1, [2,3,5] as list2
RETURN list1+list2 as final
```

This code concatenates two lists and creates a single list that contains all the elements in the order they are appended.

Let's execute it in the browser to see what the response looks like:

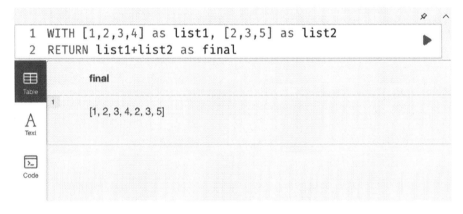

Figure 7.4 – Concatenating two lists

We can see from the screenshot that a single list is created by concatenating two lists. We can also see that it does not remove any duplicates from the list.

It is also possible to concatenate lists with multiple types to create a single list with objects with different data types. We have seen this already in *Figure 7.2*.

Let's look at the IN operator next.

The IN operator lets us check whether a given value is in the list or not. Let's look at an example usage:

```
WITH [1, 2, 3, 4, 5] as list
UNWIND list as n
WITH n
WHERE n IN [2,4,8]
RETURN n
```

The preceding code snippet shows the usage of the IN operator. From given a list of numbers, it checks whether the number is in another list and returns the matching numbers.

Let's execute it in the browser to see what the response looks like:

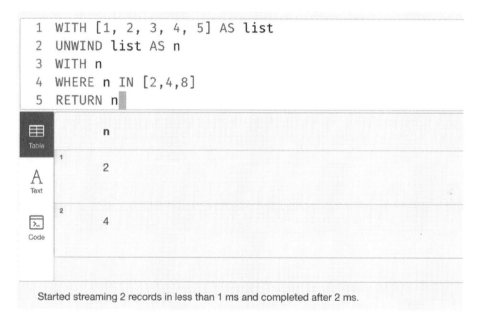

Figure 7.5 – Usage of the IN operator

The screenshot shows the usage of the IN operator and the query response.

It is also possible to look for the existence of list values using the IN operator. Let's look at this example:

```
WITH [1,2,3,[11,12], 3,4] as list
RETURN [2, 1] IN list as wrong, [11,12] in list as right
```

This code snippet shows how to check for the existence of a list in another list.

Let's execute it in the browser to see what the response looks like:

```
1  WITH [1,2,3,[11,12], 3,4] as list
2  RETURN [2, 1] IN list as wrong, [11,12] in list as right
```

	wrong	right
Table		
1	false	true
Text		
Code		

Figure 7.6 – Usage of the IN operator to check for lists

The screenshot shows the usage of the IN operator to check for the existence of a list in another list and the response.

We will take a look at the [ ] index operator next.

You can access the elements of a list using the [ ] operator. Let's look at a few examples:

```
WITH [1,2,3,[11,12], 3,4] as list
RETURN list[0] as e1
```

This code segment shows how to return the first element in a list.

Let's execute it in the browser to see what the response looks like:

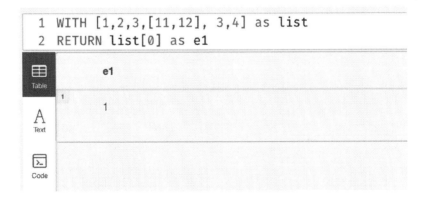

```
1  WITH [1,2,3,[11,12], 3,4] as list
2  RETURN list[0] as e1
```

	e1
Table	
1	1
Text	
Code	

Figure 7.7 – Accessing the first element of the list using the [ ] operator

We can see from the screenshot that it returns the first element of the list.

You can also use the value -1 to get the last element of a list without knowing the size of the list:

```
WITH [1,2,3,[11,12], 3,4] as list
RETURN list[-1] as e1
```

This code snippet shows how to get the last element in a list.

Let's execute it in the browser to see what the response looks like:

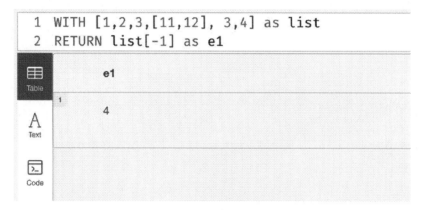

Figure 7.8 – Accessing the last element of the list using the [ ] operator

The screenshot shows we got the last element using -1 as the index value.

The indexing continues with negative values with indexing starting from -1 and traversing backward with each value going backward. Let's look at an example of this usage:

```
WITH [1,2,3,[11,12], 3,4] as list
RETURN list[-1] as last, list[-2] as prevLast
```

This code snippet shows how a -1 index gives us the last element and a -2 index gives us the element that is before the last element.

Let's execute it in the browser to see what the response looks like:

```
1  WITH [1,2,3,[11,12], 3,4] as list
2  RETURN list[-1] as last, list[-2] as prevLast
```

	last	prevLast
1	4	3

Figure 7.9 – Accessing the last element of the list using the [ ] operator and negative indices

From the screenshot, we can see the negative index values traverse the list from the last element to the first. This gives us easier means to iterate the list from first to last or last to first.

When we try to access the list beyond its length, the [ ] operator returns a null value.

Let's look at an example of this:

```
WITH [1,2,3,[11,12], 3,4] as list
RETURN size(list) as length, list[10] as e
```

This code snippet returns the list length and the *10th* element of the list, which is beyond the length of the list.

Let's execute it in the browser to see what the response looks like:

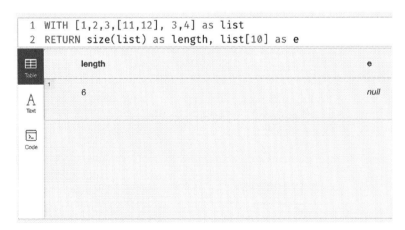

```
1  WITH [1,2,3,[11,12], 3,4] as list
2  RETURN size(list) as length, list[10] as e
```

	length	e
1	6	null

Figure 7.10 – The [ ] operator usage beyond list length

From the screenshot, we can see that the list length is 6, and when we try to access the *10th* element, we get a `null` value as the response.

It is also possible to use the index operator by using a dynamic parameter. Let's look at an example of this:

```
:param index=>1;
WITH [1,2,3,[11,12], 3,4] as list
RETURN list[$index] as e
```

This code segment shows two queries. You would need to execute them one by one to see the response in the browser:

1. First, the `:param` statement needs to be executed. This is a browser directive to define parameterized variables.

2. Then, execute the next two lines that use the parameter we defined earlier.

Let's execute it in the browser to see what the response looks like:

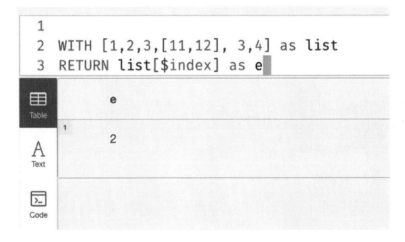

Figure 7.11 – Using a parameterized variable as an index for the list

From the screenshot, we can see that we are getting the first element as the response when we used `$index` as the index value since we defined its value as 1 beforehand.

Next, we will revisit all the list functions we worked with in earlier chapters. This will give us a more comprehensive understanding of lists.

Revisiting the list functions

In this section, we will revisit the list functions we worked with in earlier chapters:

- The range function provides a way to create a list with numbers. It takes a start value, an end value, and an optional step parameter and returns a list of all integer values bound by start and end. The syntax of the range function is as follows:

```
range(start, end [, step])
```

The step value is optional. When step is not provided, it defaults to 1. If you provide a *negative* step value, this function returns an empty list. A sample usage of the range function would be as follows:

```
RETURN range(1,10)
```

This returns a list with values from 1 to 10 in increments of 1. Let's review the head function next.

- The head function returns the first element of the list:

```
WITH [1,2,3,4] as list
RETURN head(list)
```

This returns a value of 1, which is at the head of the list. Let's review the tail function next.

- The tail function returns a list with all the elements except the first element of the list:

```
WITH [1,2,3,4] as list
RETURN tail(list)
```

This returns a list with the values 2,3, and 4 in it. Let's review the last function next.

- The last function returns the last element in the list:

```
WITH [1,2,3,4] as list
RETURN last(list)
```

This returns a value of 4, which is the last element in the list. Let's review the size function next.

- The size function returns the size of the list:

```
WITH [1,2,3,4,10,15] as list
RETURN size(list)
```

This returns a value of 6, which is the length of the list. Let's review the reverse function next.

- The reverse function returns the list in reverse order:

```
WITH [1,2,3,4,10,15] as list
RETURN reverse(list)
```

This returns a list that reads [15, 10, 4, 3, 2, 1], which is the original list in reverse order. Let's review the reduce function next.

- The reduce function is used to aggregate a result by traversing a list. This function goes through each item in the list and passes it to an expression and the resultant value is assigned to an intermediate variable. Once all the items in the list are processed, the final value is returned.

  The syntax of this function looks as follows:

  ```
  reduce(accumulator = initial, variable IN list |
  expression)
  ```

  The following table explains the arguments of the function.

Name	Description
accumulator	This variable holds the initial value and the partial result as we iterate through the list and find all results.
initial	This expression assigns the initial value to the accumulator variable.
list	The expression that returns a list.
variable	This is the variable that is assigned to the current value in the list as we iterate through it.
expression	This expression is evaluated once per item in the list and the resultant value is assigned to accumulator.

  Table 7.12 – The reduce function's parameters

  Let's take a look at an example query that uses this function:

  ```
  WITH [1,2,3,4,10,15] as list
  RETURN reduce(sum=0, x in list | sum + x) as total
  ```

  This returns the sum of all the values in the list, which is 35.

Next, we will take a look at COLLECT and UNWIND.

Working with COLLECT and UNWIND

COLLECT and UNWIND are the means to build a list or iterate a list and perform a set of operations.

The COLLECT function allows data to be collected into a list. Let's look at an example of this:

```
MATCH (d:Drug)
WITH d
```

```
LIMIT 10
RETURN COLLECT(d.code)
```

This query returns the codes of 10 drugs as a list.

Let's execute it in the browser to see what the response looks like:

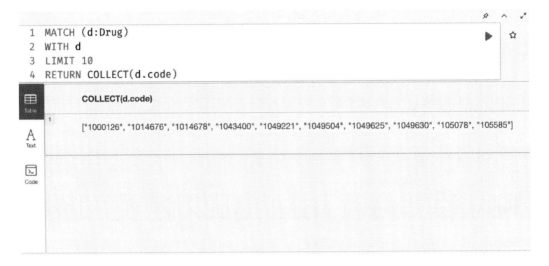

Figure 7.13 – Basic COLLECT usage

We can see from the screenshot that the response contains the list with the drug codes as a single value returned.

UNWIND is a Cypher clause that can convert a list into rows so that it can be processed one row at a time.

Let's start with a basic usage first:

```
WITH [1,2,3,4] as list
UNWIND list as e
RETURN e
```

This query converts a list into rows and returns each row.

Let's execute it in the browser to see what the response looks like:

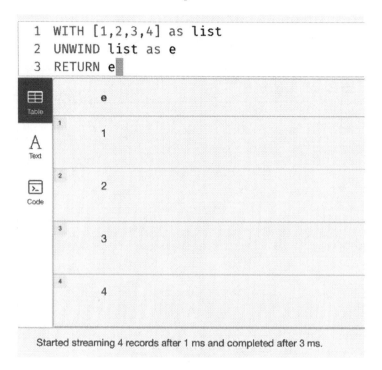

Figure 7.14 – Basic UNWIND usage

From the screenshot, we can see that we have four rows returned, one row for each element in the list.

Let's take a look at another example where there are duplicates in the list:

```
WITH [1,2,3,3,4] as list
UNWIND list as e
RETURN e
```

This query returns five rows as there are duplicates in the data. We can combine the DISTINCT clause with UNWIND to work with unique rows of data.

Let's look at this aspect:

```
WITH [1,2,3,3,4] as list
UNWIND list as e
RETURN DISTINCT e
```

This query returns only the distinct values from the list.

Let's execute it in the browser to see what the response looks like:

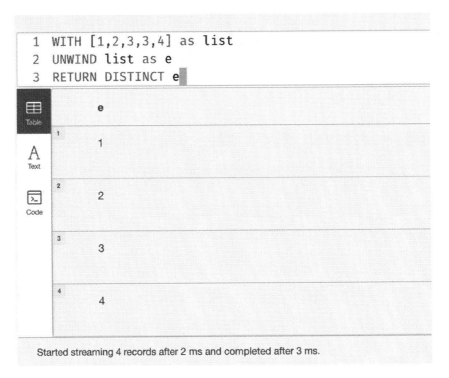

Figure 7.15 – Combining UNWIND with DISTINCT

From the screenshot, we can see that the response contains only four rows, while there are five elements in the list.

It is also possible to use UNWIND along with any expression that returns a list. Let's look at an example of this:

```
WITH [1,2] as list1, [3,4] as list2
UNWIND (list2+list1) as e
RETURN e
```

This query creates a new list by combining two lists and performs UNWIND on it.

Let's execute it in the browser to see what the response looks like:

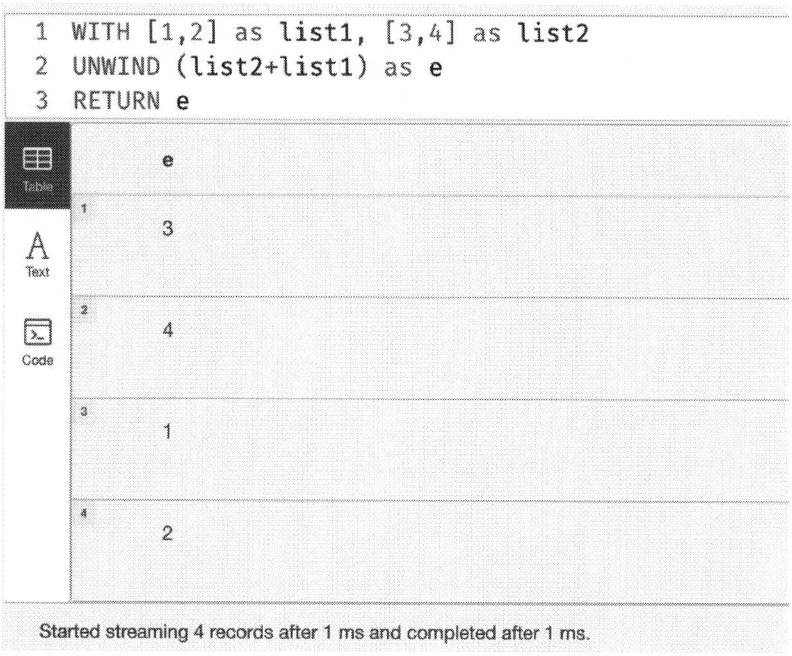

Figure 7.16 – Using list expressions with UNWIND

From the screenshot, we can see that `list2` and `list1` are combined first and `UNWIND` returns the rows of the combined list values.

It is also possible to work with nested lists using `UNWIND`. Let's look at an example of this:

```
WITH [[1,2], [3,4]] as list
UNWIND list as inner
UNWIND inner as e
RETURN e
```

With nested lists, you also need to nest the `UNWIND` statements to process them as shown in the preceding query.

Let's execute the preceding code in the browser to see what the response looks like.

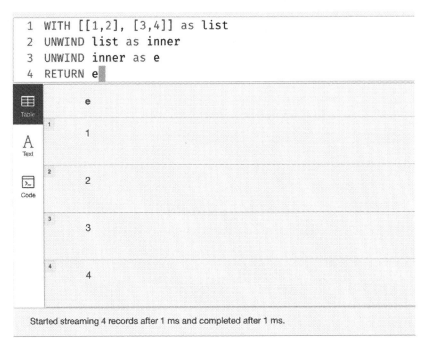

```
1  WITH [[1,2], [3,4]] as list
2  UNWIND list as inner
3  UNWIND inner as e
4  RETURN e
```

Figure 7.17 – Handling nested lists with UNWIND

We can see from the screenshot that we iterated the nested list and got all the individual elements from all the inner lists.

Now that we have taken a look at the various aspects of lists in Cypher, we will take a look at working with maps in Cypher next.

Working with maps

In this section, we will take a look at working with maps in Cypher. Maps in Cypher represent key-value pairs. The keys must be strings and values can be any object. Maps can be defined in Cypher inline, where they are called literal maps, or they can be passed as parameters. Every node and relationship object can also be treated as a map in Cypher, so that we can access all the properties using dot (.) notation or index ([ ]) notation.

A map is like a **JavaScript Object Notation (JSON)** object. A sample JSON object looks like this:

```
{
    "firstName": "John",
    "lastName": "Smith",
```

```
    "isAlive": true,
    "age": 27
}
```

If we represented the same map in Cypher, it would look like this:

```
WITH {
    firstName: "John",
    lastName: "Smith",
    isAlive: true,
    age: 27
} as map
RETURN map
```

We can see from the code that the keys in this map representation are not enclosed by double quotes as they are being represented as JSON. These are called literal maps in Cypher.

Let's execute it in the browser to see what the response looks like.

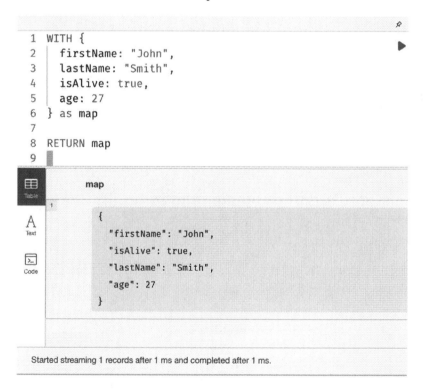

Figure 7.18 – Map representation in Cypher

As we can see from the preceding screenshot, while in Cypher we are not using double quotes for keys, in the data returned there are double quotes for keys, which is exactly what the actual JSON object looks like.

In Cypher, this is called a **literal map**. These literal maps can be as simple as the ones we have seen in the preceding figure, or they can be complex nested objects. Let's look at an example:

```
WITH {
    firstName: "John",
    lastName: "Smith",
    isAlive: true,
    age: 27,
    address: {
        line1: "1 address ln",
        city: "Newark",
        state: "NJ",
        country: "USA"
    },
    aliases: ["Johny", "John"]
} as map
RETURN map.firstName, map.lastName, map.address.state, map.
aliases[0]
```

We can see that in this map object that we have a nested map and a list of values in the outer map. Also, in the RETURN statement, we can see that we are able to refer to the keys in the map using the dot notation, similar to how JSON objects are used.

Let's execute it in the browser to see what the response looks like.

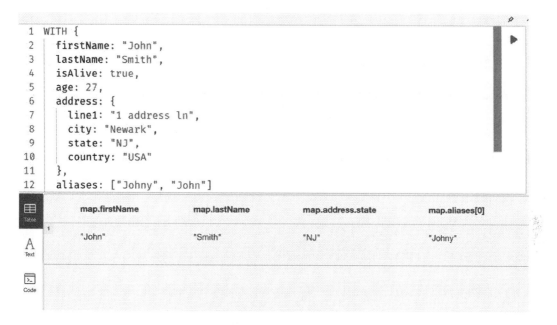

Figure 7.19 – Nested map usage in Cypher

From the screenshot, we can see that the values from the map related to the keys referred are returned. We can also see that not only can we get values of basic types that are accessible directly from the map, such as `firstName` and `lastName`, but we can also access nested content, such as a `state` key from the `address` object in the source map, along with the first element of the list identified by the `aliases` key.

In the previous query, we access the values using dot notation. We can also retrieve values using the [ ] syntax. Let's take a look at this:

```
WITH {
    firstName: "John",
    lastName: "Smith",
    isAlive: true,
    age: 27,
    address: {
        line1: "1 address ln",
        city: "Newark",
        state: "NJ",
        country: "USA"
```

```
  },
  aliases: ["Johny", "John"]
} as map
RETURN map["firstName"], map["lastName"], map["address"]
["state"], map["aliases"][0]
```

We can see in the preceding query that we are able to access the values using the [ ] syntax.

Let's execute it in the browser to see what the response looks like.

Figure 7.20 – Map value access using the [ ] syntax

We can see that the response is the same for accessing values from the map using dot notation or the [ ] syntax. This syntax is more useful when there are special characters or spaces in the key names. In that case, dot notation cannot be used to refer to those keys as it would cause syntax errors. Index notation can help us to avoid this issue and still be able to access the map values.

One more thing to note in Cypher is that for string literals, you can either use double quotes or single quotes.

Now, let's look at how we can work with map projections of data in Cypher.

Working with map projections

Cypher provides a concept called map projections. Map projections are a very useful tool to build a simple response from node or relationship entities to return only the content we need. They are maps built using nodes, relationship properties, and other values.

Let's take a look at an example of this:

```
MATCH (d:Drug)
WITH d
LIMIT 10
RETURN d{.code, .description, label: labels(d)[0]}
```

This query will retrieve the first 10 drug nodes and create a map projection with the code and description properties for the Drug node and the first label of that node.

Let's execute it in the browser to see what the response looks like.

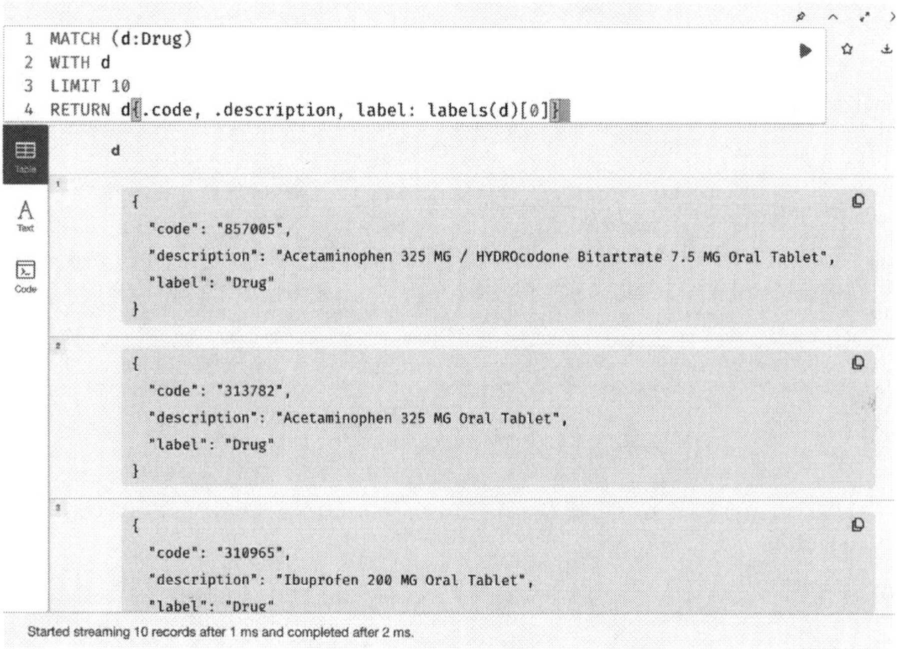

Figure 7.21 – Using map projections from Cypher

From the screenshot, we can see that the response is rows of maps with the codes, descriptions, and labels we built in the query. The response returned is a simple map with values and not a node entity.

Let's take a look at another simpler usage of map projections:

```
MATCH (d:Drug)
WITH d
LIMIT 10
RETURN d{.*}
```

This returns only the properties of the drug nodes as a map, and not all the other metadata associated with the node. This kind of usage is very useful when we don't need all the node metadata.

Let's execute it in the browser to see what the response looks like.

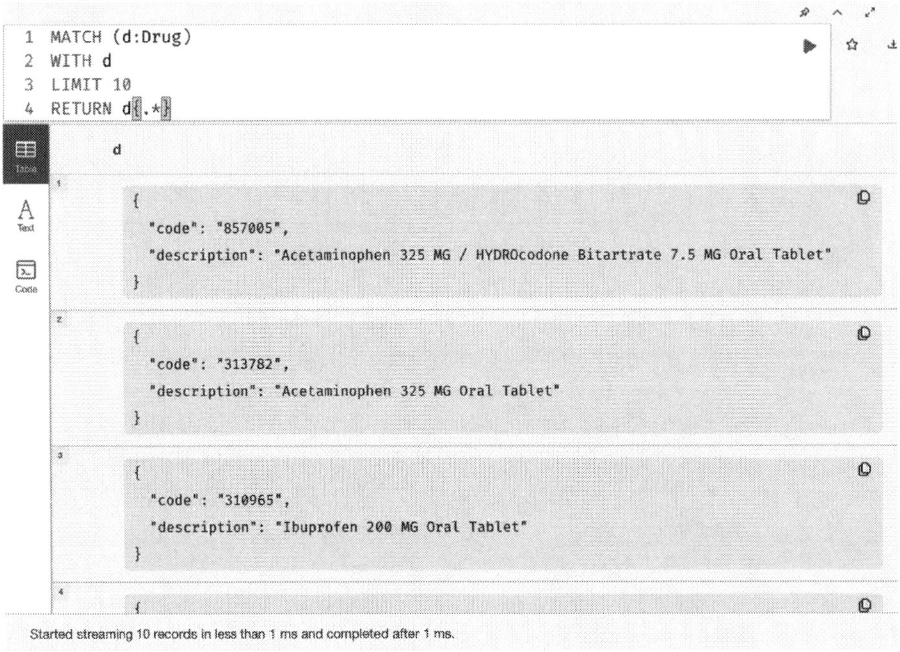

```
1  MATCH (d:Drug)
2  WITH d
3  LIMIT 10
4  RETURN d{.*}
```

```
d

{
    "code": "857005",
    "description": "Acetaminophen 325 MG / HYDROcodone Bitartrate 7.5 MG Oral Tablet"
}

{
    "code": "313782",
    "description": "Acetaminophen 325 MG Oral Tablet"
}

{
    "code": "310965",
    "description": "Ibuprofen 200 MG Oral Tablet"
}

{
```

Started streaming 10 records in less than 1 ms and completed after 1 ms.

Figure 7.22 – Basic map projections of node properties

From the screenshot, we can see that we have just the properties of the node as a map projection. There is no node metadata returned here.

For reference purposes, let's take a look at what the response would have been if we returned the node:

```
MATCH (d:Drug)
WITH d
LIMIT 10
RETURN d
```

This query returns the node.

Let's execute it in the browser to see what the response looks like.

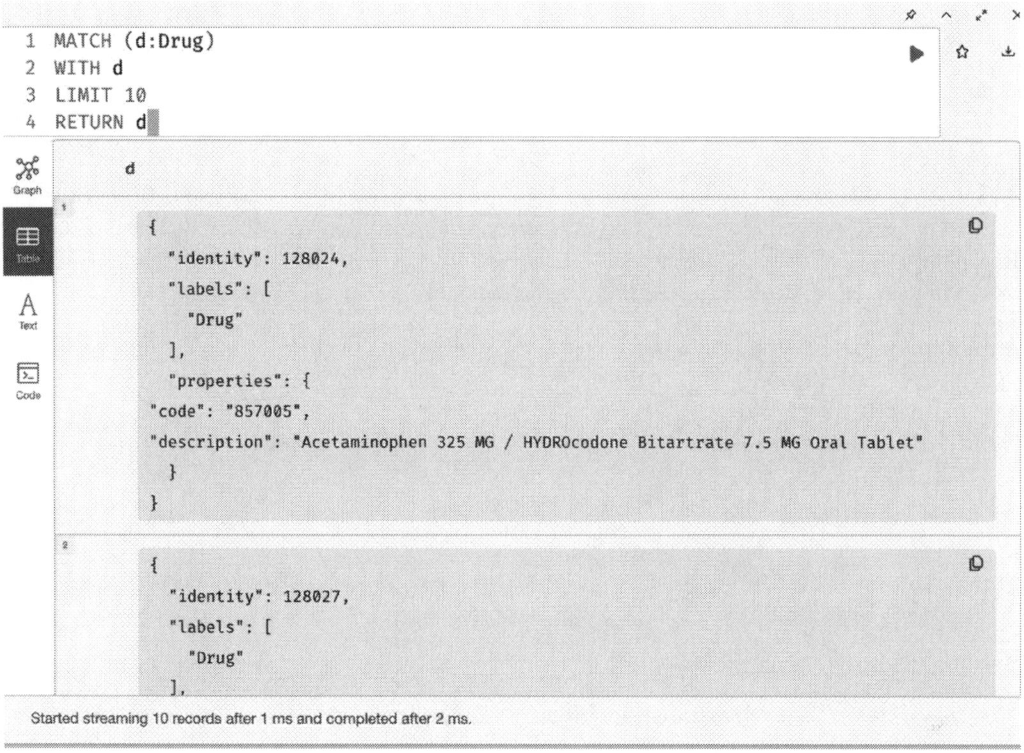

```
1  MATCH (d:Drug)
2  WITH d
3  LIMIT 10
4  RETURN d
```

```
d

{
    "identity": 128024,
    "labels": [
       "Drug"
    ],
    "properties": {
"code": "857005",
"description": "Acetaminophen 325 MG / HYDROcodone Bitartrate 7.5 MG Oral Tablet"
    }
}

{
    "identity": 128027,
    "labels": [
       "Drug"
    ],
```

Started streaming 10 records after 1 ms and completed after 2 ms.

Figure 7.23 – Node data return data for comparison

From the screenshot, we can see that when we return the node, we get the node identity labels as the list along with properties as a separate map. This could be very useful for graph visualizations, but for basic applications that are interested only in the property content, using map projections can reduce the network traffic and be more efficient.

Now, let's look at working with lists and maps together.

Combining lists and maps

Most of the time when we are loading batch data, we use lists of maps as data input to Cypher. We saw this in *Chapter 3*, *Loading Data with Cypher*, when we were loading data using LOAD CSV.

LOAD CSV turn each row in the *CSV* file into a map and we then process each row. Let's review this:

```
LOAD CSV WITH HEADERS from "file:///data.csv" AS row
WITH row
```

```
MERGE (p:Person {id:row.id})
SET p.firstName = row.firstName,
p.lastName = row.lastName
```

Here, the LOAD CSV clause reads the CSV file and converts each line into a map value and assigns it to a variable named row. We process one line at a time, which is the map assigned to the variable named row in the next steps of the query. Since the list of values in the line is converted into a map, we can access the values in the map using dot notation. In this query, we are accessing the keys, which are part of CSV headers, such as id, firstName and lastName. We will get one row object per line in the CSV file, excluding the header line, and we process in sequence one row at a time. If there are 100 lines in the CSV, then the last three lines of code will be executed 100 times.

If the same data is being sent as a parameter to the query using the driver, then the query will look like this:

```
UNWIND $data as row
WITH row
MERGE (p:Person {id:row.id})
SET p.firstName = row.firstName,
p.lastName = row.lastName
```

The $data variable holds the list of maps. We are unwinding the list to process one record at a time.

Now that we have taken a deeper look at how maps can be consumed, let's look at a summary of what we covered in this chapter.

Summary

In this chapter, we have looked at how lists and maps are core data types in Cypher for data manipulation and processing data. We looked at creating basic lists, how they can store different data types, and how we can access data using operators and functions. Also, we looked at how maps work in Cypher and how to use them when we are returning data. We also looked at how LOAD CSV creates a map for each row to be processed. Also, we took a look at lists of maps that are provided by applications using the driver to be processed to ingest data similar to LOAD CSV.

In the next chapter, we will take a deep dive into advanced querying using WITH, FOREACH, CASE, and other Cypher clauses.

8

Advanced Query Patterns

In the last chapter, we looked at working with lists and maps. In this chapter, we will explore some advanced query patterns using Cypher clauses. We will discuss query chaining using the `WITH` clause, iterate lists to modify the graph using the `FOREACH` and `UNWIND` clauses, and leverage count stores for building optimal queries. We will also take a look at simulating if condition using the `FOREACH` clause. We will take a deeper look at these clauses and discuss how they can help us in building more advanced and complex queries.

In this chapter, we will be covering the following aspects:

- Working with the `WITH` clause
- Working with the `CASE` clause
- Working with the `FOREACH` clause
- Working with the `UNWIND` clause
- Working with count stores

First, we will start by exploring the `WITH` clause. This is a very powerful paradigm that helps us build complex and performant queries with ease.

Working with the WITH clause

In Cypher, the `WITH` clause allows individual queries to be chained together by streaming the results from the first part of the query to the next part of the query. It allows you to manipulate the query result before it is passed on to the next part of the query.

We will take a look at different ways in which we can work with the `WITH` clause. We will start by introducing the variables at the beginning of the Cypher query.

Introducing variables at the start

When a query starts with the `WITH` clause, we need to introduce the variables for the next part of the query.

Let's look at an example:

```
WITH range(1,5,1) as list
RETURN list
```

In this query, we are introducing a variable called `list` and returning it.

The following screenshot shows how to prepare a new variable using the `WITH` clause and return values based on that variable.

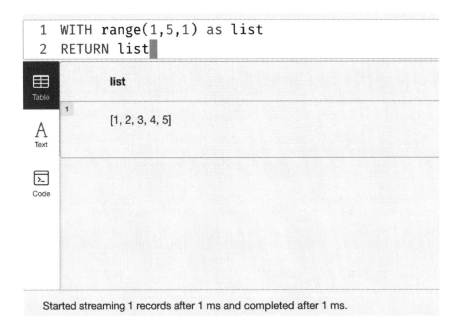

Figure 8.1 – Basic WITH usage introducing a new variable at the start

Now, let's look at using the new variable defined to perform `MATCH`:

```
WITH '313820' as code
MATCH (d:Drug {code:code})
RETURN d
```

In this query, we are defining a new variable using the `WITH` clause and then using that variable to perform other tasks in the next part of the query.

The following screenshot shows that we can retrieve the node by referring to the variable defined using the `WITH` clause.

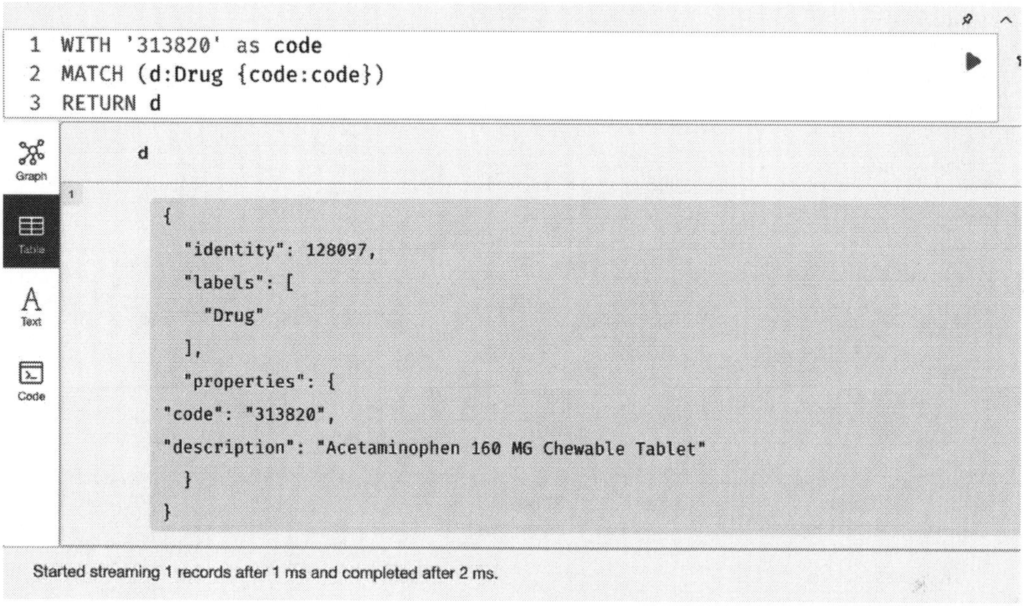

```
1  WITH '313820' as code
2  MATCH (d:Drug {code:code})
3  RETURN d
```

```
d

{
    "identity": 128097,
    "labels": [
        "Drug"
    ],
    "properties": {
        "code": "313820",
        "description": "Acetaminophen 160 MG Chewable Tablet"
    }
}
```

Started streaming 1 records after 1 ms and completed after 2 ms.

Figure 8.2 – Using a new variable to perform MATCH in the next part of the query

Now, let's look at getting some data in the first part of the query and passing it to the next part of the query:

```
MATCH (p:Patient {ssn:'999-10-9496'})-[:HAS_ENCOUNTER]->()-
[:HAS_DRUG]->(d:Drug)
WITH d
RETURN d.code, d.description
```

In this code, we are performing a `MATCH` query to get a `Patient` node and all the drugs they are prescribed in the first part of the query, and then we are passing only the drug nodes we found in this part of the query to the next query.

From the following screenshot, we can see that we are getting all the drug values with the RETURN clause using the variable passed with the WITH clause. We need to remember that all the other variables in the first part of the query are not available in the next part of the query.

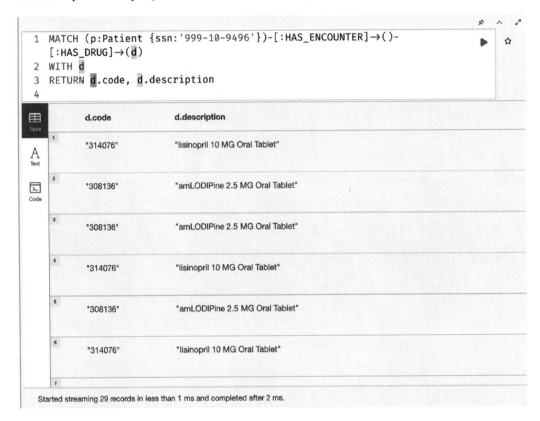

Figure 8.3 – Passing variables from one part of the query to another

Let us see what happens when we try to use the variables defined in the first part of the query in the second part of the query:

```
MATCH (p:Patient {ssn:'999-10-9496'})-[:HAS_ENCOUNTER]->()-
[:HAS_DRUG]->(d)
WITH d
RETURN p.ssn, d.code, d.description
```

This query tries to access the `Patient` node in the second part of the query that was retrieved in the first part of the query.

As we can see from the following screenshot, we get an error saying that the variable is not defined. This is because the `WITH` clause defines a new scope and only the variables passed using that clause are available in the new scope of the second part of the query.

```
1  MATCH (p:Patient {ssn:'999-10-9496'})-[:HAS_ENCOUNTER]→()-[:HAS_DRUG]→
   (d)
2  WITH d
3  RETURN p.ssn, d.code, d.description
4
```

ERROR Neo.ClientError.Statement.SyntaxError

```
Variable `p` not defined (line 3, column 8 (offset: 90))
"RETURN p.ssn, d.code, d.description"
        ^
```

Figure 8.4 – Using a variable in the second part of the query not passed using WITH

Say we want to pass all the variables we have retrieved in the first part of the query to the second part of the query without referring to each of them manually; we can use a wildcard, *, to do that. Let's look at how this is done:

```
MATCH (p:Patient {ssn:'999-10-9496'})-[:HAS_ENCOUNTER]->()-
[:HAS_DRUG]->(d)
WITH *
RETURN p.ssn, d.code, d.description
```

In this query, we are passing all the variables we have defined in the first part of the query to the second part of the query.

As we can see from the following screenshot, there are no more errors now. Data is returned from the query.

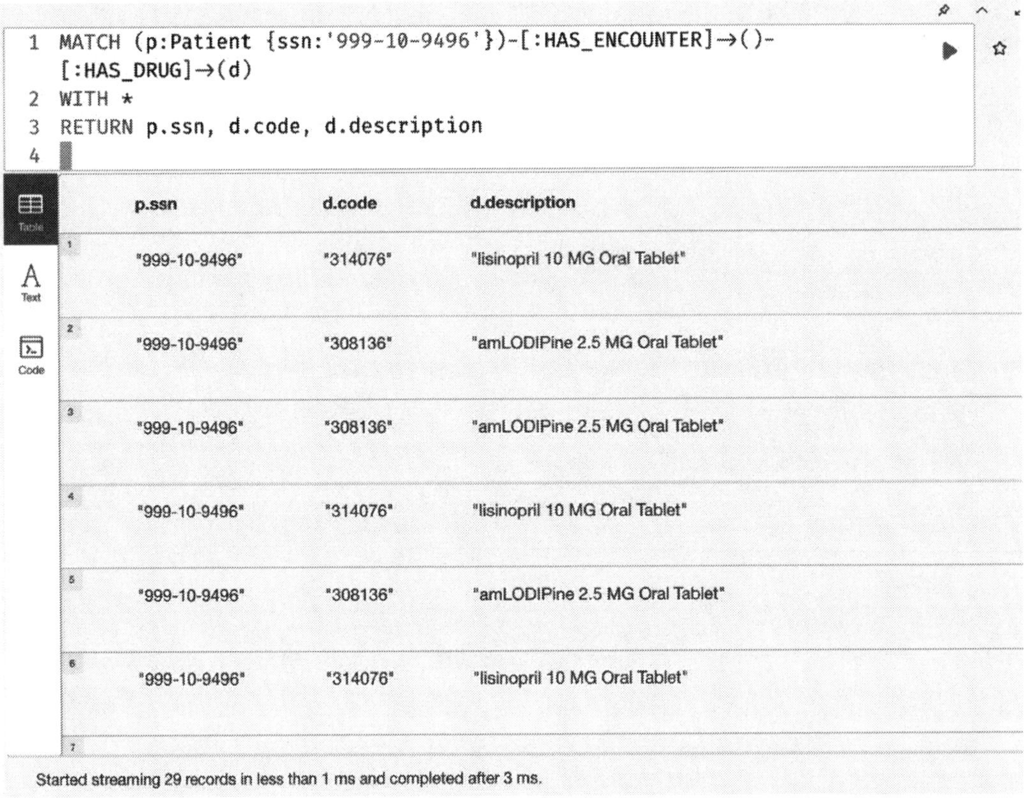

```
1  MATCH (p:Patient {ssn:'999-10-9496'})-[:HAS_ENCOUNTER]→()-
   [:HAS_DRUG]→(d)
2  WITH *
3  RETURN p.ssn, d.code, d.description
4
```

p.ssn	d.code	d.description
"999-10-9496"	"314076"	"lisinopril 10 MG Oral Tablet"
"999-10-9496"	"308136"	"amLODIPine 2.5 MG Oral Tablet"
"999-10-9496"	"308136"	"amLODIPine 2.5 MG Oral Tablet"
"999-10-9496"	"314076"	"lisinopril 10 MG Oral Tablet"
"999-10-9496"	"308136"	"amLODIPine 2.5 MG Oral Tablet"
"999-10-9496"	"314076"	"lisinopril 10 MG Oral Tablet"

Started streaming 29 records in less than 1 ms and completed after 3 ms.

Figure 8.5 – Passing all the variables from the first part of the query to the second using a wildcard

Using the WITH clause, we can not only return the variables from the first part of the query, but we can introduce new variables using aggregate functions, such as count and collect, or other clauses.

Let's take a look at a query that uses aggregation functions as well as the WITH clause:

```
MATCH (p:Patient {ssn:'999-10-9496'})-[:HAS_ENCOUNTER]->()-
[:HAS_DRUG]->(d)
WITH d, count(d) as prescriptions
RETURN d.code, d.description, prescriptions
```

This query returns the drug code, name, and the number of times it has been prescribed for the given patient. We can see that we have introduced a new variable called `prescriptions` by using the `count` method.

From the following screenshot, we can see that we are getting the distinct drug codes and names, along with the number of times the drug has been prescribed to this patient.

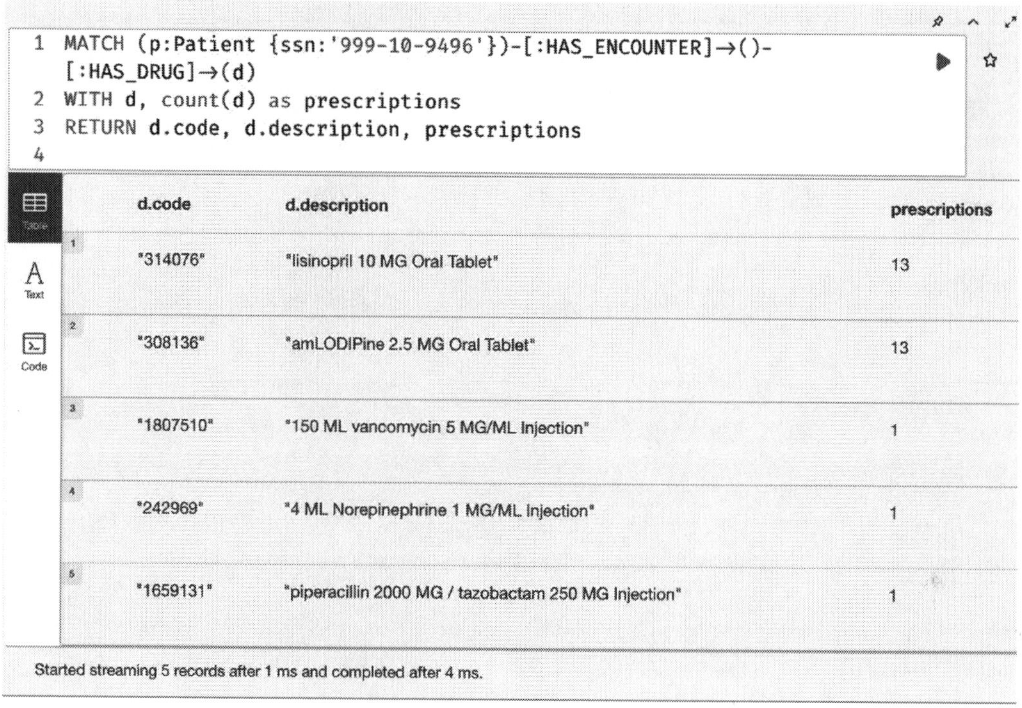

```
1  MATCH (p:Patient {ssn:'999-10-9496'})-[:HAS_ENCOUNTER]→()-
   [:HAS_DRUG]→(d)
2  WITH d, count(d) as prescriptions
3  RETURN d.code, d.description, prescriptions
4
```

d.code	d.description	prescriptions
"314076"	"lisinopril 10 MG Oral Tablet"	13
"308136"	"amLODIPine 2.5 MG Oral Tablet"	13
"1807510"	"150 ML vancomycin 5 MG/ML Injection"	1
"242969"	"4 ML Norepinephrine 1 MG/ML Injection"	1
"1659131"	"piperacillin 2000 MG / tazobactam 250 MG Injection"	1

Started streaming 5 records after 1 ms and completed after 4 ms.

Figure 8.6 – Introducing a new variable along with an existing variable

Along with the new variables, we can also introduce a WHERE condition to continue to the next part of the query only when certain conditions have been met. Let's look at an example of this:

```
MATCH (p:Patient {ssn:'999-10-9496'})-[:HAS_ENCOUNTER]->()-
[:HAS_DRUG]->(d)
WITH d, count(d) as prescriptions
WHERE prescriptions > 10
RETURN d.code, d.description, prescriptions
```

In this query, we are trying to return only the drugs that have been prescribed more than 10 times.

From the following screenshot, we can now see that only two drugs have been prescribed more than 10 times.

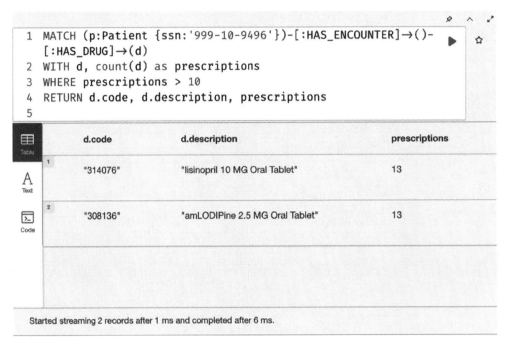

Figure 8.7 – Adding a WHERE clause along with new variables

We can also apply ORDER BY to the first part of the query result set along with the WITH clause before processing them in the next part of the query. Let's look at an example of this:

```
MATCH (p:Patient {ssn:'999-10-9496'})-[:HAS_ENCOUNTER]->()-
[:HAS_DRUG]->(d)
WITH d, count(d) as prescriptions
ORDER BY d.code
RETURN d.code, d.description, prescriptions
```

In this query, we are ordering the first query results by drug code and then passing the results to the next part of the query.

Let's execute the query and review the results.

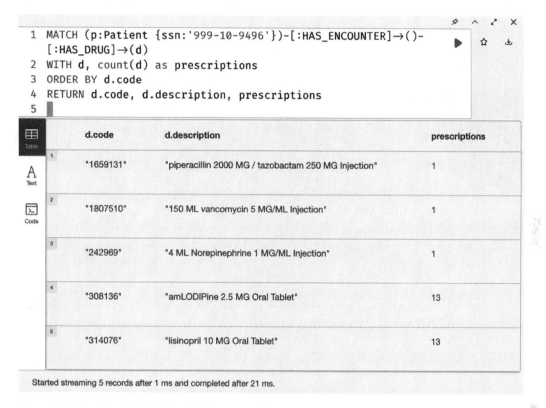

```
1  MATCH (p:Patient {ssn:'999-10-9496'})-[:HAS_ENCOUNTER]→()-
   [:HAS_DRUG]→(d)
2  WITH d, count(d) as prescriptions
3  ORDER BY d.code
4  RETURN d.code, d.description, prescriptions
5
```

d.code	d.description	prescriptions
1	"1659131"	"piperacillin 2000 MG / tazobactam 250 MG Injection"	1
2	"1807510"	"150 ML vancomycin 5 MG/ML Injection"	1
3	"242969"	"4 ML Norepinephrine 1 MG/ML Injection"	1
4	"308136"	"amLODIPine 2.5 MG Oral Tablet"	13
5	"314076"	"lisinopril 10 MG Oral Tablet"	13

Started streaming 5 records after 1 ms and completed after 21 ms.

Figure 8.8 – Applying ORDER BY to the first part of the query results and passing them on to the next part

We can see from the screenshot that the response has now ordered the results by drug code. It is also possible to apply the LIMIT clause to the first part of the query results. Let's look at this in the following code block:

```
MATCH (p:Patient {ssn:'999-10-9496'})-[:HAS_ENCOUNTER]->()-
[:HAS_DRUG]->(d)
WITH d, count(d) as prescriptions
ORDER BY d.code
LIMIT 4
RETURN d.code, d.description, prescriptions
```

Here, we are limiting the results from the first part of the query to 4, using these four results, and returning the required data in the next part of the query.

As we can see from the following screenshot, we are only getting the first four results from the ordered data from the first part of the query.

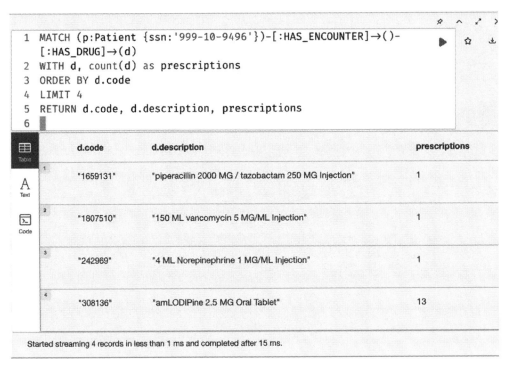

Figure 8.9 – Limiting the results from the first part of the query

Similarly, it is also possible to apply the SKIP clause and a combination of the SKIP and LIMIT clauses to the result set.

It is also possible to take the results from the first query and perform a different set of queries to do something completely different. Let's take a look at this:

```
WITH '999-10-9496' as ssn
MATCH (p:Patient {ssn:ssn})-[:HAS_ENCOUNTER]->()-[:HAS_DRUG]-
>(d)
WITH d, count(d) as prescriptions
WHERE prescriptions > 10
MATCH (other)-[:HAS_ENCOUNTER]->()-[:HAS_DRUG]->(d)
WITH  other, d, count(d) as otherPrescriptions
WHERE otherPrescriptions > 10
RETURN other.ssn as otherPatients, d.code as drug,
d.description as name, otherPrescriptions
```

In this query, we are finding the most prescribed drugs for the given patient and finding other patients to whom these drugs were prescribed most.

We can see from the following screenshot that we are able to branch after the first part of the query using the most prescribed drug node, which is passed to the second part of the query, which is retrieving the other patients who also had these drugs prescribed often. Another aspect we can notice is that we can keep the WITH chain going. In the previous query, we used WITH four times to keep passing the data to the next step while filtering for the desired results.

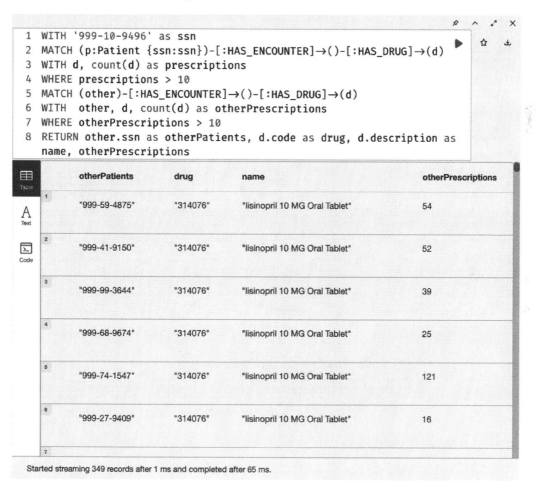

Figure 8.10 – Branching path in the second part of the query using WITH

In this section, we have discussed various ways to use the WITH clause to build advanced cypher queries. We will take a look at the CASE WHEN clause next and review various usage scenarios for building queries.

Working with the CASE clause

The CASE clause is an expression constructed that is used to transform results. There are two different forms of CASE expression and they are as follows:

- A simple CASE form to compare against multiple values
- A generic CASE form to express multiple conditional expressions

We will take a look at the simple CASE expression first.

Working with simple CASE expressions

In simple CASE expressions, the expression is evaluated and compared to the WHEN clauses. The corresponding expression is then evaluated and the resulting value is returned. If no value is found, the ELSE clause expression is evaluated and the corresponding value is returned. If there is no ELSE clause, then a null value is returned.

The syntactic representation of this looks like this:

```
CASE test
  WHEN value THEN result
  [WHEN ...]
  [ELSE default]
END
```

We can see from this syntax that the first CASE expression is evaluated and its value is compared to the WHEN clause. We can describe each variable or argument in this syntax in the following way:

- test – A valid expression. This can be evaluated into different values based on the data.
- value – An expression that will be compared against test.
- result – The value we want to return if value matches test.
- default – The value that will be returned when none of the value expressions match test.

Let's take a look at an example usage:

```
MATCH (p:Patient)
RETURN p.ssn as patient, CASE p.marital
    WHEN "S" THEN "Single"
    WHEN "M" THEN "Married"
    ELSE "UNKNOWN"
END as status
```

In this query, we are getting all the patients' statuses based on the `marital` property code and then returning an elaborate string as the response.

As we can see from the following screenshot, we are getting detailed text as the statuses instead of code.

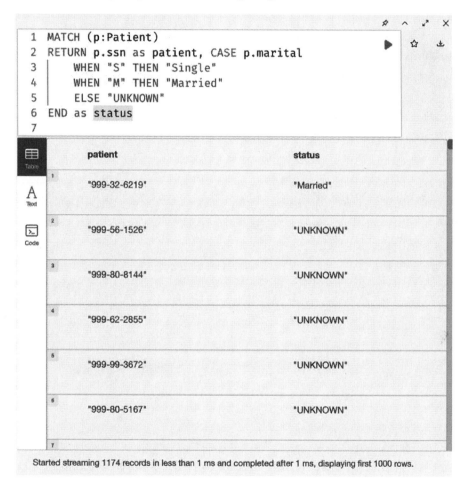

Figure 8.11 – Simple CASE expression

It is also possible to combine the `WITH` clause and apply the `CASE` expression after filtering data. Let's look at an example usage of this:

```
MATCH (p:Patient)
WITH p.ssn as patient, CASE p.marital
    WHEN "S" THEN "Single"
    WHEN "M" THEN "Married"
```

```
     ELSE "UNKNOWN"
END as status
WHERE p.marital IS NOT NULL
RETURN patient, status
```

In this query, we are combining the CASE expression and the WITH clause and retrieving only those patients' statuses who have a certain value for the marital property.

We can see from the following screenshot that we are not getting the UNKNOWN value returned anymore.

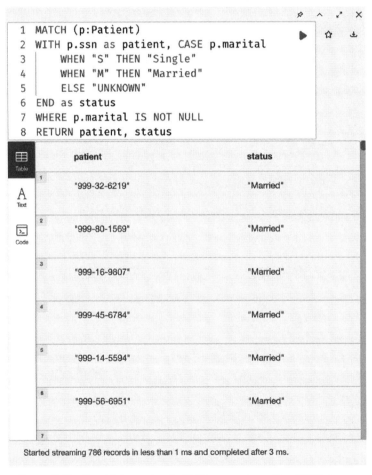

Figure 8.12 – Combining a simple CASE expression with a WITH clause

Also, we can see we are only getting 786 records returned from 1174 records, compared to the previous query we tried, as the WITH clause is eliminating all the patients who do not have a marital property value.

Working with generic CASE expressions

In generic CASE expressions, we do not have a default expression but each WHEN statement is a separate condition that is evaluated in order.

The syntax of a generic case expression looks as follows:

```
CASE
  WHEN predicate THEN result
  [WHEN …]
  [ELSE default]
END
```

We can see that we don't have a value expression after the CASE clause here. Since there is nothing to evaluate here, the WHEN clause predicates take over.

We can describe each variable or argument in this syntax in the following way:

- predicate – This is the predicate or expression that is evaluated and then returns true or false. If this predicate returns true, then the corresponding result is returned.

- result – The expression whose output is returned when predicate is evaluated to true.

- default – The expression whose output is returned when all the predicates return false. Remember that since ELSE is optional, there is no need to have this expression. When this is missing, a null value is returned if all the predicates return false.

Let's take a look at this:

```
WITH date().year as currentYear
MATCH (p:Patient)
RETURN p.ssn,
    CASE
        WHEN currentYear-p.birthDate.year < 16 THEN 'Child'
        WHEN 16 < currentYear-p.birthDate.year < 22 THEN 'Young
Adult'
        WHEN 22 < currentYear-p.birthDate.year < 60 THEN
'Adult'
        WHEN 60 < currentYear-p.birthDate.year THEN 'Old'
    END as ageGroup
```

We can see in this query that we are taking the patients' birth dates and categorizing them into age groups. While it is possible to build the same logic with a simple CASE expression, it would be very difficult and elaborate. We would need to have an individual WHEN clause for every value we could possibly have for the age value. A generic CASE expression can make it easier in this case.

As we can see from the following screenshot, we get the final value from the CASE expression returned as the age group value in the response.

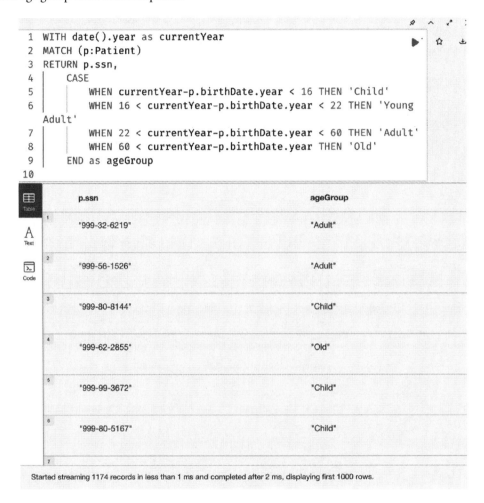

```
 1  WITH date().year as currentYear
 2  MATCH (p:Patient)
 3  RETURN p.ssn,
 4      CASE
 5          WHEN currentYear-p.birthDate.year < 16 THEN 'Child'
 6          WHEN 16 < currentYear-p.birthDate.year < 22 THEN 'Young
    Adult'
 7          WHEN 22 < currentYear-p.birthDate.year < 60 THEN 'Adult'
 8          WHEN 60 < currentYear-p.birthDate.year THEN 'Old'
 9      END as ageGroup
10
```

p.ssn	ageGroup
"999-32-6219"	"Adult"
"999-56-1526"	"Adult"
"999-80-8144"	"Child"
"999-62-2855"	"Old"
"999-99-3672"	"Child"
"999-80-5167"	"Child"

Started streaming 1174 records in less than 1 ms and completed after 2 ms, displaying first 1000 rows.

Figure 8.13 – A generic CASE expression usage

Another common use case for a generic CASE expression is to evaluate input data and then set the properties on the nodes dynamically. Since this is an expression, it can be used anywhere, as an expression is used to evaluate values.

Let's look at how we can use a CASE expression to set the properties on a node. We can use the same expression we used in the previous query to create a new property on the patient node called ageGroup.

```
WITH date().year as currentYear
MATCH (p:Patient)
```

```
SET p.ageGroup =
    CASE
        WHEN currentYear-p.birthDate.year < 16 THEN 'Child'
        WHEN 16 < currentYear-p.birthDate.year < 22 THEN 'Young
Adult'
        WHEN 22 < currentYear-p.birthDate.year < 60 THEN
'Adult'
        WHEN 60 < currentYear-p.birthDate.year THEN 'Old'
    END
RETURN p.ageGroup
```

In this query, we are reusing the CASE expression we used in an earlier query, setting the value created as a new property on the patient node, and then returning the final value.

As we can see from the following screenshot, we have set the ageGroup property on the patient node using the CASE expression value and the returned property value contains the new value.

Figure 8.14 – Using a generic CASE expression to set a property value on a node

We can see that a CASE expression can be a very powerful tool when manipulating data that makes sense either while writing data to a graph or when we are returning data.

We will explore the FOREACH clause next.

Working with the FOREACH clause

The FOREACH clause can be used to process a list and update the data in a graph. It can only be used to update data using the CREATE, MERGE, SET, DELETE, REMOVE, and FOREACH clauses. It is not possible to use the MATCH clause within FOREACH. Also, the variables in the context of the FOREACH clause are limited to its scope only and there is no option to remove those variables to be used after FOREACH.

Let's look at an example usage:

```
MATCH (p:Patient)
WHERE p.marital IS NULL
WITH collect(p) as nodes
FOREACH( n in nodes | SET n:UNKNOWN_STATUS)
```

In this query, we are finding all the patients whose marital status is null, collecting all those patients into a list, and then using the FOREACH clause to add an UNKNOWN_STATUS label.

We can see from the screenshot that we have updated 388 patient nodes with the new label.

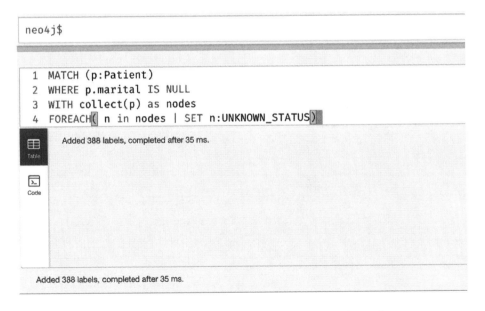

Figure 8.15 – Using FOREACH to add a new label to the node

Another usage of the FOREACH clause is to simulate an IF condition. Since there is no support for IF conditions in Cypher, we can leverage the way FOREACH works to simulate an IF condition.

Let's build a query to get all the patient nodes and use the FOREACH clause to check for the new UNKNOWN_STATUS label and remove it. To achieve this, we need to leverage a CASE expression:

```
MATCH (p:Patient)
FOREACH(
    ignoreME in CASE WHEN p:UNKNOWN_STATUS THEN [1] ELSE [] END
|
    REMOVE p:UNKNOWN_STATUS
)
```

In this query, we are leveraging FOREACH by preparing a list using the CASE expression first. The CASE expression applies the predicate. When it is true, it returns a list with one element, and when it is false, it returns an empty list. When a list with a single value is returned, the next set of statements is executed once. In this part, we are accessing the variable in the outer scope and removing the label on it.

From the following screenshot, we can see we have removed the label from exactly 388 nodes to whom we added this label in an earlier query.

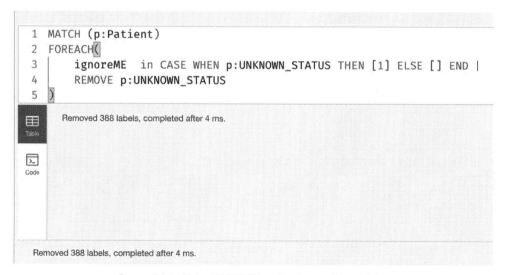

Figure 8.16 – Using FOREACH to simulate an IF condition

FOREACH is a convenient way to process the lists to update the graph. But, when we need to do some extra work, such as finding other nodes before processing, this could be limiting. In that case, UNWIND is the best option to build the query.

With that in mind, now let's explore the UNWIND clause.

Working with the UNWIND clause

We saw the usage of FOREACH in the previous section and explored how we can iterate a list and update the graph. But, its usage is limited. If we want to retrieve data from a graph based on the data in a list before we can update the graph, then it is not possible with FOREACH. The UNWIND clause allows us to be able to do this. Also, if we want to return some data while processing a list, then UNWIND is the option to do this.

Let's take a look at the query we built to add a label in the previous section and build it using UNWIND:

```
MATCH (p:Patient)
WHERE p.marital IS NULL
WITH collect(p) as nodes
UNWIND nodes as n
SET n:UNKNOWN_STATUS
```

This does exactly what the FOREACH query did earlier. We find the patients who do not have a marital property set, and then we collect those nodes into a list and unwind that list to process one node at a time.

We can see from the screenshot that we updated 388 nodes, which is exactly what happened when we used FOREACH to process the list.

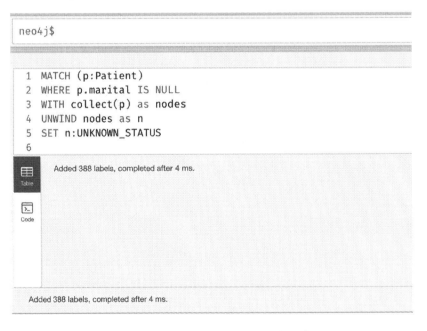

Figure 8.17 – Using UNWIND to process a list

When we want to process a list based on a condition, UNWIND provides good options. Let's build a query using UNWIND to remove the label we added in the previous query:

```
MATCH (p:Patient)
WITH collect(p) as nodes
UNWIND nodes as n
WITH n
WHERE n:UNKNOWN_STATUS
REMOVE n:UNKNOWN_STATUS
```

We can see in this query that we have combined UNWIND and WITH to be able to process the data conditionally.

We can see from the following screenshot that we removed the label from exactly 388 nodes.

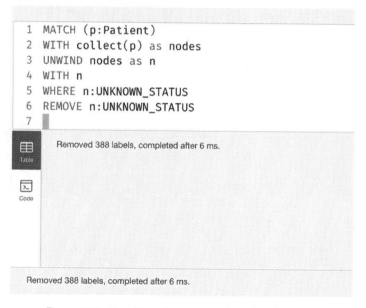

Figure 8.18 – Conditional processing data after UNWIND

From the last two sections, we can see that if we are doing some simple list processing and updating data, then FOREACH is the best and most simple option, as it isolates the processing. In this case, the UNWIND clause might be overkill, as it executes all the Cypher code below the UNWIND statement. If we want to elaborate data processing some more while iterating through the list and returning the data, then UNWIND is the best option.

We will take a look at using count stores next to build performant queries.

Working with count stores

Neo4j maintains certain data statistics as count stores. For example, there are node count stores that maintain the counts of nodes for each label type. Since our dataset is small, we will use PROFILE to understand how much work the database would be doing in terms of db hits, with and without count stores, for a given type of work. We will also take a look at how to leverage count stores to build more performant queries.

Let's look at a sample node count store query:

```
PROFILE MATCH (n:Patient)
RETURN count(n)
```

This is a very basic query, and it leverages count stores instead of counting the nodes that have the Patient label.

We can see from the screenshot, the database uses **NodeCountFromCountStore@neo4j**, which looks for the totals from the count store. We can see that it takes one db hit. The performance is constant, no matter how large the database grows.

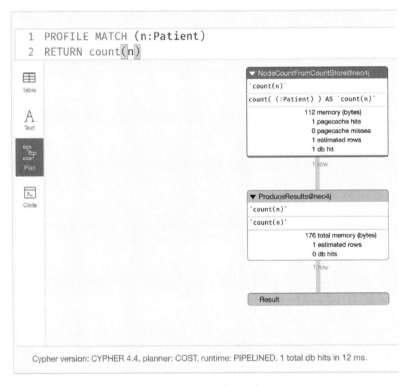

Figure 8.19 – A query using the node count store

We can see the performance gains when we are looking at traversals.

Let's look at how most users try to build a query to count paths. We will take a look at the query that leverages the count stores to do the same work optimally.

Let's look at the query first:

```
PROFILE MATCH p=(:Drug {code:'313820'})<--()
RETURN count(p)
```

In this query, we are searching for the drug node identified with the 313820 code and counting all the paths with incoming relationships to this node.

From the following screenshot, we can see that there are 115 incoming relationships to the node and it took 119 db hits to complete this query.

Figure 8.20 – Query to count incoming relationships to a node

Let's rewrite this query using the size function:

```
PROFILE RETURN size((:Drug {code:'313820'})<--())
```

We can see this query is much simpler and leverages the expressive nature of Cypher combined with the size function to return the response.

We can see from the following screenshot that the performance of this query is exactly the same as the previous version.

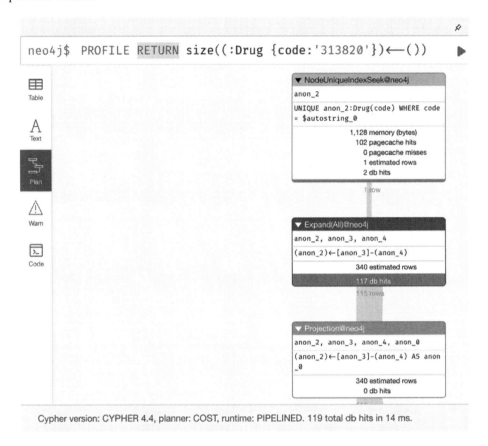

neo4j$ PROFILE RETURN size((:Drug {code:'313820'})←())

NodeUniqueIndexSeek@neo4j

anon_2

UNIQUE anon_2:Drug(code) WHERE code = $autostring_0

1,128 memory (bytes)
102 pagecache hits
0 pagecache misses
1 estimated rows
2 db hits

1 row

Expand(All)@neo4j

anon_2, anon_3, anon_4

(anon_2)←[anon_3]-(anon_4)

340 estimated rows

117 db hits

115 rows

Projection@neo4j

anon_2, anon_3, anon_4, anon_0

(anon_2)←[anon_3]-(anon_4) AS anon_0

340 estimated rows
0 db hits

Cypher version: CYPHER 4.4, planner: COST, runtime: PIPELINED. 119 total db hits in 14 ms.

Figure 8.21 – Using the size function to count the paths

Now, let us look at how to leverage the count stores to perform this operation more effectively:

```
PROFILE MATCH (d:Drug {code:'313820'})
RETURN size((d)<--())
```

We can see that we have changed our approach in this query. First, we wrote a query for the node and then we used the `size` function to find all the incoming relationships this node has.

From the screenshot, we can see it took only three db hits to perform the same activity to count the number of relationships.

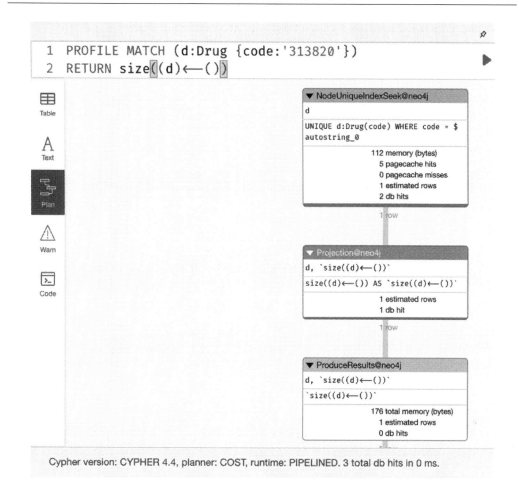

Figure 8.22 – Optimal way to count the relationships

We are not using the count stores here as we are looking at data for a single node. If we look for incoming relationships for all the Drug nodes, it should leverage the count store.

Let's try that:

```
PROFILE MATCH (:Drug)<-[r]-()
RETURN count(r)
```

This query returns the count of all incoming relationships of the Drug node.

We can see from the screenshot that it uses relationship count stores to return the data and it takes only one db hit.

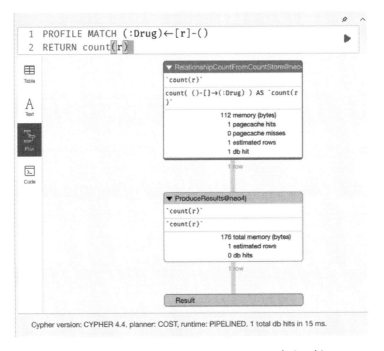

Figure 8.23 – Leveraging count stores to count relationships

There is a knowledgebase article (`https://neo4j.com/developer/kb/fast-counts-using-the-count-store/`) that talks about how to use count stores. This is updated with proper advice on how to leverage count stores and is kept updated with all the new releases.

We have looked at various aspects of Cypher used for building advanced queries. Let's summarize what we have learned.

Summary

In this chapter, we explored using the WITH, CASE, FOREACH, and UNWIND clauses to build some advanced query patterns. We looked at chaining queries using the WITH clause to introduce new variables to the next part of the query, reducing the scope of the variables, and performing some conditional query executions. We looked at using a CASE expression to manipulate data to either write a graph or when returning a response. We looked at using the FOREACH and UNWIND clauses to iterate lists either to write a graph or to return data and discussed where graphs are appropriate to use and where not to use them. Finally, we looked at count stores, how we can leverage them in queries, and the optimal query patterns for counting the relationships of a single node.

In the next chapter, we will take a look at using the EXPLAIN and PROFILE keywords to identify query performance pain points and how to address them.

9
Query Tuning

Till now, we have looked at various aspects of building Cypher queries. In this chapter, we will take a look at which options are available to profile and tune queries.

We have two options available to tune queries. The first one is the `EXPLAIN` clause, which takes the Cypher query and provides an estimated amount of work the database might do. It does not execute the query. The other one is the `PROFILE` clause. This will execute the query and gives the exact amount of work the database is doing. We will review both of these options in detail to understand how to leverage them to tune queries.

We will be taking a look at these aspects:

- Working with `EXPLAIN`
- Working with `PROFILE`
- Reviewing plan operators
- Using index hints

First, let's take a look at how to use `EXPLAIN` to tune queries.

Working with EXPLAIN

The `EXPLAIN` clause returns a query execution plan as the database sees it. It does not actually execute the query and does not return data. It does not make any changes to the database itself. It can be used to easily identify missing indexes or query plans not using existing indexes, and so on. Also, it tells us how a query is traversing relationships to do its work.

Let's look at a basic example of `EXPLAIN` usage:

```
EXPLAIN MATCH (d {code:'313820'})
RETURN d
```

This query is trying to find a node with a code property matching the provided value. Notice that we did not provide a label in the query. This is intentional to showcase how a query plan can be used to identify issues.

We can see from the following screenshot that the first step we are doing is `AllNodesScan`. What this means is that we are looking at the whole database to find the node we want and that we either have a mistake in the query or we are missing an index:

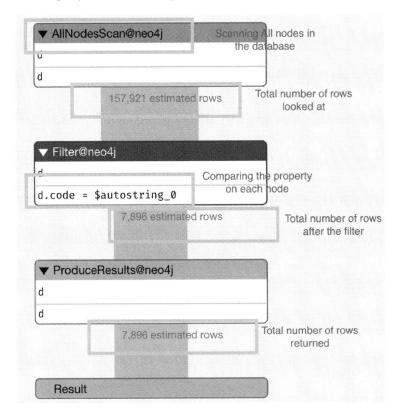

Figure 9.1 – Basic EXPLAIN plan

We can also see that the query plan provides estimated rows returned in each step. These are approximate values based on statistics collected by the database and not exact values.

Now, let's add the missing label and retry the plan again:

```
EXPLAIN MATCH (d:Drug {code:'313820'})
RETURN d
```

We added a label to the query here.

From the following screenshot, we can see that the query plan is using `NodeUniqueIndexSeek` to find the node now:

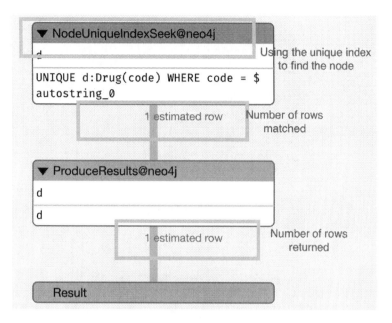

Figure 9.2 – EXPLAIN plan with node label present

This is better—even though we don't know exact performance benchmarks as such, this indicates the database query planner knows there is a unique index on the `Drug` label and the `code` property and tells the database to use it when it executes the query.

Let us try a slightly more complex query and see its plan:

```
EXPLAIN MATCH (p:Patient)-[:HAS_ZIPCODE]->(zip)
WITH p, zip
MATCH (p)-[:HAS_ENCOUNTER]->()-[:HAS_PROVIDER]->
      (prov)-[:HAS_ZIPCODE]->(zip)
WITH DISTINCT p,prov, zip
RETURN p.firstName as patientFirst,
       p.lastName as patientLast,
       prov.name as provider,
       zip.zip as zipcode
```

We can see this is a bit more complex query than what we tried before. The plan is big, so we will explore it in sections.

We can see that the first step here is to do something called NodeByLabelScan. Since we did not provide any property or WHERE clause to limit the results in the first line of the query, it is finding all nodes identified by the Patient label:

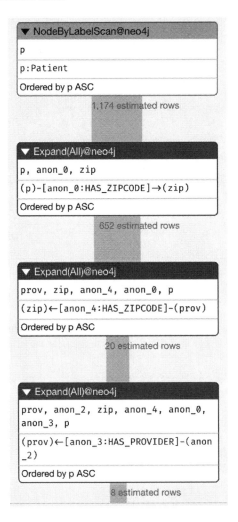

Figure 9.3 – Part 1 of query plan of complex query

The reason it is starting from the Patient label is that we have not specified a label for the other node in the query. Due to this, the query planner starts from a known label first. If it had to start from zip, it would have to do AllNodesScan, which is a costlier operation than NodeByLabelScan. Another thing we notice here is that once it finds the patient nodes, it is ordering them in ascending order. If we notice in the query, we do not have ORDER BY anywhere.

Then, why is the query planner looking to order the nodes?

If we go to the next part of the query, we are doing this:

```
WITH DISTINCT p,prov, zip
```

Since we want the distinct values, it is trying to order by the patient nodes first so that it can eliminate duplicates easily. Sorting the dataset when it is small and exploring from there could be more cost-effective than collecting all the data and trying to sort; considering all the different combinations could be costlier. The query planner could be considering this aspect and sorts the patient nodes immediately.

Next, it traverses the HAS_ZIPCODE relationship and collects the zip codes:

```
MATCH (p)-[:HAS_ENCOUNTER]->()-[:HAS_PROVIDER]->
      (prov)-[:HAS_ZIPCODE]->(zip)
```

We can see from *Figure 9.3* that the query planner is planning for the query snippet shown previously. In the query, we are starting from the patient node, but the query planner is starting from the zip code node. This is because the total number of zip code nodes is a lot less, so it is trying to start from there and going backward. It is traversing this way and collecting all the providers.

The next step that is planned is finding all the anonymous nodes connected to these provider nodes.

Let's look at the query plan image in the next screenshot:

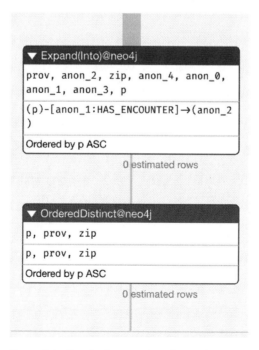

Figure 9.4 – Part 2 of query plan of complex query

The next step in the query plan is to check the patient node is connected to the anonymous nodes and only pick those nodes. Once all the conditions are satisfied, we collect the patient, provider, and zip nodes.

Let's look at the query plan image for the next part here:

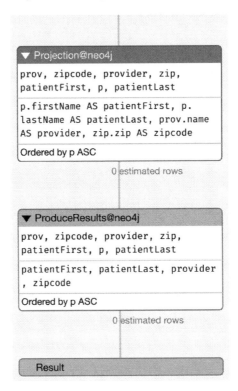

Figure 9.5 – Part 3 of query plan of complex query

We can see in the last step of the plan that we are now collecting all the return data and returning the result.

We will take a look at the profile of these queries to gain more insight into the amount of work the database is doing.

Working with PROFILE

The PROFILE clause executes as per the plan created by the database and provides the exact cost of the query. It will keep track of how many rows pass through the operators and the amount of work the database is doing that is measured as database hits.

Let's look at a basic example and compare the EXPLAIN and PROFILE plans:

```
PROFILE MATCH (d {code:'313820'})
RETURN d
```

In the query, we can see that the only difference is we are using PROFILE instead of EXPLAIN:

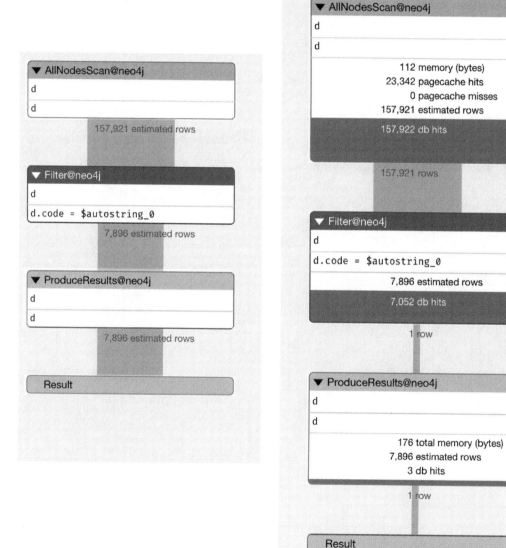

Figure 9.6 – Basic query without EXPLAIN and PROFILE label comparison

We can see that the plan remained exactly the same, but we are seeing the db hits, which are the measurement of how much work the database is doing. You can think of 1 db hit as a unit of work the database is doing. More db hits mean a plan step is taking more work than the database is doing to complete that step in the query. Also, more db hits mean that it's taking more time to execute the query. The total amount of db hits required to execute this query is 164968, and the time taken is 76 milliseconds.

Let's look at the profile of the query with a label:

```
PROFILE MATCH (d:Drug {code:'313820'})
RETURN d
```

We are using PROFILE here with a Drug label in the query. We will compare the EXPLAIN and PROFILE plans for this query in the following screenshot:

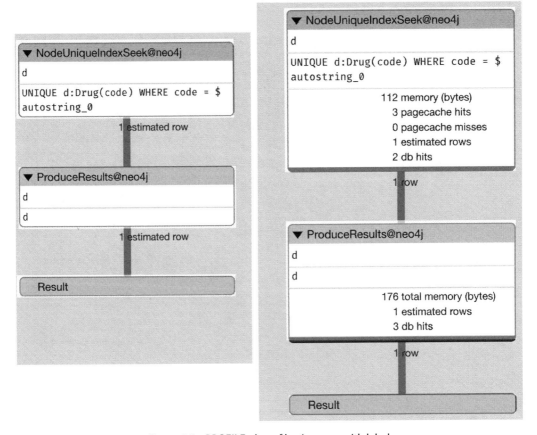

Figure 9.7 – PROFILE plan of basic query with label

From the preceding screenshot, we can see again the plans are exactly the same and PROFILE has the db hits. By adding the label, we can see that the first operation took only 2 db hits. If we remember, in the earlier query, this step took 157,913 db hits. Also, here we are missing one step when compared to the previous query without a label. There is a step with 7,052 db hits, which is comparing the property value of the node found to the input value. This is not needed here because the index lookup gives up the node for the matching index value. The last step is exactly the same, with 3 db hits, which returns the node we found.

If we look at the results, this query takes 5 db hits and takes less than 1 ms (reported by the browser as 0 ms).

Let's look at the profile of the complex query:

```
PROFILE MATCH (p:Patient)-[:HAS_ZIPCODE]->(zip)
WITH p, zip
MATCH (p)-[:HAS_ENCOUNTER]->()-[:HAS_PROVIDER]->
      (prov)-[:HAS_ZIPCODE]->(zip)
WITH DISTINCT p,prov, zip
RETURN p.firstName as patientFirst,
       p.lastName as patientLast,
       prov.name as provider,
       zip.zip as zipcode
```

We will compare the EXPLAIN plan and the profile of that plan in the next steps:

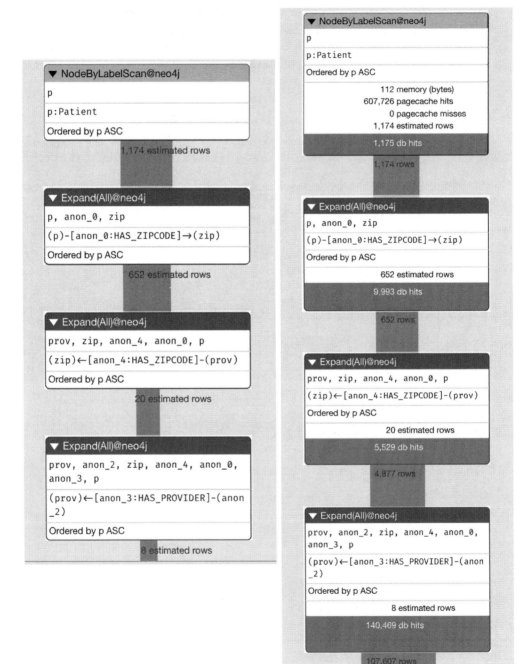

Figure 9.8 – Part 1 of query plan and profile of complex query

We can see again the plan steps are the same. We can see here clearly how the row estimations can be wildly different from the EXPLAIN plan and the actual PROFILE plan. For the first two steps, we can see the estimated rows do match the actual rows processed. This is where the data differs, as we are traversing the relationships, and the actual number of relationships cannot be captured in the query plan as count stores do not have that granular information:

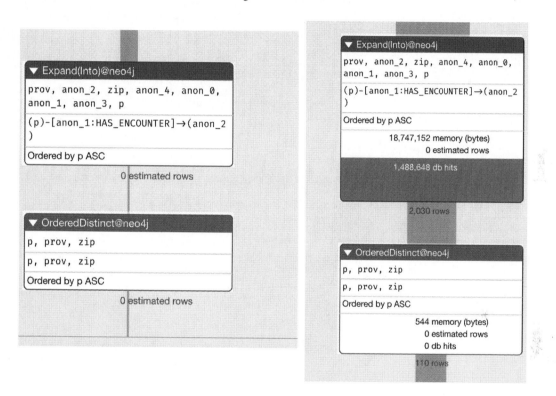

Figure 9.9 – Part 2 of query plan and profile of complex query

We can see again in the following screenshot how the plan thinks there are zero estimated rows and the actual execution provides actual rows:

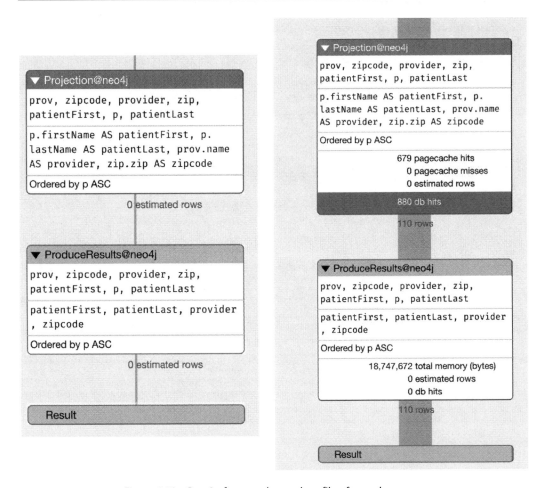

Figure 9.10 – Part 3 of query plan and profile of complex query

We can observe the same pattern again here. PROFILE gives us the actual amount of work that the database is doing. When we look at the total db hits for the query, they are 1,646,694 db hits, and the actual time taken is 228 ms.

The EXPLAIN and PROFILE plans of these queries show us how we can use EXPLAIN to understand how the database is planning to execute the query and PROFILE to tell us exactly how much work it is doing. To identify basic issues such as missing indices or not using an index, and so on, EXPLAIN is useful. As the data grows, PROFILE is very important to understand exactly how much work the database is doing to execute the query.

Next, we will take a look few important plan operators.

Reviewing plan operators

We will take a look at a few important operators that we will encounter most often while tuning queries.

These operators impact query performance the most and are listed as follows:

- `AllNodesScan`: This means the database is looking at all the nodes. Most often than not, this means the user forgot to provide a label. There are scenarios where this might be the intention. Most users when they are beginning with Cypher add the label name but forget to add " : " before the label. An example looks like this:

```
MATCH (Drug {code: '1234'} RETURN *
```

We might have thought we provided the label name, but since we don't have " : " before the label, it will be treated as a variable, and we will see all nodes are being looked at.

- `CartesianProduct`: This is a scenario when we have multiple `MATCH` statements without the `WITH` clause between them. A sample of such a scenario looks like this:

```
MATCH (p:Patient)
MATCH (d:Drug)
RETURN p,d
LIMIT 10
```

In this scenario, we are creating a Cartesian product of the response. Unless we are sure we need this scenario, when `CartesianProduct` appears in the query plan, we want to take a look at the query and see how we can avoid it.

- `NodeUniqueIndexSeek`: This means we are finding a unique node leveraging the index. As much as possible, this should be the approach to find the initial node and then traverse from there. This also means for the node label and property, there is a unique constraint that exists.

- `NodeIndexScan`: This means we are trying to find all nodes that match the label and property by looking at the whole index. This means we have an index created, but it is not a unique constraint. This is going to be way faster than a label scan. If a node has a primary key, we should strive to create a unique constraint rather than a simple index.

- `NodeByLabelScan`: This means we have provided the label, but either we are not providing any property or there is no index on the label and property combination. The most common mistake users make is not creating an index on the node label and property, and the query performance keeps degrading as the data keeps growing.

Now, let us look at index hints that can assist us with query performance.

Using index hints

Index hints are used to specify which indexes the planner should try to use. This can change how the query gets executed. There might be a trade-off compared to the default planning when using index hints.

We can provide index hints to the planner with a USING clause. Let's take a sample query that uses multiple entities and review a basic query profile and index hint driver query profile:

```
MATCH path=
(p:Patient {id:'7361ce15-cf67-ae76-88e6-bcbdca19ce0b'})
-[:HAS_ENCOUNTER]->()
-[:HAS_DRUG]->(d:Drug {code:'1190795'})
RETURN path LIMIT 1
```

We will take the preceding query and get a basic query profile first:

```
PROFILE MATCH path=
(p:Patient {id:'7361ce15-cf67-ae76-88e6-bcbdca19ce0b'})
-[:HAS_ENCOUNTER]->()
-[:HAS_DRUG]->(d:Drug {code:'1190795'})
RETURN path LIMIT 1
```

The following screenshot represents a basic query profile:

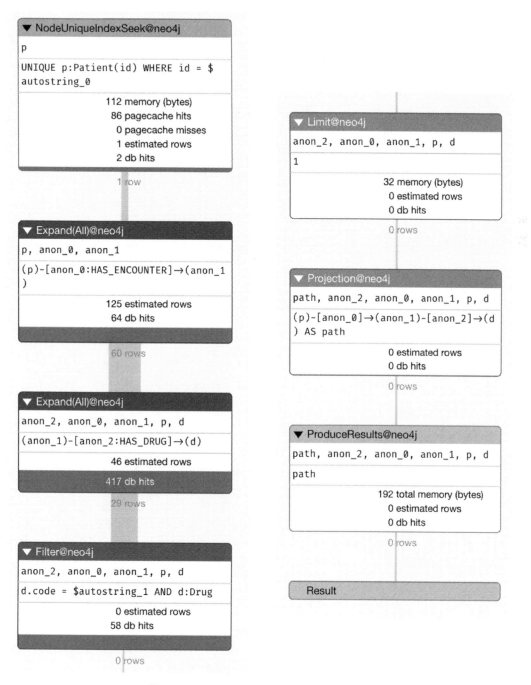

Figure 9.11 – Basic query profile without hints

From the preceding screenshot, we can see that the query planner is starting with the Patient node first, even though we also have an index on the Drug node, as it tries to optimize based on the statistics available. The Patient node has a smaller number of outgoing relationships when compared to the Drug node's incoming relationships, so it is cheaper to start from the Patient node. We can also see that we retrieve the Drug node and check for the label and compare the code property values. We can see that it takes a total of 541 db hits and uses 192 bytes of total memory to execute the query. It also takes 1 ms to execute.

Now, let's get a profile for the query with an index hint. The query would look like this:

```
PROFILE MATCH path=
(p:Patient {id:'7361ce15-cf67-ae76-88e6-bcbdca19ce0b'})
-[:HAS_ENCOUNTER]->()
-[:HAS_DRUG]->(d:Drug {code:'1190795'})
USING INDEX d:Drug(code)
RETURN path LIMIT 1
```

In the query, we can see the usage of an index hint. We are telling the query planner to use the index we have on the code property of the Drug node.

Let's take a look at the profile of the query in the following screenshot:

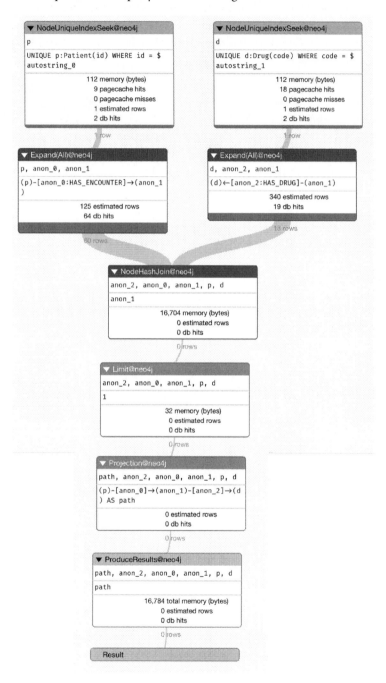

Figure 9.12 – Query profile with index hint

From the profile, we can see that there is a difference in the execution here. We have two starting points now. The first one is the `Patient` node with a specified `id` property and the second one is the `Drug` node with the specified `code` value. We take both the starting and ending points and traverse both ways to meet in the middle. We can see that we only take 87 db hits here, but we are using 16,784 bytes of memory. Also, it takes 2 ms to execute the query.

While the second profile is using a smaller number of db hits, it is using up more memory and CPU time. This is because of the way the query is executed. If we have enough page cache for the database to be loaded into memory, then the basic query profile gives us better results as it is straightforward to execute the query. When the database is big and the page cache is not enough to load the whole database into memory, then the second query can work better as it avoids page faults, due to a smaller number of db hits.

You can read more about planner hints at `https://neo4j.com/docs/cypher-manual/current/query-tuning/using/`.

Now, let us summarize what we have learned in this chapter.

Summary

In this chapter, we looked at using `EXPLAIN` and `PROFILE` to understand how queries will be executed by the database by looking at a plan and actual work done by the database in terms of db hits. We looked at some query plans for some basic queries and a complex query to understand the difference between `EXPLAIN` and `PROFILE` plans.

We looked at using index hints and how these affect the query execution time, along with the amount of work the database is doing to execute the query. We also reviewed a few important plan operators we need to look out for.

In the next chapter, we will take a look at **Awesome Procedures on Cypher** (**APOC**) functions and procedures and how they help us with querying.

10
Using APOC Utilities

APOC is an acronym for **Awesome Procedures On Cypher**. It is an add-on library for Neo4j that provides a lot of procedures and functions that can extend Cypher to perform more complex operations. It's built and maintained by Neo4j Labs. This chapter talks about using APOC utilities to extend the built-in capabilities of Cypher. It gives you more options to load CSV and JSON data, schedule timers, carry out ad hoc batch data modifications, and more.

We will cover these topics in this chapter:

- Installing APOC
- Working with data import and export
- Viewing database schema
- Executing dynamic Cypher
- Working with advanced path finding
- Connecting to other databases
- Using other useful methods

We will start with APOC plugin installation. We will take a look at the Neo4j Desktop plugin installation as well as installation on a server.

Installing APOC

APOC is a custom add-on library for Neo4j. We need to follow the appropriate installation process to make sure we can access all the capabilities provided by the APOC library. Since it uses core database APIs, we need to make sure we install the version of the library that matches the server version. If we do not follow these steps, the Neo4j server instance may not start:

1. First, we need to match the version of the library with the server we are running.

   APOC releases use a consistent versioning scheme in the format `<neo4j-version>.<apoc>`. The trailing `<apoc>` version is incremented with each release.

The following table shows the compatibility of the APOC library with server versions. This table is partly taken from the APOC GitHub repository (`https://github.com/neo4j-contrib/neo4j-apoc-procedures`), which contains the full list:

APOC Version	Neo4j Server Version
4.4.0.1	4.4.0 (4.3.x)
4.3.0.4	4.3.7 (4.3.x)
4.2.0.9	4.2.11 (4.2.x)
4.1.0.10	4.1.11 (4.1.x)
4.0.0.18	4.0.12 (4.0.x)

Table 10.1 – APOC version to Neo4j version mapping

We will look at installing the plugin in Neo4j Desktop first.

2. When we click on the database in Neo4j Desktop, we can see the **Plugins** tab, as shown in the following screenshot:

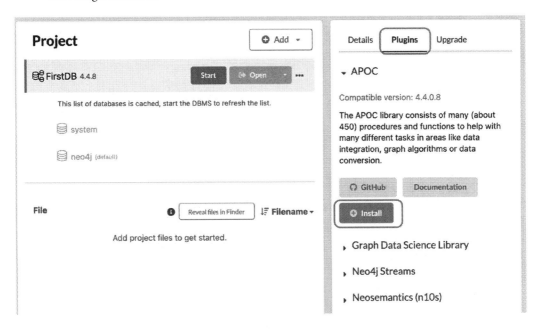

Figure 10.1 – Neo4j Desktop – the Plugins tab

3. When you click the **Plugins** tab, it shows all the available plugins. To install the APOC plugin, click on **APOC** to show the option to install it. Click on the **Install** button to install the plugin. The advantage of Neo4j Desktop installation is that it updates the config file, `neo4j.conf`, automatically to enable all the features of APOC.

Next, we will take a quick look at how to install the plugin on the server.

The following screenshot shows a tar install of the Neo4j server. We can see a list of directories that are part of the installation. The highlighted `plugins` directory is where we can install the plugins:

```
bash-3.2$
bash-3.2$
bash-3.2$ ls -l
total 328
-rw-r--r--     1 ravianthapu  staff     22701 Jun 25 17:58 LICENSE.txt
-rw-r--r--     1 ravianthapu  staff    124566 Jun 25 17:58 LICENSES.txt
-rw-r--r--     1 ravianthapu  staff       135 Jun 25 17:58 NOTICE.txt
-rw-r--r--     1 ravianthapu  staff      1499 Jun 25 17:58 README.txt
-rw-r--r--     1 ravianthapu  staff        96 Jun 25 17:58 UPGRADE.txt
drwxr-xr-x     9 ravianthapu  staff       288 Jun 25 17:58 bin
drwxr-xr-x     4 ravianthapu  staff       128 Jun 25 17:58 certificates
drwxr-xr-x     5 ravianthapu  staff       160 Jun 25 17:58 conf
drwxr-xr-x     7 ravianthapu  staff       224 Jun 25 17:58 data
drwxr-xr-x     2 ravianthapu  staff        64 Jun 25 17:58 import
drwxr-xr-x     5 ravianthapu  staff       160 Jun 25 17:58 labs
drwxr-xr-x   226 ravianthapu  staff      7232 Jun 25 17:58 lib
drwxr-xr-x     2 ravianthapu  staff        64 Jun 25 17:58 licenses
drwxr-xr-x    13 ravianthapu  staff       416 Sep 23 12:16 logs
drwxr-xr-x    76 ravianthapu  staff      2432 Jun 25 18:03 metrics
drwxr-xr-x     5 ravianthapu  staff       160 Oct  1 19:12 plugins
drwxr-xr-x     4 ravianthapu  staff       128 Jun 25 17:58 plugins-pre-upgrade
drwxr-xr-x     5 ravianthapu  staff       160 Jun 25 17:58 products
-rw-r--r--     1 ravianthapu  staff       853 Sep 26 13:26 relate.dbms.json
drwxr-xr-x     2 ravianthapu  staff        64 Sep 26 13:26 run
bash-3.2$
```

Figure 10.2 – Neo4j server installation directory

We can download the JAR file from the APOC releases at `https://github.com/neo4j-contrib/neo4j-apoc-procedures/releases` and copy it to the `plugins` directory. Once the JAR file is copied, we need to edit the `neo4j.conf` file found in the `conf` directory. For security reasons, all the procedures that use internal APIs are disabled by default. We can enable them by adding or updating the configuration:

```
dbms.security.procedures.unrestricted=apoc.*
```

The following screenshot shows the updated configuration highlighted. Once the configuration is changed, you need to restart the server for the changes to take effect:

```
# Only allow read operations from this Neo4j instance. This mode still requires
# write access to the directory for lock purposes.
#dbms.read_only=false

# Comma separated list of JAX-RS packages containing JAX-RS resources, one
# package name for each mountpoint. The listed package names will be loaded
# under the mountpoints specified. Uncomment this line to mount the
# org.neo4j.examples.server.unmanaged.HelloWorldResource.java from
# neo4j-server-examples under /examples/unmanaged, resulting in a final URL of
# http://localhost:7474/examples/unmanaged/helloworld/{nodeId}
#dbms.unmanaged_extension_classes=org.neo4j.examples.server.unmanaged=/examples/unman
aged

# A comma separated list of procedures and user defined functions that are allowed
# full access to the database through unsupported/insecure internal APIs.
dbms.security.procedures.unrestricted=jwt.security.*,apoc.*

# A comma separated list of procedures to be loaded by default.
# Leaving this unconfigured will load all procedures found.
#dbms.security.procedures.allowlist=apoc.coll.*,apoc.load.*,gds.*

# For how long should drivers cache the discovery data from
# the dbms.routing.getRoutingTable() procedure. Defaults to 300s.
#dbms.routing_ttl=300s

#****************************************************************
# JVM Parameters
#****************************************************************

# G1GC generally strikes a good balance between throughput and tail
# latency, without too much tuning.
```

Figure 10.3 – Editing neo4j.conf to add the APOC configuration

Working with data import and export

APOC allows us to load data from various file formats, including CSV, JSON, Excel, XML, HTML, and GraphML. It can also export graph data as CSV or JSON. We will take a look at how to import data in each format.

First, we will take a look at importing CSV data.

Importing CSV data

We can use the apoc.load.csv method to load CSV data into a graph. It is very similar to the LOAD CSV command, but it provides a lot more options and is more tolerant of failures.

It provides these extra options when loading CSV files:

- It provides line numbers so that we can trace issues
- Both map and list representations for each CSV line are available

- The data is automatically converted to the correct data type and the data can be split into arrays as needed
- It is also possible to keep the original string-formatted values they are in the file
- There is an option to ignore fields, thus making it easier to assign a full line as properties
- It provides the ability to process headerless files
- It provides the ability to replace certain values with `null`
- You can also read compressed files

> **Note**
>
> Please note that if you are using Neo4j 5.0 or above database, the APOC library is split into Core, which is packaged with database and extended which user has to download manually and install. The method apoc.load.csv is moved to extended APOC library. Neo4j Desktop is not handling this aspect correctly. So to use this method you might have to manually download the plugin and copy it to plugins directory.

To load a CSV file from the local filesystem on the server, we need to follow these steps:

1. Let's add this configuration first:

   ```
   Apoc.import.file.enabled=true
   ```

2. As shown in the following screenshot, click on **...** and select **Settings...** to update the configuration. It will bring up the settings screen:

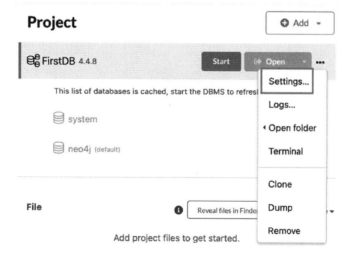

Figure 10.4 – Selecting Settings... to update the configuration

3. As shown in the following screenshot, add the configuration and click on **Apply** to apply the changes. If the database has not started, then start the database. If it was already running, then it will be automatically restarted by Neo4j Desktop:

Edit settings

Figure 10.5 – Updating the configuration

> **Note**
>
> With this configuration enabled, you can only read the files from the import directory, as identified in the configuration.

4. Let's create a sample test CSV file in the `import` directory with this content:

```
id,firstName,lastName
1,Tom,Hanks
2,Meg,Ryan
```

Let's look at an example.

The following statement loads a CSV file and returns the data as one row for each line. The returned data will have a line number, data as a list, and data as a map:

```
CALL apoc.load.csv("test.csv")
```

We can see in the screenshot that in each row, we have the line number of the CSV file, data as a list, and data as a map as well:

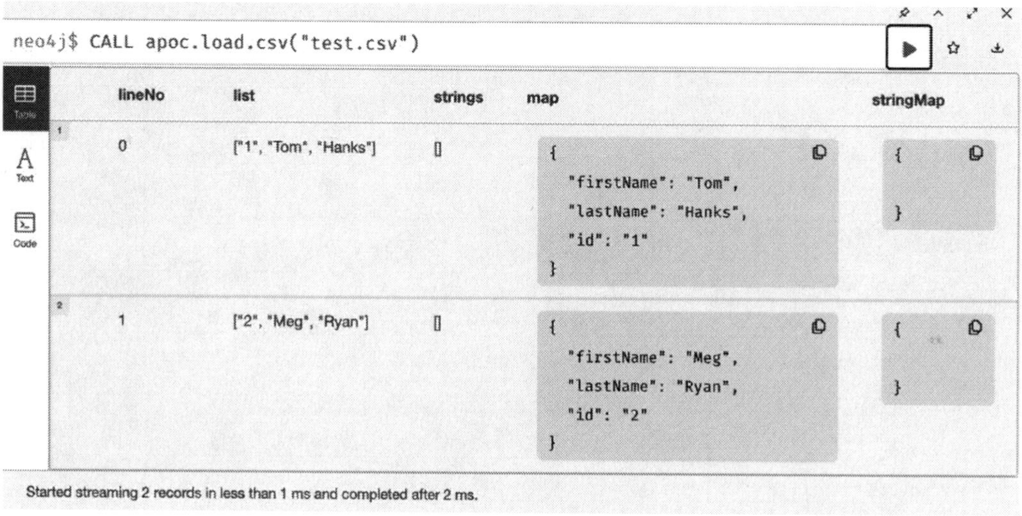

Figure 10.6 – apoc.load.csv sample usage

If we want to be able to load data from anywhere in the filesystem of the server, then we need to add this configuration:

1. First, let's try without adding this configuration to understand how it behaves:

```
apoc.import.file.use_neo4j_config=false
In this case we are trying to load the file using the
absolute path "/tmp/test.csv". CALL apoc.load.csv("/tmp/
test.csv")
```

2. In the following screenshot, we can see that when we use the absolute path, it prepends the `import` directory location to it automatically and fails to load the file:

Figure 10.7 – Loading from an absolute path

Let's update the configuration now:

3. Once we change the configuration and click on **Apply** button, the database will restart. Once it is restarted, we can try the command again:

Figure 10.8 – Adding the configuration to ignore neo4j_config for apoc

In the screenshot, we can see that we can load the file from `/tmp/test.csv`:

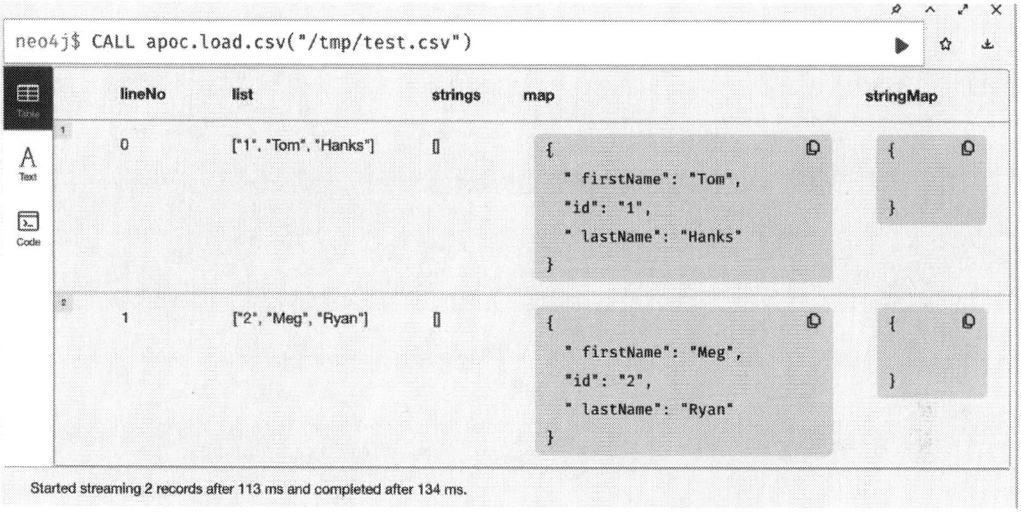

Figure 10.9 – Loading the CSV from an absolute path

> **Note**
>
> With neo4j configuration disabled, we can read any file in the whole file system that we have access to. *This can be a security concern and should be done with the consultation of security team.* Also, note that when you have this enabled, to read the files from neo4j import directory, you need to provide the full path. The previous command we tried to read the file from import directory will fail with this configuration added.

So far, we have only read a CSV file. Now let's look at how to load it into a graph.

We will leverage the map output, as it has key/value pairs of the data:

```
CALL apoc.load.csv("/tmp/test.csv") YIELD lineNo, map
CREATE (p:Person {id:map.id, firstName: map.firstName,
lastName: map.lastName})
RETURN lineNo
```

We can see from the query that we are taking the lineNo and map values returned by apoc.load. csv and using them to add data to a graph. As a response, we are returning the line numbers of the rows we have processed:

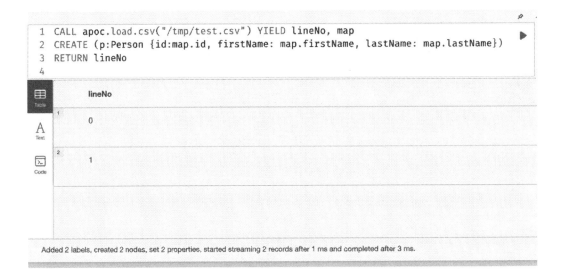

Figure 10.10 – Updating the data into a graph using apoc.load.csv

> **Note**
>
> One thing to note here is that this is a single transaction. If we have large amounts of data, then we must use `apoc.periodic.iterate` to process the data in batches. We will discuss this aspect later in the chapter.
>
> Also, note that the directory names might be bit different for different operating systems. In windows the directory name could be "C:/temp" and in unix systems it could be "/tmp". Please verify the file system and update the URL appropriately.

We can also use URLs to load CSV data. We will take a look at loading JSON data next.

Importing JSON data

Loading JSON data is similar to loading CSV data. We can use the `apoc.load.json` method.

JSON data should look like this for this to work:

```
{ " firstName": "Tom", "id": "1", " lastName": "Hanks" }
{ " firstName": "Meg", "id": "2", " lastName": "Ryan" }
```

We can see each line is a JSON object. This format is mandatory if you want to use this method.

Let's look at a simple example.

This reads the JSON file from /tmp/test.json and returns each line as a map. One thing that is different from reading CSV files is that we do not have the line number or a list representation of the data here. We will only have the map:

```
CALL apoc.load.json("/tmp/test.json")
```

We can see from the following screenshot that with this method, we only have a map representation of each line:

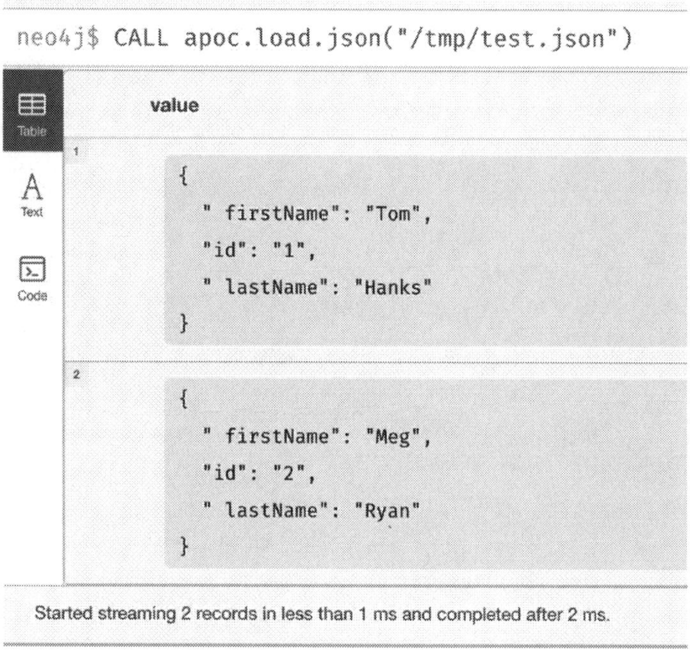

```
neo4j$ CALL apoc.load.json("/tmp/test.json")
```

	value
1	`{ " firstName": "Tom", "id": "1", " lastName": "Hanks" }`
2	`{ " firstName": "Meg", "id": "2", " lastName": "Ryan" }`

Started streaming 2 records in less than 1 ms and completed after 2 ms.

Figure 10.11 – Loading JSON

Let's look at an example of loading JSON from a URL.

This code reads the JSON response from a URL and creates a map from it:

```
CALL apoc.load.json("https://api.stackexchange.com/2.2/question
s?pagesize=5&order=desc&sort=creation&tagged=neo4j&site=stacko
verflow&filter=!5-i6Zw8Y)4W7vpy91PMYsKM-k9yzEsSC1_Uxlf") YIELD
value
UNWIND value.items AS i
RETURN i.title as title, i.owner as owner, keys(i) as keys
LIMIT 10
```

In the following screenshot, we can see the returned data. Also, we can see that some of the data can be nested JSON, and it is returned as a proper map instead of a string. This makes it easier to process nested JSON content easily:

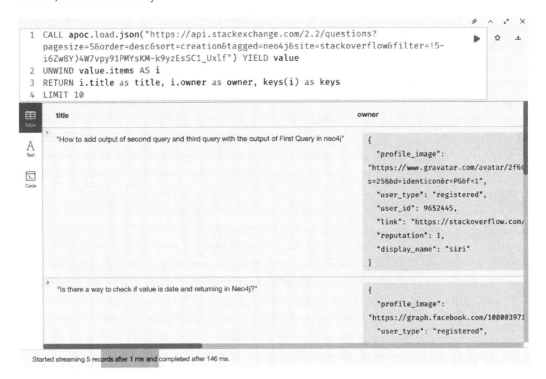

Figure 10.12 – Loading JSON with a URL

It's also possible to use JSON PATH to limit what data we can try to process. The following table describes all the operators we can use to use JSON PATH expressions. The following table is from the APOC documentation (please see this link for the latest options https://neo4j.com/labs/apoc/4.1/import/load-json/):

Operator	Description	Example
$	The root element of the top level	$ - retrieve all data in a top-level object
@	The current node processed by a filter predicate	$.items[?(@.answer_count > 0)] – retrieve the item if the answer_count is greater than 0

Operator	Description	Example
`*`	Wildcard. Available anywhere a name or number is required	`$.items[\*]` – retrieve all items in the array
`..`	Deep scan. Wherever a name is required it can be used	`$..tags[\*]` – find substructure named tags and pull all the values
`.<name>`	Dot-notated child	`$.items[0:1].owner.user_id` – retrieve `user_id` of the first owner object
`[<number> (,<number>)]`	Array index	`$.items[0,-1]` – retrieve the first and last item from an array
`[start:end]`	Array slice	`$.items[0:5]` – retrieve the first through fifth items from the array
`[?(<expression>)]`	Filter expression. It must be a Boolean value	`$.items[?(@.is_answered == true)]` – retrieve items where the is answered value is `true`

Table 10.2 – JSON PATH expressions

Let's look at an example of this.

The following query fields are identified by the `owner` key and return them from the JSON data:

```
CALL apoc.load.json("https://api.stackexchange.com/2.2/questio
ns?pagesize=5&order=desc&sort=creation&tagged=neo4j&site=stack
overflow&filter=!5-i6Zw8Y)4W7vpy91PMYsKM-k9yzEsSC1_Uxlf", "$..
owner") YIELD value
RETURN value
LIMIT 10
```

```
1  CALL apoc.load.json("https://api.stackexchange.com/2.2/questions?
   pagesize=5&order=desc&sort=creation&tagged=neo4j&site=stackoverflow&filter=!5-
   i6Zw8Y)4W7vpy91PMYsKM-k9yzEsSC1_Uxlf", "$..owner") YIELD value
2  RETURN value
3  LIMIT 10
```

```
value

{
  "result": [
    null,
    {
      "profile_image": "https://www.gravatar.com/avatar/9049df96b6596236925b5a0222625b27?
s=256&d=identicon&r=PG&f=1",
      "user_type": "registered",
      "user_id": 4788979,
      "link": "https://stackoverflow.com/users/4788979/dominus",
      "reputation": 708,
      "display_name": "Dominus",
      "accept_rate": 47
    },
    {
      "profile_image": "https://i.stack.imgur.com/0cqzy.jpg?s=256&g=1",
      "user_type": "registered",
```

Started streaming 1 records after 1 ms and completed after 222 ms.

Figure 10.13 – Using JSON PATH to get fields at nested level

In the screenshot, we can see that we get a single JSON with a result field that represents the owner values for each entity. We can see that if there is no owner value in a given entity, we get a null value at that index. This pattern tries to find the values identified by a specific key at any depth. If we want to traverse the data exactly and get the values, we can try this approach.

This query traverses the JSON data with the exact path. First, it finds items values, which should be an array, and the owner value in each of those JSON values:

```
CALL apoc.load.json("https://api.stackexchange.com/2.2/quest
ions?pagesize=5&order=desc&sort=creation&tagged=neo4j&site=st
ackoverflow&filter=!5-i6Zw8Y)4W7vpy91PMYsKM-k9yzEsSC1_Uxlf",
"$.items[*].owner") YIELD value
RETURN value
```

We can see in the screenshot that the data returned is a bit different from the earlier query, even though we are requesting the data identified by the `owner` key. The first query tries to find the values at any depth for the specified key, and the second one traverses the exact path:

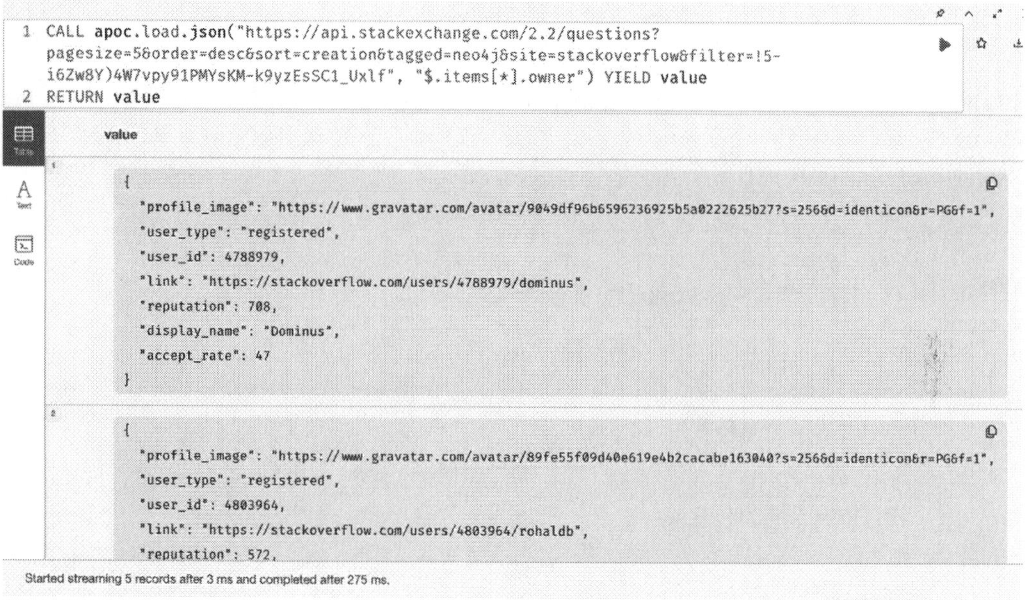

```
1  CALL apoc.load.json("https://api.stackexchange.com/2.2/questions?
   pagesize=5&order=desc&sort=creation&tagged=neo4j&site=stackoverflow&filter=!5-
   i6Zw8Y)4W7vpy91PMYsKM-k9yzEsSC1_Uxlf", "$.items[*].owner") YIELD value
2  RETURN value
```

```
{
    "profile_image": "https://www.gravatar.com/avatar/9049df96b6596236925b5a0222625b27?s=256&d=identicon&r=PG&f=1",
    "user_type": "registered",
    "user_id": 4788979,
    "link": "https://stackoverflow.com/users/4788979/dominus",
    "reputation": 708,
    "display_name": "Dominus",
    "accept_rate": 47
}
```

```
{
    "profile_image": "https://www.gravatar.com/avatar/89fe55f09d40e619e4b2cacabe163040?s=256&d=identicon&r=PG&f=1",
    "user_type": "registered",
    "user_id": 4803964,
    "link": "https://stackoverflow.com/users/4803964/rohaldb",
    "reputation": 572,
```

Started streaming 5 records after 3 ms and completed after 275 ms.

Figure 10.14 – JSON PATH with specific path traversal

There are scenarios when we want to load JSON from a URL and it requires authentication. In those cases, it might not be wise to have the credentials hardcoded in the query. We can use `apoc.load.jsonParams` to define the values in the `apoc.conf` file and have them referred in the Cypher.

Let's look at the usage of this.

This configuration defines a value called `mylink` that can be retrieved with all the values in it as a map:

```
apoc.static.mylink.bearer=XXXX
apoc.static.mylink.url=https://test.mytest.com/data
```

This query will fetch the data from the URL specified in the configuration with an access token value, which also comes from the configuration and returns the data. If there is a payload that the URL requires, that can also be passed using this method:

```
WITH apoc.static.getAll("mylink") AS linkData
CALL apoc.load.jsonParams(
    linkData.url,
```

```
    {Authorization:"Bearer "+ linkData.bearer},
    null // payload
)
YIELD value
RETURN value
```

It is possible to load the data from other data formats, as mentioned earlier. We will not be discussing all these topics in this book, but you can read more at https://neo4j.com/labs/apoc/4.4/ import/web-apis/.

We will now take a look at how we can see the database schema details using APOC.

Viewing database schema

Procedures with the apoc.meta suffix provide the functionality to inspect the metadata about graph, such as viewing the current schema or database statistics or inspecting the types. We will take a look at some important procedures:

The first one we will explore is the procedure to display the schema graph.

This displays the metadata graph that represents the schema of how nodes are related to each other:

```
CALL apoc.meta.graph()
```

In the following screenshot, we can see that the metadata graph seems very busy. This is because this representation does not understand nodes with multiple labels correctly and they are represented independently:

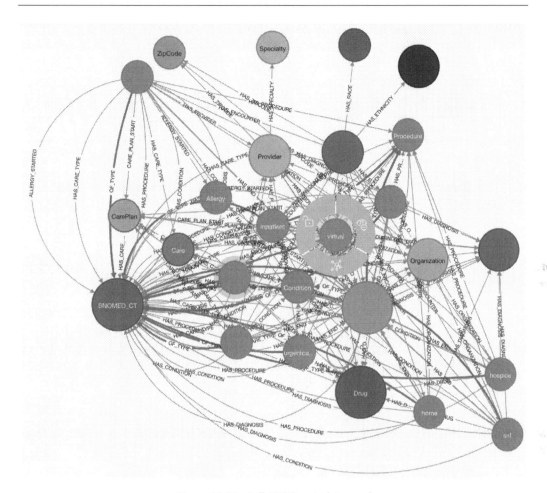

Figure 10.15 – Full APOC metadata graph

The nodes with the labels home, hospice, and so on are the secondary labels on the Encounter nodes.

We can have a cleaner representation using apoc.meta.subGraph. When we call this method, we can use, include, or exclude the node labels so that we can get the metadata graph the way we want with desired nodes and relationships.

The signature of this method is as follows:

```
apoc.meta.subGraph(config :: MAP?) :: (nodes :: LIST? OF NODE?,
relationships :: LIST? OF RELATIONSHIP?)
```

The configuration options for this method are as follows:

- `includeLabels`: A list of the node labels to include in the graph. The default is to include all labels.

- `includeRels`: A list of the relationship types to include in the graph. The default is to include all relationship types.

- `excludeLabels`: A list of labels to exclude from the graph. The default is to not exclude any labels.

- `Sample`: The number of nodes to sample per label. The default is to scan `1000` nodes.

- `maxRels`: The number of relationships to be analyzed by the type of relationship and the start and end label. The default is 100 per type.

Let's look at the usage of this method:

```
CALL apoc.meta.subGraph({
    excludeLabels:
        ['home', 'hospice',
        'virtual', 'wellness',
        'emergency', 'outpatient',
        'inpatient','urgentcare',
        'snf','ambulatory' ]})
```

In the query, we are only trying to exclude the node labels, as we know these are secondary labels. It is also possible to use include and not to exclude labels.

We can see in the screenshot that this graph is much cleaner than the other schema. This represents the actual database schema by removing the secondary nodes from the schema diagram:

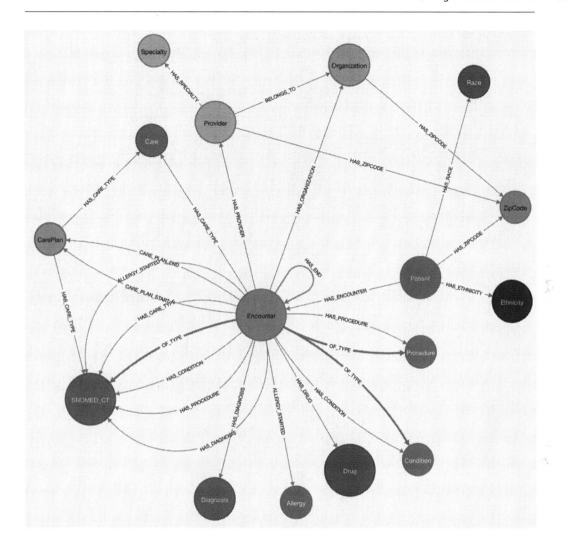

Figure 10.16 – Clean database schema

Now we will take a look at the `apoc.meta.stats` method to display the database statistics:

```
CALL apoc.meta.stats()
```

This will display database statistics such as the number of node labels, relationship types, and the number of nodes per label.

We can see in the following screenshot that this procedure displays the database statistics at a very granular level. It shows the number of nodes by label, the number of relationships by type, the number of relationships by start node label and relationship type, and so on:

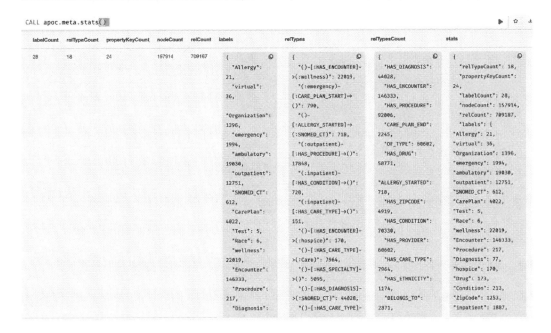

Figure 10.17 – Database statistics

This can be very useful for keeping track of now how the graph is growing by executing and keeping the results at regular intervals.

The next procedure, `apoc.meta.data`, provides property-level statistics. We can see from the name that it provides data-level statistics. The response is in tabular format; the previous procedure returns JSON:

```
CALL apoc.meta.data()
```

In the screenshot, we can see how the data is distributed at the property level. For each property, it shows at the node or relationship level how many times it is present in the graph:

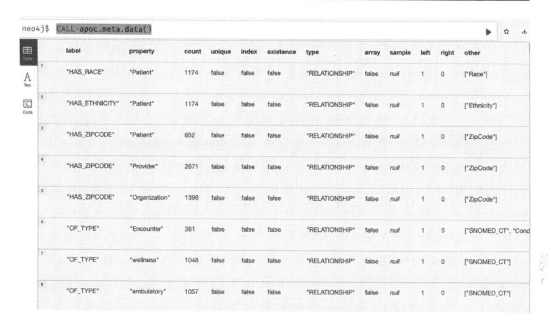

Figure 10.18 – Property-level statistics

If you would like to read more about these procedures and other schema-related procedures, visit https://neo4j.com/labs/apoc/4.4/database-introspection/meta/.

Next, we will take a look at how we can execute dynamic Cypher.

Executing dynamic Cypher

Cypher does not allow dynamic query execution. If you are getting a value in the data that you want to use as a label on the node, or you need to create a relationship with that name, that is not easy to do in Cypher. It is possible to use the FOREACH trick to check for the value and make the code deterministic, but this is not a practicable solution if the number of combinations is more than five, for example. In these scenarios, APOC procedures can help us to either to build a string and execute it or add or create nodes and relationships with dynamic values:

1. First, we will take a look at how to add a new label to a node using a dynamic value:

```
WITH {label: "MyTest", id:10 , name: 'Another'} as data
MERGE(p:Person {id:data.id})
SET p.name=data.name
WITH data, p
CALL apoc.create.addLabels([p], [data.label])
YIELD node
RETURN node
```

2. This query creates a `Person` node with the data and appends the label from the input data using the `apoc.create.addLabels` method. You may have noticed here that we are preparing a list with a `Person` node and a new label because this method takes a list as its input parameter. The following screenshot shows that we have created the new node, and the node has the label from the data:

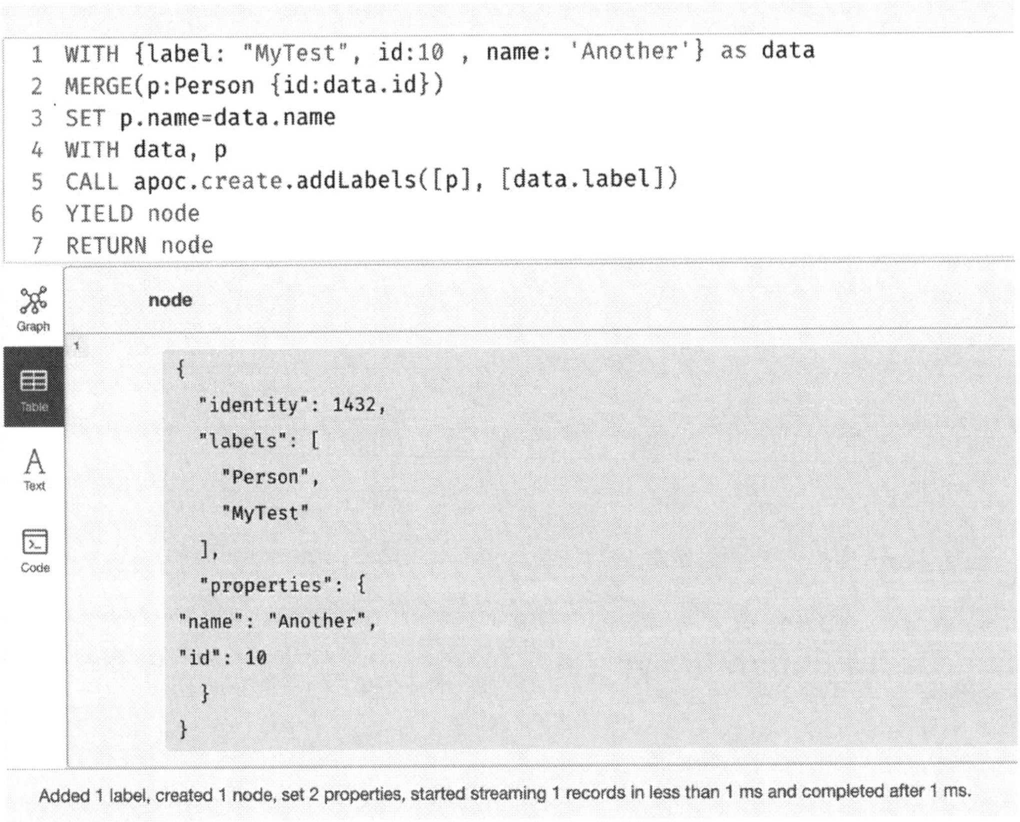

```
1  WITH {label: "MyTest", id:10 , name: 'Another'} as data
2  MERGE(p:Person {id:data.id})
3  SET p.name=data.name
4  WITH data, p
5  CALL apoc.create.addLabels([p], [data.label])
6  YIELD node
7  RETURN node
```

```
node
{
    "identity": 1432,
    "labels": [
      "Person",
      "MyTest"
    ],
    "properties": {
  "name": "Another",
  "id": 10
    }
}
```

Added 1 label, created 1 node, set 2 properties, started streaming 1 records in less than 1 ms and completed after 1 ms.

Figure 10.19 – Adding a label from the data

We needed to use the APOC method because if we try to add the label using a variable in Cypher, it will give a syntax error because Cypher does not support dynamic label addition. The following query shows a way to add a label dynamically, which will throw a syntax error:

```
WITH {label: "MyTest", id:10 , name: 'Another'} as data
MERGE(p:Person {id:data.id})
SET p.name=data.name, p:data.label
```

If we are getting all the labels from the data, then we can use the apoc.create.node or apoc.merge.node method to create the node as required. Let's take a look at an example of this.

3. This query creates a node with labels "MyTest" and "Person" with an id value of 12, and we set the name to "Another":

```
WITH {labels: ["MyTest", "Person"], id:12 , name:
'Another'} as data
CALL apoc.merge.node(data.labels, {id:data.id},
{name:data.name}, null )
YIELD node
RETURN node
```

You can also create relationships dynamically using the apoc.create.relationship or apoc.merge.relationship method. You can read more about these methods at https://neo4j.com/labs/apoc/4.4/overview/apoc.merge/ and https://neo4j.com/labs/apoc/4.4/overview/apoc.create/.

When you need to execute a whole Cypher query as a string, then we can use apoc.cypher.doIt for write queries and apoc.cypher.run for read queries.

Let's look at an example of this:

```
WITH {label: "MyTest", id:20 , name: 'Another'} as data
CALL apoc.cypher.doIt(
    "WITH $data as data MERGE(p:Person {id:data.id})
    SET p.name=data.name, p:" + data.label +
    " RETURN p",
    {data: data}
) YIELD value
RETURN value
```

This query does what we did before with the addLabels method, but we are building a dynamic Cypher query and executing it. In the screenshot, we can see that we are building a Cypher string from the data and executing it. This could be useful in a few scenarios where data is more dynamic:

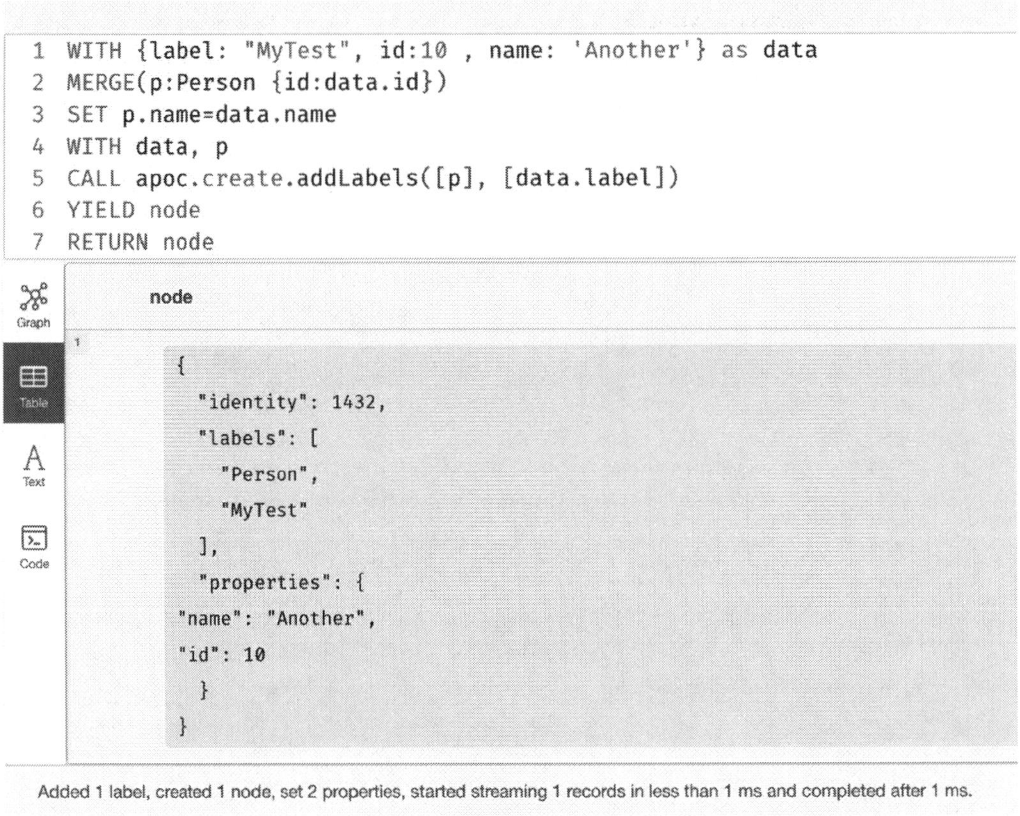

```
1  WITH {label: "MyTest", id:10 , name: 'Another'} as data
2  MERGE(p:Person {id:data.id})
3  SET p.name=data.name
4  WITH data, p
5  CALL apoc.create.addLabels([p], [data.label])
6  YIELD node
7  RETURN node
```

Graph

Table

A
Text

Code

node

```
{
    "identity": 1432,
    "labels": [
        "Person",
        "MyTest"
    ],
    "properties": {
"name": "Another",
"id": 10
    }
}
```

Added 1 label, created 1 node, set 2 properties, started streaming 1 records in less than 1 ms and completed after 1 ms.

Figure 10.19 – Dynamic Cypher query execution

We are not going to discuss all the available options for dynamic Cypher execution; you can read more about them at https://neo4j.com/labs/apoc/4.4/overview/apoc.cypher/.

Working with advanced path finding

Cypher provides means for variable pathfinding. But it has some limitations, as it is path distinct to make sure we don't miss any paths. When there are loops in the graph, Cypher can be very memory intensive when we use variable-length paths. Also, if we need to change directions in the traversal or have node label filters, it is not possible in Cypher. This is where APOC provides an option with apoc.path.expandConfig that provides a lot of options with variable-length path expansion.

The syntax for this procedure looks like this:

```
apoc.path.expandConfig(
    startNode <id>|Node|list, ConfigMap
    ) YIELD path
```

The config map can have these values:

```
        minLevel
        maxLevel
        uniqueness
        relationshipFilter
        labelFilter
        uniqueness
        bfs:true,
        filterStartNode
        limit
        optional:false,
        endNodes

terminatorNodes
        sequence
        beginSequenceAtStart
```

All of these values are optional in the configuration, and we will take a look at how each of these values affects the path expansion. It starts from the start node or the list of nodes provided and traverses based on the configuration options provided. All the configuration options are optional. If you provide an empty configuration, then the equivalent Cypher query would look as follows:

```
MATCH path=(n)-[*]-() RETURN path
```

Let's take a detailed look at the configuration options for this procedure:

- `minLevel`: The minimum path size to traverse. The default value is -1.

- `maxLevel`: The maximum path size to traverse. The default value is -1. The path expansion happens until all the other conditions are satisfied.

- `relationshipFilter`: The relationships to take into account when traversing the path. It can be one or more list of relationship types with optional directions separated by the | delimiter. Here are some examples:

  - `CONNECTED>`: Traverse only outgoing `CONNECTED` relationships.

  - `<CONNECTED`: Traverse only incoming `CONNECTED` relationships.

  - `CONNECTED`: Traverse the `CONNECTED` relationships irrespective of direction.

  - `>`: Traverse any outgoing relationship.

- `<`: Traverse any incoming relationship.

- `CONNECTED>|<KNOWS`: Traverse outgoing `CONNECTED` or incoming `KNOWS` relationships. *This option is not possible with Cypher.*

- `labelFilter`: A list of node labels separated by the `|` delimiter to include or exclude, or a termination of traversal or end node in the path. Let's look at some examples:

  - `-Test`: Blacklisted label. This means this node should not exist in any of the paths that are returned. The default is that no label is blacklisted.

  - `+Test`: Whitelisted label. When we use this option, then all the node labels in the path should exist in the white label list. The default is that all labels are whitelisted.

  - `>Test`: End node in the path. Every path returned should have the end node label in this list. When we encounter an end label during traversal, we take that path and add it to the return list, but we continue traversing that path to see if there are other nodes with these labels to return a longer path. We can only traverse beyond the end node if the next node labels are whitelisted.

  - `/Test`: Terminate traversal once you encounter node labels in the termination list. We terminate our path expansion at the first occurrence of the labels in the termination list.

- Uniqueness:

  - `RELATIONSHIP_PATH`: This is the default and matches how Cypher works with variable-length paths. For each end node returned, there is a unique path from a start node, in this case in terms relationships traversed to reach the end node.

  - `NODE_GLOBAL`: A node cannot be traversed more than once in the whole graph.

  - `NODE_LEVEL`: All the node entities at the same level are guaranteed to be unique.

  - `NODE_PATH`: For each end node returned, there is a unique path from a start node, in this case in terms nodes traversed to reach the end node.

  - `NODE_RECENT`: This is very similar to `NODE_GLOBAL`, except for the fact that it only checks the last few recent nodes whose number can be specified by the configuration. This can be very useful when traversing large graphs.

  - `RELATIONSHIP_GLOBAL`: A relationship cannot be traversed more than once.

  - `RELATIONSHIP_RECENT`: This is very similar to `NODE_RECENT` but at the relationship level.

  - `NONE`: No restrictions in traversal, and results have to be managed by the user.

- Bfs: Use breadth-first search if true or depth-first if false. The default value is true.

- filterStartNode: This determines whether labelFilter and sequence apply to the start nodes. The default value is false.

- Limit: This determines how many paths are returned. The default value is -1, which means all paths should be returned.

- Optional: This determines whether the path expansion is like an optional match. If this is true, then a null value is returned if no paths are found, instead of there being no return value. The default is false.

- endNodes: A list of nodes that can be at the end of the path returned. This is optional as this information can also be provided in labelFilter. Providing those nodes here instead of in the labelFilter syntax could be more readable for users.

- terminatorNodes: A list of terminator nodes. Similar to the endNodes configuration option, this can be done using labelFilter.

- sequence: This tells the path expansion procedure the exact sequence of node labels and relationship types that have to appear in a sequence. Every path returned should start with this sequence and end with this sequence. When you use sequence, labelFilter and relationshipFilter are ignored.

- beginSequenceAtStart: This determines whether the sequence configuration should be applied to the start node or not.

Now let's see a few examples of using this procedure. The PATIENT data model we have built may not benefit much from this procedure, so we will create some sample data and load it into a graph to see how this procedure can help us when traversing large graphs.

We can use this Cypher to create a test graph:

```
CREATE (:Test {id: 1})-[:CONNECTED]->(n1:Test {id: 2})
    -[:CONNECTED]->(n2:Test {id: 3})
    -[:CONNECTED]->(n3:Test {id: 4})
    -[:CONNECTED]->(n2)-[:CONNECTED]->(n5:Test {id: 6})
    -[:CONNECTED]->(n1),
    (n2)-[:CONNECTED]->(n7:Test {id: 8})
    <-[:CONNECTED]-(n3)-[:CONNECTED]->(n4:Test {id:
5})-[:CONNECTED]->(n1),
    (n7)-[:CONNECTED]->(n4)-[:CONNECTED]->(n5)
    -[:CONNECTED]->(:Test {id: 7})
```

The graph looks like this:

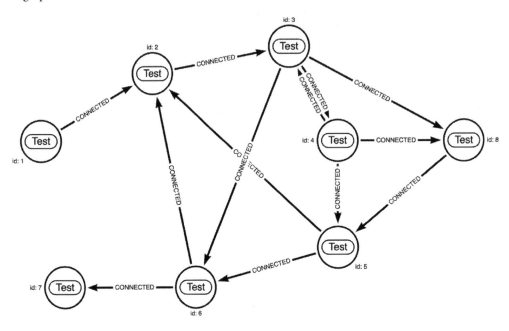

Figure 10.20 – Sample graph to test the APOC expandConfig procedure

This graph has a lot of loops. We will take a look at Cypher and APOC's expand procedure to see how much work each query is doing, and how much data is returned:

- First, we will look at the Test node with id 1 and expand all the way. The Cypher looks like this:

```
MATCH path=(:Test {id:1})-[:CONNECTED*]->()
RETURN count(path)
```

- We are returning only the number of paths we have traversed instead of the actual graph. When browser displays the graph, it merges the duplicate data, meaning a node that appears in multiple paths will be shown only once:

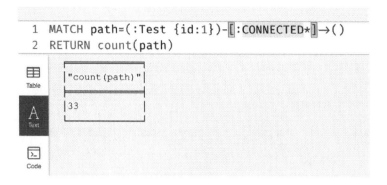

Figure 10.21 – Cypher variable length expansion

The screenshot shows that 33 paths are returned.

- Let's look at the graph returned. We can see in the following screenshot that it is the complete test graph that we have created:

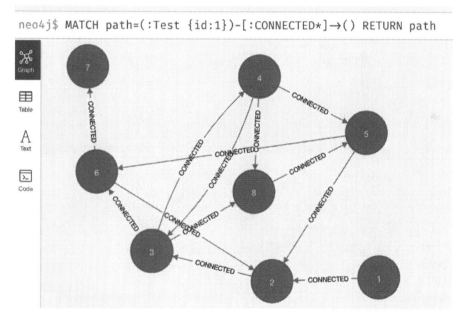

Figure 10.22 – Cypher variable length expansion graph

- Let's look at the APOC expand procedure with the default configuration:

```
MATCH (t:Test {id:1})
WITH t
```

```
CALL apoc.path.
expandConfig(t,{relationshipFilter:"CONNECTED>"}) YIELD
path
RETURN count(path)
```

The original Cypher is much more readable and succinct than this query. Here, we have to get the node using MATCH first and then invoke the procedure.

- In the following screenshot, we can see that the number of paths is 34, which is one higher than previously, which is probably due to the start node being returned as a separate path:

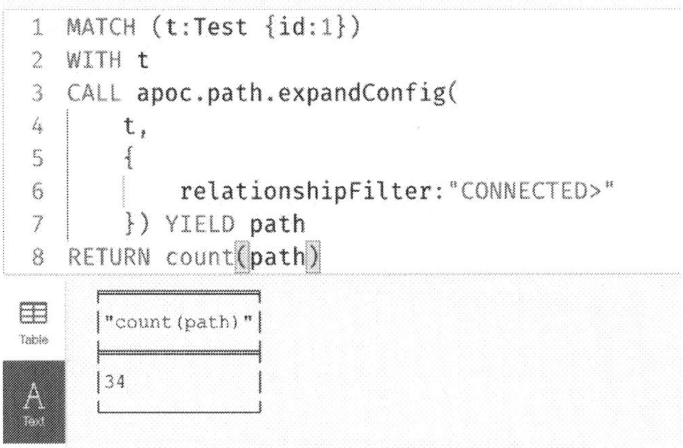

```
1  MATCH (t:Test {id:1})
2  WITH t
3  CALL apoc.path.expandConfig(
4      t,
5      {
6          relationshipFilter:"CONNECTED>"
7      }) YIELD path
8  RETURN count(path)
```

"count(path)"
34

Figure 10.23 – Variable expansion path with the default APOC expand configuration

Now, let's look at using more configuration options and see how the procedure behaves.

We will take a look at the NODE_GLOBAL uniqueness option:

```
MATCH (t:Test {id:1})
WITH t
CALL apoc.path.expandConfig(
    t,
    {
        relationshipFilter:"CONNECTED>",
        uniqueness: "NODE_GLOBAL"
    }) YIELD path
RETURN count(path)
```

We have added NODE_GLOBAL to the configuration. Let's look at the response.

In the following screenshot, we can see only eight paths being returned. Let's see if the graph returned is the same:

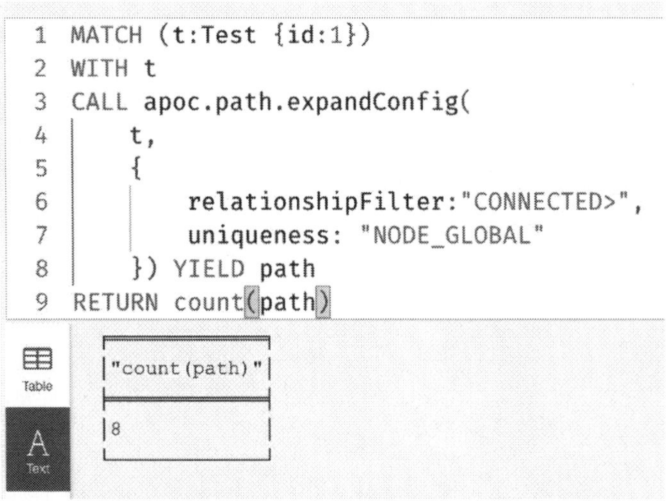

```
1  MATCH (t:Test {id:1})
2  WITH t
3  CALL apoc.path.expandConfig(
4      t,
5      {
6          relationshipFilter:"CONNECTED>",
7          uniqueness: "NODE_GLOBAL"
8      }) YIELD path
9  RETURN count(path)
```

Table

|"count(path)"|

| 8 |

Text

Figure 10.24 – Using the NODE_GLOBAL configuration

We can see from the graph that we have all the nodes but are missing the loop-back relationships here. This is because once we reach a node, we do not traverse those relationships. That's why this graph is different from the other graph. If we are only interested in the nodes in the paths, then this option will not only be faster but use less memory as well:

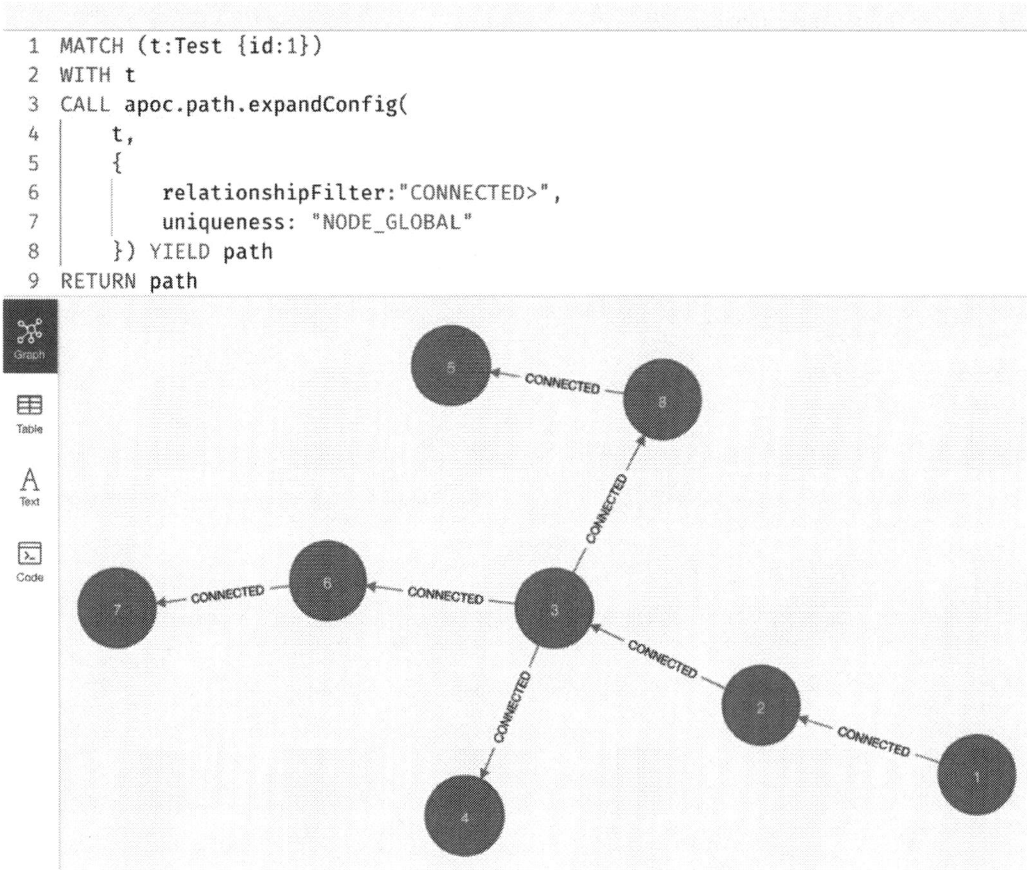

```
1  MATCH (t:Test {id:1})
2  WITH t
3  CALL apoc.path.expandConfig(
4      t,
5      {
6          relationshipFilter:"CONNECTED>",
7          uniqueness: "NODE_GLOBAL"
8      }) YIELD path
9  RETURN path
```

Figure 10.25 – Graph returned with the NODE_GLOBAL configuration

Let's take a look at the RELATIONSHIP_GLOBAL configuration:

```
MATCH (t:Test {id:1})
WITH t
CALL apoc.path.expandConfig(
    t,
    {
        relationshipFilter:"CONNECTED>",
        uniqueness: "RELATIONSHIP_GLOBAL"
    }) YIELD path
RETURN count(path)
```

In this query, we are using RELATIONSHIP_GLOBAL as the configuration option.

Let's look at the query response:

```
1  MATCH (t:Test {id:1})
2  WITH t
3  CALL apoc.path.expandConfig(
4      t,
5      {
6          relationshipFilter:"CONNECTED>",
7          uniqueness: "RELATIONSHIP_GLOBAL"
8      }) YIELD path
9  RETURN count(path)
```

"count(path)"
14

Figure 10.26 – Using the RELATIONSHIP_GLOBAL configuration

We can see in the following screenshot that we now have 14 paths returned. Let's look at the graph being returned:

```
1  MATCH (t:Test {id:1})
2  WITH t
3  CALL apoc.path.expandConfig(
4      t,
5      {
6          relationshipFilter:"CONNECTED>",
7          uniqueness: "RELATIONSHIP_GLOBAL"
8      }) YIELD path
9  RETURN path
```

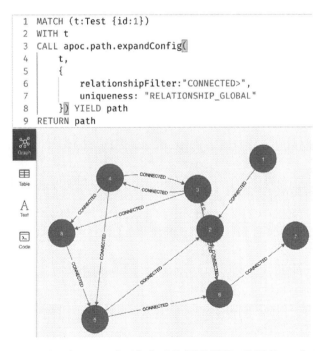

Figure 10.27 – Graph returned with the RELATIONSHIP_GLOBAL configuration

We can see the graph returned is the same in terms of nodes and relationships returned. In terms of graph visualization, this option can be faster and less memory intensive than the Cypher variable path expansion.

Let's look at an example of termination node filter usage:

```
MATCH (t:Test {id:1})
WITH t
CALL apoc.path.expandConfig(t,
    { relationshipFilter:"CONNECTED>", labelFilter: "/Test"})
YIELD path
RETURN path
```

We are providing the termination nodes using the `labelFilter` option here.

In the screenshot, we can see that it is returning only one path because the first node it encountered was the `Test` node:

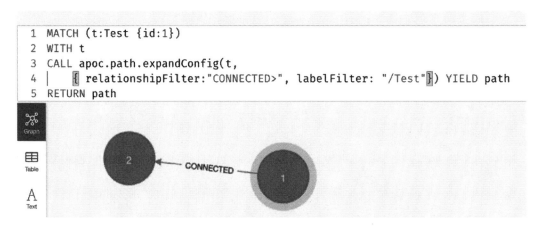

Figure 10.28 – Using the termination node filter

From the usage of the procedure, we can see that `apoc.path.expandConfig` is a very powerful way to traverse a graph using various conditional traversals and can be a very good utility to be aware of when we are writing complex Cypher queries.

APOC also provides utility procedures to enable you to connect to other databases. We will take a look at those procedures in the next section.

Connecting to other databases

APOC provides ways to integrate with various databases to read or modify data. We will take a look at each of these methods to see how we can interact with other databases from Cypher:

- **JDBC**: To connect to JDBC-compliant data using a JDBC driver, we need to make sure to add the required JARs to the `plugins` directory. Once you have added the JARs to the `plugins` directory, restart the server instance.

  To make sure the `jdbc` driver is loaded, we need to execute the load driver method first as shown here:

  ```
  CALL apoc.load.driver("com.mysql.test.Driver")
  ```

  Once the driver is loaded, we can query the data using the `load.jdbc` method. We will take a look at an example query here:

  ```
  WITH "jdbc:mysql://localhost:3306/mydb?user=root" as url
  CALL apoc.load.jdbc(url,"person") YIELD row
  RETURN row
  ```

  This query returns each row as a map from the person table in the `mydb` database. You can take this row and add it to a graph or do other work.

- **Elasticsearch**: APOC provides a lot of functions to interact with Elasticsearch to read, write, and query. Similar to JDBC drivers, you need to copy the required JAR files to the `plugins` directory. Some of the methods available are as follows:

  - `apoc.es.get`: This retrieves documents from the specified server and index.
  - `apoc.es.query`: This method executes the specified query against the provided server.
  - `apoc.es.post`: This performs the POST function against the specified server.
  - `apoc.es.put`: This performs the PUT action against the specified server.

  You can read more about these methods and examples at `https://neo4j.com/labs/apoc/4.4/database-integration/elasticsearch/`.

- **MongoDB**: Similar to the other database integration, you would need to copy the required JAR files to the `plugins` directory. Some of the methods provided are as follows:

  - `apoc.mongodb.find`: Finds documents of a given type
  - `apoc.mongodb.insert`: Inserts the specified document into MongoDB
  - `apoc.mongodb.update`: Updates the specified document
  - `apoc.mongodb.delete`: Deletes the specified document

  You can read more about these methods and examples at `https://neo4j.com/labs/apoc/4.4/database-integration/mongodb/`.

We talked about a few of the database integrations available in APOC. For a full list of functionality and documentation, please visit `https://neo4j.com/labs/apoc/4.4/database-integration/`. A complete discussion on the usage with examples is beyond the scope of this book.

> **Note**
>
> While it is convenient for these functions to talk to other databases from Cypher, you need to keep in mind that they are running on Neo4j server instances and using the heap on the server. The quality of those queries can have a negative impact on graph database performance. In some scenarios, these queries can even crash the server.

We will take a look at some other useful procedures next.

Using other useful methods

There are a few other procedures that are useful when we are manipulating graphs. One of the most widely used procedures in this regard is `apoc.periodic.iterate`. Before the `CALL` subquery capability was added to Cypher, this was the only way to manipulate a graph in a batch manner.

Please note that this syntax is provided by the APOC documentation (`https://neo4j.com/labs/apoc/4.4/overview/apoc.periodic/apoc.periodic.iterate/`). You can visit that link for the latest syntax. The syntax of this procedure looks like this:

```
apoc.periodic.iterate(cypherIterate :: STRING?, cypherAction
:: STRING?, config :: MAP?) :: (batches :: INTEGER?, total
:: INTEGER?, timeTaken :: INTEGER?, committedOperations ::
INTEGER?, failedOperations :: INTEGER?, failedBatches ::
INTEGER?, retries :: INTEGER?, errorMessages :: MAP?, batch
:: MAP?, operations :: MAP?, wasTerminated :: BOOLEAN?,
failedParams :: MAP?, updateStatistics :: MAP?)
```

This procedure takes two Cypher strings and a configuration as parameters. The first Cypher statement is called the data statement. We execute this query, and the returned data is passed to the second action statement. The action statement is executed with data collected in batches from the first statement.

Let's look at an example. The following query shows a simple query that adds a new label to a node in a batch manner:

```
CALL apoc.periodic.iterate(
    "MATCH (person:Person) WHERE (person)-[:ACTED]->() RETURN
person ",
    "SET person:Actor",
    {batchSize:100, parallel:true})
```

We can see the data query, action query, and configuration details here.

The data query returns all the people who have an ACTED relationship. In the action query, we are adding an extra label, Actor, to it. It collects 100 people at a time (the batch size) and executes the second action query with that batch. If we have 1,000 people, then the action query is executed 10 times, with 100 people per batch.

Another thing we should mention here is that we are using the parallel: true option in the configuration. This means that the action query can be run in parallel.

This is the most common usage of this procedure. While the CALL subquery can still be used, most of this it is not possible to execute the action queries in parallel in subqueries.

> **Note**
>
> When you are using the parallel: true option, you need to be aware of locking.
>
> If you are creating relationships or deleting them, parallel: true can be troublesome depending on how you get the data from the data query.
>
> When adding/updating/deleting properties or labels, parallel: true can be safe.

Another useful procedure is apoc.do.when. We know Cypher does not have an IF/ELSE construct. This procedure fills in that gap. The syntax of this procedure is as follows:

```
apoc.do.when(
    condition :: BOOLEAN?,
    ifQuery :: STRING?,
    elseQuery =  :: STRING?,
    params = {} :: MAP?) :: (value :: MAP?)
```

We can see that this works pretty similarly to an IF - THEN - ELSE construct. We can simulate an IF condition using a FOREACH clause in Cypher. But one disadvantage is that we cannot do a MATCH inside a FOREACH clause or invoke other procedures. Even the nodes or relationships created or updated in a FOREACH clause are not visible outside of it. This procedure removes these obstacles. We can perform any Cypher query and provide the response to be processed in the next steps.

Let's summarize our understanding of APOC procedures.

Summary

We have looked at installing the APOC plugin, using various APOC procedures to review the database schema and statistics, loading data into graphs using CSV or JSON files, executing dynamic Cypher statements, traversing graphs using path expansion with various configuration options, and connecting to other databases from Cypher. We have also reviewed a few important procedures that we can use to build complex queries easily. What we have covered in this chapter are only a few representative procedures. To take a look at what other procedures and functions are available, along with examples, please visit `https://neo4j.com/labs/apoc/4.4/`. There, you can find extensive documentation about all the functionality provided, along with detailed examples.

In the next chapter, we will take a look at the ecosystem surrounding Cypher.

11

Cypher Ecosystem

In the previous chapters, we looked at all the aspects of querying graph databases using Cypher. This chapter focuses on the Cypher ecosystem. You will be introduced to a selection of tools and packages available for more advanced data processing, along with visualizing the results as graphs, tables, and more.

We will look at the following topics in this chapter:

- Using Neo4j extensions
- Using visualization tools
- Using Kafka and Spark connectors
- Using Graph Data Science
- Using Neo4j Workspace

First, we will take a look at the Neo4j extensions.

Using Neo4j extensions

While Cypher is a very powerful language for expressing graph traversal in a simple manner, it is difficult to implement complex graph analytics or handle different kinds of data effectively. This is where Neo4j extensions come into the picture. Neo4j provides the ability to build and register plugins with procedures that can be invoked from Cypher to perform more complex operations.

In the following screenshot, we can see the plugins available to install for the selected database in Neo4j Desktop:

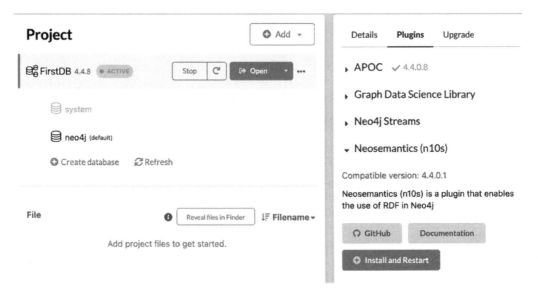

Figure 11.1 – Plugin management in Neo4j Desktop

Let's review what these plugins provide in the following list:

- **APOC**: APOC is short for **Awesome Procedures On Cypher** and is an add-on library that provides a lot of functions and procedures that add useful functionality to Cypher. We discussed the important features of this extension in detail in *Chapter 10, Using APOC Utilities*.

  You can find more details on this at `https://neo4j.com/labs/apoc/`.

- **Graph Data Science library**: The Neo4j **Graph Data Science (GDS)** library provides a lot of analytical capabilities to analyze the data in graph databases by leveraging graph algorithms and machine learning workflows. Some of the graph algorithms provided are as follows:

  - Community detection

  - Centrality

  - Node similarity

  - Path finding

  - Link prediction

  It also provides a catalog of procedures to support data science workflows and machine learning tasks on graph data. All these procedures are built for massive scale and parallelization. You can read more about graph algorithms and machine learning capabilities at `https://neo4j.com/product/graph-data-science/`.

- **Neo4j Streams**: The Neo4j Streams plugin integrates Neo4j with Apache Kafka to act as a source or sink. There are two different aspects to this connector. There is a version called **Kafka Connect**, which only works with Neo4j as the sink. This is deployed on Kafka servers. This works with Confluent Cloud as well. You can read more about this at `https://neo4j.com/labs/kafka/4.1/kafka-connect/`. The second version is a Neo4j extension that needs to be deployed on a Neo4j server. In this aspect it can work with Neo4j as the source or the sink. It provides some **change data capture** (**CDC**) capabilities also. While this can make it easy to do certain things, it also means a certain percentage of CPU will be used by this plugin, thus reducing the processing capability available for the database server to carry out its usual functionalities. You can read more about the features and capabilities at `https://neo4j.com/labs/kafka/4.1/`.

- **Neosemantics (n10s) Neo4j RDF and Semantics toolkit**: This plugin enables the processing of **Resource Description Framework** (**RDF**, `https://www.w3.org/RDF/`) datasets and mapping them to property graph format for storage in Neo4j. It supports **RDF** vocabularies, such as **OWL**, **RDFS**, **SKOS**, and others, in a seamless manner. You can use this plugin to consume or generate RDF data. It can also validate graphs against defined constraints expressed in **Shapes Constraint Language** (**SHACL**, `https://www.w3.org/TR/shacl/`). You can read more about this plugin at `https://neo4j.com/labs/neosemantics/`.

We have introduced these extensions so that developers are aware of external plugins that can expand Cypher's functionality. It is out of the scope of this book to go deeper than this, but feel free to visit the sites provided to understand more about these extensions and how they can help us to build better solutions.

We will take a look at visualization tools available for Cypher to present results next.

Using visualization tools

We will take a look at the visualization tools available to present the results. The visualization tools available from Neo4j are already installed in Neo4j Desktop by default. These are as follows:

- **Neo4j Browser**: We have looked at using Neo4j Browser to interact with databases in *Chapter 1, Introduction to Neo4j and Cypher*. It is a very good tool for developers to interact with databases.

- **Bloom**: Bloom is a more powerful graph visualization tool than Neo4j Browser. While Neo4j Browser is aimed more at developers, Bloom is aimed at end users exploring graphs using more natural language queries. It provides the following capabilities:

  - High-performance, GPU-powered rendering to create large graphs with physics-based layouts.

  - Data exploration functionality without needing to learn Cypher with the ability to use near-natural language search phrases.

- The ability to selectively expand the nodes and relationships along with inspecting the properties.

- The ability to visually edit existing records and add new records.

- The ability to create different views and perspectives of the same graph and share those perspectives with different users. This can be customized to meet different business requirements from the same data.

Along with these visualization tools, Neo4j Desktop also provides options to explore other visualization aspects via graph apps. You can install graph apps at `https://install.graphapp.io/`.

Let's take a look at a few of the graph apps and utilities available at the preceding link:

- **Graph Gallery**: This graph app provides a lot of example graphs that developers can play with to familiarize themselves with graph databases and Cypher. You can find more details at `https://medium.com/neo4j/meet-the-graph-gallery-3666a127efee`.

- **Charts**: This graph app provides functionality to build charts using graph data. It provides a visual query builder, so that the user does not need to know Cypher fully to use it. It gives options to developers as well as business users to build simple dashboards with charts to provide insights from graphs. You can read more at `https://medium.com/neo4j/creating-charts-from-your-graphs-2f5b4e86fd6c`.

- **GraphXR** provides the ability to explore graph data in **virtual reality** (**VR**). To learn more about this, please visit `https://neo4j.com/blog/graphxr-graph-app-neo4j-desktop/`.

- **NeoDash** is a no-code utility to quickly build dashboards with Neo4j as the backend database. It is a lightweight app that hooks into Neo4j to build dashboard widgets quickly. You can read more about this at `https://nielsdejong.nl/neo4j%20projects/2020/11/16/neodash.html`.

- **Graphlytic Desktop**: Graphlytic is capable of building a graph data model from scratch by combining various data sources. It also provides pattern-searching functionality and visual analytical exploration of graphs. You can find out more about this at `https://graphlytic.biz/blog/how-to-install-graphlytic-in-neo4j-desktop`.

- **SemSpect**: This is another visualization tool that can assist the exploration of large graphs without using Cypher to get intelligence and perform analytics. It instead explores graphs using the model semantics. You can read more about it at `https://neo4j.com/blog/semspect-different-approach-graph-visualization/`.

- **NeoMap Map Visualizer**: This visualization tool overlays data onto geographical maps. It leverages the geographical coordinates (point properties) in the data to display the nodes on a map. You can learn more about this tool at `https://medium.com/neo4j/introducing-neomap-a-neo4j-desktop-application-for-spatial-data-3e14aad59db2`.

- **Neo4j Commander 3**: This tool provides an intuitive way to edit the data in a graph without relying on Cypher. You can read more about this tool at `https://medium.com/neo4j/editing-data-in-neo4j-graphs-doesnt-have-to-be-hard-8e9791c731bc`.

We have only discussed the tools available for Neo4j Desktop here. There are other visualization tools such as **Linkurious**, **yWorks**, and **KeyLines**, among others.

Let's take a look at Kafka and Spark connectors next.

Using Kafka and Spark connectors

Neo4j has official support for Kafka and Spark connectors that can read and write data to graphs. The Kafka connector makes it easy to ingest data into Neo4j at scale, without needing to build custom client code. Spark connector simplifies the reading and writing of data to graphs using dataframes. Let's take a look at the core features provided by these connectors:

- Kafka connector:

  - Provides the capability to ingest data into Neo4j using templatized Cypher queries

  - Can handle streaming data efficiently

  - Runs as a plugin on existing Kafka installations

  - You can read more about this connector at `https://neo4j.com/labs/kafka/4.1/kafka-connect/`

- Spark connector:

  - Makes it easier to read nodes and relationships into a dataframe

  - Makes it possible to take the data from dataframes and write it into Neo4j easily

  - Supports using Python or R as the language of choice in Spark

  - Makes it easier to leverage all the capabilities of Spark to massage the data before writing it to Neo4j

  - You can read more about this connector at `https://neo4j.com/docs/spark/current/overview/`

Now let's look at the Graph Data Science plugin.

Using Graph Data Science

Neo4j's **Graph Data Science** (**GDS**) library implements a lot of graph algorithms to help users derive intelligence from data. They are implemented to run in parallel, allowing algorithms to run fast and provide results quickly.

The algorithms included are as follows:

- Node centrality algorithm

- Community detection algorithm

- Similarity algorithms including the Jaccard, Cosine, Pearson, Euclidean and k-nearest neighbor algorithms

- Path-finding algorithms including the Dijkstra, A* shortest path, Yen's shortest path, breadth-first, depth-first, and random walk algorithms

- Node embedding algorithms including FastRP, GraphSAGE, and Node2Vec

- Link prediction algorithms

Along with these graph algorithms, this library also provides the following machine learning pipelines:

- Node classifications

- Link predictions

This library is a must-have tool in any data scientist's toolkit to process graph data effectively and extract intelligence and outcomes from the data.

Next, let's look at Neo4j Workspace, which is a new feature released recently to help developers work with Neo4j without needing to write any code.

Using Neo4j Workspace

Neo4j Workspace is a new tool to help developers quickly map and load the data and analyze it with visual tools such as Neo4j Browser and Bloom without needing any coding experience. It makes it easy for graph enthusiasts, explorers, and data scientists who lack coding experience or knowledge of Cypher to get started very quickly. It includes other tools such as Data Importer, which provides a UI to map CSV/TSV data to a graph model and load the data into a graph. Browser and Bloom are also included to help explore the data visually in a single place. Workspace is still in early access; users can register for access at `https://neo4j.com/product/workspace/`.

Now, let's summarize what we've learned in this chapter.

Summary

In this chapter, we took a brief look at Neo4j extensions including APOC, the Graph Data Science library, Neosemantics, and Neo4j streams, which can enhance Cypher's capabilities to handle complex activities in Neo4j. We also talked about visualization tools such as Bloom, NeoDash, and others that are available to explore graph data using charts and maps, among other things.

In the next chapter, we will take a look at some tips and tricks to help you get the most out of Cypher.

12

Tips and Tricks

We have looked at Cypher syntax, how to load data into a graph, and retrieving data and APOC in the previous chapters. In this chapter, we will discuss the best practices to get the most out of Cypher queries, including how to leverage data modeling and patterns by looking under the hood to understand how Neo4j stores data. We will also discuss the tips and tricks to identify performance bottlenecks and how to go about addressing them. We will take a look at the following topics:

- Understanding the internals of Neo4j

- Reviewing querying patterns

- Troubleshooting a few common issues

- Reviewing the new 5.0 changes

We will also take a look at a few tips and tricks for good query patterns and identifying issues and what to look out for when we are building queries.

First, we will look at understanding the internals of Neo4j.

Understanding the internals of Neo4j

Having a good understanding of how Neo4j stores data can help us to build better queries. There are a few files that are important to understand how Neo4j stores data.

They are given in the following list:

- `nodestore.db`: This is the file that stores all the nodes. The internal node ID is indexed in this file.

- `relationshipstore.db`: This is the file that stores all the relationships. The internal relationship ID is indexed in this file.

- `propertystore.db`: This is the file that stores all the properties, whether they are on a node or relationship. This file does not store the large string values or array values, as they may not fit into the property record.

- `propertystore.db.strings`: This file stores the large string values.

- `propertystore.db.arrays`: This file stores the array property values.

- `Schema`: This directory stores the indexes.

Let's take a look at these store sizes for a database.

```
bash-3.2$ du -h *
   0B    database_lock
 8.0K    neostore
  48K    neostore.counts.db
  48K    neostore.indexstats.db
 832K    neostore.labelscanstore.db
 8.0K    neostore.labeltokenstore.db
  40K    neostore.labeltokenstore.db.id
 8.0K    neostore.labeltokenstore.db.names
  40K    neostore.labeltokenstore.db.names.id
 4.5M    neostore.nodestore.db
 248K    neostore.nodestore.db.id
 8.0K    neostore.nodestore.db.labels
  40K    neostore.nodestore.db.labels.id
  24M    neostore.propertystore.db
 8.0K    neostore.propertystore.db.arrays
  40K    neostore.propertystore.db.arrays.id
 312K    neostore.propertystore.db.id
 8.0K    neostore.propertystore.db.index
  48K    neostore.propertystore.db.index.id
 8.0K    neostore.propertystore.db.index.keys
  40K    neostore.propertystore.db.index.keys.id
  11M    neostore.propertystore.db.strings
 144K    neostore.propertystore.db.strings.id
 216K    neostore.relationshipgroupstore.db
  48K    neostore.relationshipgroupstore.db.id
 216K    neostore.relationshipgroupstore.degrees.db
  33M    neostore.relationshipstore.db
 584K    neostore.relationshipstore.db.id
 3.1M    neostore.relationshiptypescanstore.db
 8.0K    neostore.relationshiptypestore.db
  40K    neostore.relationshiptypestore.db.id
 8.0K    neostore.relationshiptypestore.db.names
  40K    neostore.relationshiptypestore.db.names.id
 8.0K    neostore.schemastore.db
  48K    neostore.schemastore.db.id
 4.0K    profiles/schema/index/native-btree-1.0/9
 4.0K    profiles/schema/index/native-btree-1.0/11
```

Figure 12.1 – Database store files

We can see from the screenshot that the store files are highlighted. These are the files that will have the most impact on the memory and performance requirements. We are discussing these aspects here because understanding how Neo4j stores and retrieves data helps us to write more optimal queries.

The reason we are discussing this aspect in this chapter instead of earlier ones is that combining this knowledge and query processing with tips can better assist you to build queries. For example, if you have been working with Cypher queries and want to look at how to improve your skills, this chapter is more beneficial.

Let's now look at node store structure.

Understanding the node store

A node store is a single file that stores all the nodes in a graph. Each node is a fixed-size data structure, as shown in the following table.

ID	Labels	Props	Rels
01	:Patient	01	01

Table 12.2 – Node data structure

From the preceding table, we can see that the node data structure contains the node ID. This is an index in the node store file (`nodestore.db`) that we looked at in the previous section. It has labels associated with it. We can see in the table that this node has a label, `Patient`. The **Props** section contains the first property of the node. If there are other properties, they are stored as a linked list, with the first property being stored in the node. The **Rels** section points to the first relationship this node has. If the number of relationships starts becoming dense, such as more than 100, then this can point toward a relationship group store. The relationships also get connected as a linked list. When it is stored as a group, it will have one entry per relationship type, with IN and OUT directions separated. The labels stored are not the actual strings but, instead, ID numbers associated with the label name, and the corresponding ID is stored in the node data structure.

Now, let's look at the relationship store.

Understanding the relationship store

The relationship data structure is a bit bigger than a node. It can be seen as follows:

ID	Type	Source node	Target node	Props	Source previous	Source next	Target previous	Target next
01	HAS_ENCOUNTER	01	03	09	6	02	4	03

Table 12.3 – Relationship data structure

The **ID** value is the index in the relationship store file (`relationshipstore.db`) that we looked at in the previous section. It has one type, which is an ID number associated with that name. It contains both **Source node** and **Target node** IDs in the data structure. This should make it clear that in Neo4j, data is connected as a doubly linked list to make it easier to traverse in any direction in an efficient manner. The *properties* section contains the ID of the first property associated with this relationship. The **Source previous** entry contains the number of relationships in the chain for the source node when this is the first relationship in the chain. Similarly, **Target previous** contains the number of relationships in the chain for the target node if this is the first relationship in the chain. This is useful to tell us the number of relationships the node is connected quickly with. If it is not the first relationship in the chain, then these entries will contain the previous relationship in the chain.

The **Source next** entry contains the next relationship for the source node in the chain. The same applies to the **Target next** entries. This should make it clear that once we have obtained the relationship, we can traverse back and forth using the previous and next entries, depending on the source or target node context.

Next, let us take a look at the property store.

Understanding the property store

The property store contains the property values for both nodes and relationships in a single stored file. It is split into three different stores to make sure the data structure size can be fixed.

Let us look at the basic property data structure:

ID	NextProp	PrevProp	Payload
01	02	-1	name | String | "Jon"

Table 12.4 – Property data structure

Similar to node and relationship stores, **ID** is the index in the property store file (`propertystore.db`). It contains the locations to store next and previous properties. The *Payload* section contains the ID for the property name, the ID for the type, and the actual value. This can store all the basic property types except lists, which are stored in a property arrays store (`propertystore.db.arrays`).

One exception is that, if the string value does not fit into the data structure here, it will be stored in the string's property store (`propertystore.db.strings`). In that case, the last value we stored in the payload points to the ID of the data structure stored in the strings property store or arrays property store. Even the strings property store and arrays property store use fixed-size data structures. If a value does not fit in one data structure, it can be split into a chain of data structures to store all the values. So, when you are storing a large string or reading it, the cost of it can be higher.

> **Note**
>
> As you can see from the previous paragraph, storing and retrieving large strings or arrays can be costly, as we may need to traverse multiple chain blocks to retrieve data. Therefore, we need to be careful about how and what we are storing and how we are retrieving the data.

You can read about data structure sizes here: `https://neo4j.com/developer/kb/understanding-data-on-disk/`.

Next, we will take a look at how Neo4j uses memory to execute queries.

Understanding Neo4j memory usage

Neo4j splits the memory into three different segments, given as follows:

- **JVM memory**: This is the memory used to load the Java classes, compiled Cypher queries, thread stacks, metaspace, GC, Lucene indices, and so on.

- **Heap**: This is the memory that is used to execute the queries. This contains the transaction state, query execution data, and graph management details. For high transactional usage, this should not exceed 31 GB because the JVM garbage collection is not efficient if the heap is more than that.

- **Page cache**: Cached graph data and indices.

When a query is executed, a transaction state is initiated in heap memory, and it goes to the page cache to retrieve the data. The query execution always goes to the page cache to get the nodes, relationships, and properties. If a node, relationship, or property is not found in the page cache, it causes a page fault that will load the required entity from the corresponding store. Since the page cache loads not just one data structure but a single page block around 4 KB, it may be reading more data than required.

You can read more about these aspects at `https://www.graphable.ai/blog/neo4j-performance/` and `https://maxdemarzi.com/2012/08/13/neo4j-internals/`.

Now that we have taken a brief look at how Neo4j stores data, let's look at some query patterns and review what a good query and a bad query are.

Reviewing querying patterns

Let's review a few query patterns and see how a database will try to execute them to understand how to write optimal queries:

- The following code segment shows one of the most common mistakes:

```
MATCH (Mango {color: 'Yellow'}) return count(*)
```

We forgot to add :, even if `Mango` is a valid label. When we look at the query, we read it as return the count of yellow mangoes. Say we have mangoes, oranges, and apples in our cart. Since a database does not know what a mango is, it is going through all the fruits and checking for a color property, which should be `Yellow`, and returns the count of that. This is because when the database sees the query, it does not see the name `Mango` as a label.

> **Tip**
>
> Look for browser warnings before running the queries. Browsers are very good at highlighting these kinds of errors.

- The following code block is another common mistake made by developers:

```
MATCH (p:Patient)--(e:Encounter) RETURN p,e
```

There are two issues here. First, no direction is provided for the relationship. Second, there is no relationship type provided. Let's see whether we can explain, in layman's terms, the work the database needs to do here. Let's say there is a junction with four incoming roads and three outgoing roads. There is a post office one block away. If someone asks us to find the post office one block away, since we don't know where it is, we have to traverse all the roads by one block to find the post office. That's what the database is doing here. It is traversing one hop in all directions and giving you data. Let's see how this changes if a direction was provided. If we are looking for the post office one block away on the outgoing roads, we would be looking at only three roads instead of seven roads. This is the same with the database. Let's see how this changes if there was more information provided. Out of the three roads, let's say two are going *east* and one is going *west*. If we are asked to find a post office one block away on eastward outgoing roads, then we will be looking at only two roads instead of three. Similarly, if we provide the relationship type, then the amount of work the database does to retrieve data is also less.

> **Tip**
>
> Look at the query profile to understand the amount of work the database is doing. We should always be using the direction and relationship type for better performant queries.

- The following query can be very expensive in terms of memory and CPU usage. Depending on the graph size, this can cause out-of-memory exceptions and can crash a database server:

```
MATCH path=(:Patient)-[*]-(:Drug) RETURN path
```

Again, if we use the layman example from before, this is like trying to find a post office from a given point. This means we have to traverse in all directions and find all the paths that connect this point and a post office. Say you are at a point in a city and traversing all the roads in all directions to find all the paths; you can imagine how much time and effort it would take. Almost the same thing is happening here with the database. These kind of queries should be avoided at all costs. This query should have used relationship types, direction, and limiting the length to be able to respond in time.

> **Tip**
>
> You can avoid having out-of-memory exceptions thus causing outage by using the `dbms.memory.transaction.global_max_size` configuration. This configuration makes sure that all queries will not use more memory than this value. This should be a bit smaller than the maximum heap size configured. Also, you can use `dbms.memory.transaction.max_size` to make sure a given query does not use more than this memory. If it tries to use more memory, it would be terminated.

Cypher queries can be termed as **anchor** and **traverse**. Anchor means we are finding a node from which we start our traversal of a graph. This is the strongest feature of Neo4j.

In general, the following rules help to write better queries.

- For the anchoring point, make sure there is an index created for the WHERE condition. Remember that in Neo4j, a node label and property name are part of the index.

- We should traverse from a node that has a fewer number of relationships.

- It is always better to use direction and relationship types in queries; unless we want to traverse all the relationships, the node has to do our work.

- Leverage count stores for performant queries.

- Avoid specifying the labels for the nodes in the path, if possible, except the anchor node. This adds one extra step to do during traversal. In general, with a good model, the relationship type indicates what the next node label would be.

- Profile queries to understand the amount of work a database is doing.

- Leverage certain properties, such as `true` or `false` or values that contain a group with a limited set of values, to labels on the node. Using these labels can be much more effective than checking for a property or relying on an index.

- Property access is the most expensive part of Neo4j queries. Delay accessing the properties as late as you can.

- Make sure you are leveraging index-based sorting in your queries.

- Do not start the traversal from a super node. You can always check whether a node is connected to a super node.

- Use constraints, such as unique constraints, for nodes if possible. This can make a query optimizer pick an optimal query plan, instead of a simple index.

- Be careful when using variable length expansion. If possible, use bounds to limit the expansion. Also, for complex traversals, leverage `apoc.path.expandConfig`.

- Leverage `apoc` procedures and functions.

- Pay attention to how your graph is growing. The most common mistake made in data modeling is relying heavily on properties, which means we will also be relying on index lookups more often. This leads to a smaller graph in terms of node and relationship store sizes, and bigger property and index stores.

Next, we will take a look at troubleshooting a few common issues.

Troubleshooting a few common issues

When you are troubleshooting, logs are your friends. You must take a look at query log and debug log files to identify any issues. Please note that query logs are not available in Community Edition of Neo4j. If you are using *Neo4j Desktop* to create a database and test it, then you are using a single-user enterprise license, so you will have access to query logs. We will take a look at what information we have to troubleshoot issues and how we can fix them here:

- *A debug log tells you a lot about how memory is being used*. Look out for JVM **garbage collection** (**GC**) pauses. If there are few GC pauses and they are smaller than 100 ms, then there should not be any issues. If there are lot of GC pauses and they are going above 100 ms, then the queries are using lot of heap. This could be due to a bad query, no indexes, or a query collecting a lot of data.

- Query logs tell you how much time a query is taking. If you enable time tracking using `dbms.logs.query.time_logging_enabled`, you can see the actual CPU time the query has taken, along with the amount of time it spent waiting for resources to become available and the time taken to create a plan. By enabling `dbms.logs.query.page_logging_enabled`, you can also see the number of page faults the query is causing:

  - If a lot of queries have a plan time greater than 0, then you might not be leveraging parameterization of queries.

  - If a query has more than zero wait time, then you may not have enough compute power to handle the queries. This, by itself, should not be an issue if the wait time is small – say, under 100 ms. When you get a burst of queries at the same time, some of the queries do have to wait for the CPU to be available. It is also possible that the query is waiting for another transaction to complete because it is trying to modify the same node or relationship and needs to acquire a lock on it. Again, if the wait time is small, then it should not be an issue.

  - If a lot of queries have page faults, then the page cache available may not be enough. We need to understand how our queries are using the page cache to make sure we reduce the page faults. Most likely, the situation here would be that your data model has evolved and your queries may not be efficient any more. Another situation could be your queries are over-reliant on properties, and the page cache is not big enough to hold a property store along with node and relationship stores.

Let's take a look at few of the common issues faced during query execution and how to address them:

- *The write query performance starts degrading as we keep writing data*: The most likely scenario here is that there are no indexes created. As the data keeps growing, the time taken to find a node for a given label linearly keeps increasing:

  - Take a look at your MERGE and MATCH statements to make sure you are leveraging indexes using EXPLAIN

- *An out-of-memory exception during writes*: This means that the heap provided is not enough to handle the request:

  - If you are using the LOAD CSV command, then use EXPLAIN to see whether there are any EAGER steps. If there are any EAGER steps, then the query engine tries to load all the CSV data into memory before it can start processing it. If you are trying to load a large file, then it can run out of memory.

    The best way to resolve this issue is to change the query to avoid any EAGER steps. Please read this article about it: https://medium.com/neo4j/cypher-sleuthing-the-eager-operator-84a64d91a452. Another option is to use client drivers and avoid using LOAD CSV in production environments. This should be your approach for stable applications.

  - Check whether the heap is good by reducing the batch size.

- *An out-of-memory exception during read queries*: This means the query is collecting a lot of data in memory before it can start returning it. This is the most common scenario if you are using COLLECT, ORDER BY, or DISTINCT clauses:

  - Reduce the number of variables in the queries

  - See whether you can filter more data before using these clauses

- *A* MERGE *query creating duplicate nodes*: MERGE is supposed to check whether the node exists and creates it only if it does not exist. However, this operation is not thread-safe. If you have two separate transactions that are executing this statement at the same time, then it is possible to have duplicate nodes:

  - If it is possible, create a unique constraint on the key used in the MERGE statements. It may cause one of the transactions to fail, but there won't be any duplicates.

- *A MERGE statement is failing with a unique constraint error:* A MERGE statement tries to create the whole path, excluding variables. Let's say your query is as follows:

```
MERGE (p:Person {id:1})-[:LIVES_AT]->(:Address {id:"A1"})
```

Here, even if the Person and Address nodes exist, if there is not a relationship between them, then MERGE will try to create the whole path, which means creating the Person and Address nodes again.

  - The best way to address this is to split the query into the following:

```
MERGE (p:Person {id:1})
MERGE (a:Address {id:"A1"})
MEGE (p)-[:LIVES_AT]->(a)
```

This query is doing MERGE on the nodes first and separates the relationship creation using another MERGE statement. Since they are separated, this query will not attempt to create duplicate nodes.

- An application shows the Unable to schedule bolt session <session_id> for execution since there are no available threads to serve it at the moment error. This means the server bolt connection thread pool is exceeded. This can be due to bad coding, where the sessions are not closed, there is burst traffic that is exceeding the thread pool configuration, or queries are taking time and the connections are not being released in time:

  - Check the client code to make sure that after the transaction is complete, session. close() is called

  - If the traffic rate is higher than the connection pool available, then increase the bolt thread pool size on the server

  - Check whether the queries are performing well and that they are not blocking the resources for a long time

- *In the cluster, all the queries are going to the leader node.* This means the client code is using the session.run() method to execute the queries. This implicitly creates a write transaction and all those transactions go to the leader. Also, the applications built using the Spring Data framework, by default, start to write transactions. In this case, again, all your queries are directed to the leader node:

  - If you are using a driver directly in the client, then you should use the session. readTranasaction() and session.writeTransaction() methods. In this case, all the read queries are directed to follower nodes and writes are directed to leader node.

  - If you are using the Spring Data framework, annotate the methods that should be executing read queries using the @Transaction(readonly=true) annotation.

- *Queries are slow in Enterprise Edition.* In some scenarios, queries work fine in Community Edition of Neo4j but are slow in Enterprise Edition:

  - Neo4j Community Edition supports only interpreted runtimes. In this mode, a basic plan is used to execute queries. In Enterprise mode, there are optimized runtimes such as pipelined and slotted. In Enterprise mode, by default, the query planner tries to use pipelined mode, which tries to optimize for faster execution. It is possible in a few scenarios that the query planner makes a mistake and the pipelined runtime is not effective. In these scenarios, it is possible to tell the planner to use other runtimes. One of the ways to force runtime is to prefix the query with `CYPHER runtime=interpreted`. When the planner sees this, it tries to use the runtime that is requested.

> **Note**
>
> This option is only available in Enterprise mode. Also, from 5.0 onward, the slotted runtime is the default option in Community Edition, and interpreted runtime is not available. You can read more about these options at `https://neo4j.com/docs/cypher-manual/4.4/query-tuning/how-do-i-profile-a-query/`.

- *Queries are slow and there are lot of page faults*: This means that the page cache is not enough to be able to execute the queries efficiently. Most likely, the situation here is that the graph data model evolved too quickly or is not in an optimal state. Another situation is that we are over-reliant on properties and indexes, and that is requiring a lot of page cache:

  - Take a look at your store sizes and your query patterns to see whether the page cache settings are optimal.

  - If the node store and relationship store are very small and the property and index stores are bigger, then we are over-reliant on properties and indexes. We need to take a step back and see whether the model can be improved. Another aspect to look at here is whether we can make the queries easy to traverse and access properties at the end.

Next, let's take a look what's new in Cypher 5.0.

Reviewing the new 5.0 changes

In version 5.0, multiple changes have been made to the Cypher language. You can read about all these changes at `https://neo4j.com/docs/cypher-manual/current/deprecations-additions-removals-compatibility/`. We will take a look few of the changes that impact the Cypher queries.

The first important change to note is index creation. In version 5.0, the indexes are separated to represent the different types so that the indexes can be more performant. The indexing types that are available in version 5.0 are listed here:

- **Fulltext index**: This is the Lucene text index
- **Lookup index**: This index is for node labels and relationship types
- **Range index**: This index replaces the B-tree index option and can be used with a single or multiple properties
- **Text index**: This index is used on string properties
- **Point index**: This index is used on point types

You can read more about the new index types at https://neo4j.com/docs/cypher-manual/current/indexes-for-search-performance/.

Another change that could be important for developers applies to label filtering and relation type filtering, along with the WHERE clause. It is possible to use logical predicates for node label and relationship types.

Here's a sample query that demonstrates this aspect:

```
MATCH (n: A&(B|C)&!D|E) RETURN n
```

You can see in this query that we want all the nodes with E or A labels, either B or C, and not D.

It is also possible to use the same syntax for relationships.

Here's a sample query that demonstrates this aspect:

```
MATCH p=()-[: A&(B|C)&!D|E]->() RETURN p
```

The logic here is also very similar to how node label filtering works.

Another change that is interesting is that we can use the WHERE clause in line with node labels and relationship types.

Here's an example of inline usage with nodes:

```
MATCH (a:Person WHERE a.name = 'Rob')
     -[:KNOWS]->(b:Person WHERE b.age > 25)
RETURN b.name
```

We can see the WHERE clause is used in line with nodes.

The same syntax also applies to relationships:

```
MATCH (a:Person {name: 'Tom'})
RETURN [(a)
-[r:KNOWS WHERE r.since < 2020]->(b:Person) | r.since] AS years
```

We can see that we are able to use the WHERE clause in line with the relationship that is inside a list comprehension. This new syntax can help us build complex queries with ease.

You can read more about this syntax and examples at https://neo4j.com/docs/cypher-manual/current/clauses/where/.

One last thing that may impact how users can add configuration to the neo4j.conf file is the introduction of a new configuration parameter called server.config.strict_validation. enabled. This is, by default, set to true. What this configuration does is not start the database instance if there are unknown configuration namespaces that are not part of the core database configuration, such as apoc, or a configuration is repeated multiple times, and then the database will fail to start. This is more of a security feature. So, when you want to add a new configuration, such as apoc. import.file.enabled=true, it would cause a problem.

There are two options available when you run into this kind of scenario:

- Modify the configuration to add or update the value to server.config.strict_ validation.enabled false, as shown here:

  ```
  server.config.strict_validation.enabled=false
  ```

- Create a separate configuration file that is appropriate for the plugin you are loading and add the configuration there. For example, for the apoc plugin, you can add all apoc-related configurations to the apoc.conf file and add it to the configuration directory.

  A sample apoc.conf configuration would look like this:

  ```
  apoc.import.file.enabled=true apoc.import.file.use_neo4j_
  config=false
  ```

  Please note that in the new configuration file, you need to add the apoc.import.file. use_neo4j_config=false config for the apoc plugin to use this new configuration file. If not, it looks for the configuration in the neo4j.conf file.

Now, let's summarize everything we have learned.

Summary

In this chapter, we took a deeper look at Neo4j internals to understand how a database works to execute queries. We also reviewed a few query patterns and saw the right and wrong ways to build queries and looked at troubleshooting common issues.

Cypher is an easy language to learn compared to SQL. However, it takes a bit of an effort to get the most out of it. One thing to remember is that Neo4j is a schemaless storage. This gives us great flexibility when it comes to data modeling. If your application use case starts changing, the current data model becomes too limiting, and your queries get slower, there is no need to create a completely new model. You can start adapting the existing model by adding new model concepts, thus keeping the same graph for the old and new functionality. Once you are satisfied with new model changes, it is possible to remove the remnants of the old model that are not required. Combining this kind of model flexibility with the simplicity and power of Cypher makes it easy to build effective and complex applications.

Furthermore, openCypher, which is the open source version of the Cypher language, is being adapted by other graph databases such as Amazon Neptune. So, by learning Cypher, your knowledge is not just limited to Neo4j but can also be leveraged to work with other databases. However, there might be subtle nuances that you need to be aware of to get the most out of different types of graph databases.

In short, to become an effective Cypher query developer, understand the domain and take a look at the graph database capabilities and graph modeling. Also, become familiar with capabilities such as EXPLAIN and PROFILE along with logs that are available to be able to identify and fix any issues.

Index

Symbols

5.0 Cypher
  changes, reviewing 299-301
  indexing types 300
  reference link, for changes 299

A

advanced path finding
  working with 268-278
aggregations
  working with 148-151
American Standard Code for Information Interchange (ASCII) 35
anchor 295
apoc.create
  reference link 267
apoc.cypher
  reference link 268
apoc.merge
  reference link 267
apoc.periodic.iterate
  reference link 280
Arrows App
  reference link 99

Arrows.app site
  reference link 60
Awesome Procedures On Cypher (APOC) 245, 284
  databases integrations 279, 280
  installing 245-247
  reference link 284
  used, for viewing database schema 260-265

B

Bloom 285, 286
browser help
  using 25-27
browser's UI
  working with 24, 25

C

CartesianProduct operator 239
CASE clause
  working with 212
change data capture (CDC) 285
Charts 286
client drivers
  data loading with 64-66

`Packt.com`

Subscribe to our online digital library for full access to over 7,000 books and videos, as well as industry leading tools to help you plan your personal development and advance your career. For more information, please visit our website.

Why subscribe?

- Spend less time learning and more time coding with practical eBooks and Videos from over 4,000 industry professionals

- Improve your learning with Skill Plans built especially for you

- Get a free eBook or video every month

- Fully searchable for easy access to vital information

- Copy and paste, print, and bookmark content

Did you know that Packt offers eBook versions of every book published, with PDF and ePub files available? You can upgrade to the eBook version at `packt.com` and as a print book customer, you are entitled to a discount on the eBook copy. Get in touch with us at `customercare@packtpub.com` for more details.

At `www.packt.com`, you can also read a collection of free technical articles, sign up for a range of free newsletters, and receive exclusive discounts and offers on Packt books and eBooks.

Other Books You May Enjoy

If you enjoyed this book, you may be interested in these other books by Packt:

Graph Machine Learning

Claudio Stamile, Aldo Marzullo, Enrico Deusebio

ISBN: 978-1-80020-449-2

- Write Python scripts to extract features from graphs

- Distinguish between the main graph representation learning techniques

- Learn how to extract data from social networks, financial transaction systems, for text analysis, and more

- Implement the main unsupervised and supervised graph embedding techniques

- Get to grips with shallow embedding methods, graph neural networks, graph regularization methods, and more

- Deploy and scale out your application seamlessly

Hands-On Graph Analytics with Neo4j

Estelle Scifo

- Become well-versed with Neo4j graph database building blocks, nodes, and relationships
- Discover how to create, update, and delete nodes and relationships using Cypher querying
- Use graphs to improve web search and recommendations
- Understand graph algorithms such as pathfinding, spatial search, centrality, and community detection
- Find out different steps to integrate graphs in a normal machine learning pipeline
- Formulate a link prediction problem in the context of machine learning
- Implement graph embedding algorithms such as DeepWalk, and use them in Neo4j graphs

Packt is searching for authors like you

If you're interested in becoming an author for Packt, please visit `authors.packtpub.com` and apply today. We have worked with thousands of developers and tech professionals, just like you, to help them share their insight with the global tech community. You can make a general application, apply for a specific hot topic that we are recruiting an author for, or submit your own idea.

Share Your Thoughts

Now you've finished *Graph Data Processing with Cypher*, we'd love to hear your thoughts! Scan the QR code below to go straight to the Amazon review page for this book and share your feedback or leave a review on the site that you purchased it from.

`https://packt.link/r/1-804-61107-7`

Your review is important to us and the tech community and will help us make sure we're delivering excellent quality content.

Download a free PDF copy of this book

Thanks for purchasing this book!

Do you like to read on the go but are unable to carry your print books everywhere? Is your eBook purchase not compatible with the device of your choice?

Don't worry, now with every Packt book you get a DRM-free PDF version of that book at no cost.

Read anywhere, any place, on any device. Search, copy, and paste code from your favorite technical books directly into your application.

The perks don't stop there, you can get exclusive access to discounts, newsletters, and great free content in your inbox daily

Follow these simple steps to get the benefits:

1. Scan the QR code or visit the link below

https://packt.link/free-ebook/9781804611074

2. Submit your proof of purchase
3. That's it! We'll send your free PDF and other benefits to your email directly

Made in the USA
Columbia, SC
27 February 2023